The Cell Phone

The Cell Phone

An Anthropology of Communication

Heather A. Horst and Daniel Miller

Oxford • New York

First published in 2006 by
Berg
Editorial offices:
1st Floor, Angel Court, 81 St Clements Street, Oxford, OX4 1AW, UK
175 Fifth Avenue, New York, NY 10010, USA

Berg is the imprint of Oxford International Publishers Ltd.

Library of Congress Cataloging-in-Publication Data
Horst, Heather A.
The cell phone : an anthropology of communication / Heather
A. Horst and Daniel Miller.
 p. cm.
Includes bibliographical references and index.
ISBN-13: 978-1-84520-401-3 (pbk.)
ISBN-10: 1-84520-401-8 (pbk.)
ISBN-13: 978-1-84520-400-6 (cloth)
ISBN-10: 1-84520-400-X (cloth)
 1. Cellular telephones—Jamaica. 2. Cellular telephones—
Social aspects—Jamaica. 3. Cellular telephones—Jamaica—
Psychological aspects. I. Miller, Daniel, 1954- II. Title.
 HE9715.J25H67 2006
 384.5'35—dc22   2006018528

British Library Cataloguing-in-Publication Data
A catalogue record for this book is available from the British Library.

ISBN-13 978 1 84520 400 6 (Cloth)
ISBN-10 1 84520 400 X (Cloth)

ISBN-13 978 1 84520 401 3 (Paper)
ISBN-10 1 84520 401 8 (Paper)

Typeset by Avocet Typeset, Chilton, Aylesbury, Bucks
Printed in the United Kingdom by Biddles Ltd, King's Lynn

www.bergpublishers.com

Contents

Acknowledgements

We have many people to thank for this book and the research underpinning its completion. In the first instance, this project would not have been possible without funding from the Department for International Development (UK), as part of the project 'Information Society: Emergent Technologies and Development Communities in the South' (2003–2005) to investigate the impact of new communication technologies amongst low-income populations in Ghana, India, Jamaica and South Africa.

Once in Jamaica Professor Barry Chevannes, (then) Dean of Social Sciences at the University of West Indies, Mona, was very hospitable and granted us appointments as visiting Professor and Research Fellow, respectively, during 2004. We are particularly indebted to Dr Aldrie-Henry-Lee, who was also extremely helpful in discussing and facilitating our work and introducing us to her colleagues. She was also central to organizing a successful workshop at the University, which provided initial feedback regarding the results of our work. Deborah Duperly-Pinks gave us important comparative information about her research with Carole Rakodi in downtown Kingston, as well as thoughtful conversation concerning the dynamics of crews and urban social formations.

Inger Boyett generously shared her data on the 'culture' of Digicel, as well as key contacts within the organization, and Don Anderson of Media Research Associates provided us with copies of his company's private research. Mrs Judith Bruce of West Indies Home Constructors Ltd (WIHCON) was particularly benevolent with her assistance in researching the history of Portmore (and WIHCON generally), which we hope to write about elsewhere. Finally, Portmore Mayor George Lee and the Office of the Municipality compiled useful information about the growing municipality.

We are thankful for the time of various representatives of the companies Digicel, Cable and Wireless and MiPhone, who agreed to interviews. Mr David Hall, the Chief Executive Officer (CEO) of Digicel, generously provided us with data on usage. A number of officers at the Ministry of Commerce, Science and Technology and especially Mr Michael Duquesnay of the Central Information Technology Office were of considerable assistance. We are also grateful to the owner of the Digicel outlet in Orange Valley, who provided us with vital figures not only within his shop but the circulation of remittances through the local

Western Union and cambio.* Although for purposes of anonymity we cannot identify them by name, many individuals, principals, civil servants and other organizations helped us with information and access throughout the course of the research. We hope they realize how deeply appreciative we are for their support and assistance.

Miss Susan Isaacs worked as a research assistant for us and we are deeply indebted to Susan for her advice, companionship and ability to open doors during our time in Portmore. We are also grateful to Emma Garner, who worked as a short-term researcher on the project, as well as Andrew Garner, who shared research data and insights from Negril. In addition, we are indebted to Antoinette Butler, Nakeisha Downer, Sharon Heron-Robinson, Kacey-Ann Kelly and Lisa Taylor-Stone for assistance and confidentiality in transcribing the expressive words of the Jamaicans we interviewed.

Mrs Icilda Cameron graciously opened her home to us and we were particularly honoured to be the co-caretakers of her house while she was in the UK. We are equally grateful to Mr Nerisander Mundle for introducing us to the Isaacs family – Mr and Mrs Isaacs, Susan, Nadine, Natalie, Rushaine, Kimberley and Imhani, as well as Diane, Devon, Kerry, Oliver, Olivia and Wendy – who graciously made room (quite literally) and welcomed us into their home and family. Without them we would have missed the many pleasures of living in Portmore and Jamaica. In addition, Heather would like to thank Miss Madge, Antoinette, Beverley, Auntie Amy, Uncle Bill and Maggie as well as Susan, Nadine, Mrs Isaacs, Mr Isaacs and Grandma and Grandpa Crowl, for the candid childcare advice and assistance, visits to the doctor and taxi rides and becoming surrogate grandparents, Aunties and Uncles for Zachary. And, as ever, Heather would like to express a heartfelt thank you to Antoinette, Simone, Beverley and 'Sister Mae', as well as Andrew Garner and Anat Hecht, who kept her focused and sane throughout the ebbs and flows of life in Jamaica.

Outside of Jamaica we appreciate the efforts of Hannah Shakespeare, Kathryn Earle, Fran Martin, Ian Critchley and Berg for assistance with the completion of the book and cover design. Our colleagues in this project, Andrew Skuse and Thomas Cousins (South Africa), Don Slater and Janet Kwami (Ghana), Jo Tacchi and Tripta Chandola (India), facilitated an insightful meeting in London during January of 2005. Our manuscript has also benefited from the critical comments of Mizuko (Mimi) Ito, Mirca Madianou, Fiona Parrot and Florian Schlichting, as well as an anonymous reviewer for Berg. Heather would also like to acknowledge the support of the Annenberg Center for Communication during her tenure as a Postdoctoral Research Associate at the University of Southern California. We take full responsibility for all errors and omissions.

* A cambio is a place in Jamaica that specializes in foreign currency exchange.

Finally, Danny thanks Ricki, Rachel and David for accepting his absences throughout the year. Heather wishes to express her deepest love and thanks to her son Zachary, who joined her on part of this excursion, as well as David Heck, who has been an unending source of support and encouragement throughout her continuing relationship with Jamaica.

Note on Orthography

Throughout the manuscript we have used extensive quotes from Jamaicans we interviewed in Standard Jamaican English as well as what would locally be termed 'patois', or Jamaican Creole. While we have attempted to follow the guidance of Cassidy and Le Page's (2003) *Dictionary of Jamaican English*, our interview data and transcriptions reflect oral practice. Because we want to retain as much of the local discourse as possible, quotes incorporating the range of Jamaican dialect spoken by our participants may appear inconsistent or grammatically inaccurate to readers.

–1–

Introduction

On a Friday evening in November of 2004,[1] an executive bus, travelling between Half-Way-Tree (the main bus terminus in central Kingston) and the suburb of Portmore, made its way down congested Hagley Park Road. As the bus stopped at a traffic light near Three Mile, an area surrounded by many of Jamaica's infamous garrison communities, four 'youths' shoved open the door.[2] Brandishing an AK-47, they boarded the bus and ordered every passenger to place their cell phone in a black scandal bag.[3] The passengers on the full bus passed up their cell phones one by one. But when only twenty-six cell phones arrived the youths became angry and demanded that the remaining three phones be passed to the front of the bus, where it is clearly stated that the bus capacity is twenty-nine passengers. Eventually the youths were able to coerce the reluctant passengers into giving up the remaining phones and got off the bus without further incident.

Although we travelled this very same route to Kingston on a regular basis in order to interview government and company officials, this particular evening we had remained in Portmore. When we heard about the hijacking, its significance for our project was obvious, but became even more so over the course of the next month as it was transformed into urban legend. When we presented a workshop at the University of the West Indies less than two weeks later, a woman recounted the incident. By that time some of the details had changed; one account added some violence and some details about the age of the youths and another version included extra guns. The story continued to travel and capture the imaginations as well as the fears of residents across Portmore and Kingston, not only because it signalled what many predicted would be a bad season for crime in the aftermath of Hurricane Ivan, but because of what it said about the cell phone – whereas just a few years ago many low-income Jamaicans had little access to any kind of phone, now these youths could simply assume that twenty-nine passengers represented twenty-nine phones.

Our project, funded by the British Department for International Development (DFID), was one of four simultaneous ethnographies devoted to a general assessment of the relationship between new information and communication technologies (ICTs) and poverty alleviation in Ghana, India, Jamaica and South Africa.[4] Our contribution involved research on the impact of ICTs among Jamaicans in two low-income communities over the course of a year (January 2004 to December 2004). As anthropologists, we viewed poverty as something more than macrostatistics of income and gross domestic product (GDP) and we were specifically concerned with documenting the experience of poverty among low-income Jamaicans. We wanted to assess the extent to which communications were felt to be of value in their own right, and the degree to which they had also become integral to people's relationship to health, crime and other people as well as to their own sense of self.

While the project was aimed at assessing the wider communication ecologies of low-income Jamaicans (e.g. the Internet, telecommunications, television, radio and the transport system), it soon became clear to us that the cell phone was dramatically changing the lives and livelihoods of low-income Jamaicans. During the same year, it was also apparent that Jamaica was not the only country where cell phones were being incorporated into people's lives with extraordinary rapidity. The integration of the cell phone in China, India and many countries in Africa raised what we considered to be urgent questions about the impact of the cell phone for development and poverty alleviation throughout much of the world. By 2003, there were already more cell phones in the world than landlines and in many European countries more than 75 per cent of the population were subscribers. China is by far the biggest market, with 200 million subscribers, although notably this comprises only 16 per cent of the population. The Caribbean country of Martinique, much like Jamaica, has 78.9 per cent penetration, compared with the USA with only 48 per cent (Ling 2004: 13–14; cf. Castells et al. 2005). Because many non-metropolitan countries did not have household landlines, the availability of cheap and accessible cell phones and cell phone towers represented the first opportunity to possess this means of communication. Given that many developing countries are superseding countries such as the USA in their use and integration of these phones, we are faced with an example of global leapfrogging and we feel compelled to obtain a sense of how these new developments in communications are transforming the world, for better or for worse, for richer or for poorer.

The increasing use of the mobile phone in countries such as Jamaica also represents a renewed opportunity for anthropologists to consider the overall impact of telephony as a form of communication, a telephony that is analogous to the original introduction of the phone within metropolitan regions nearly a century ago or the introduction of the cell phone within metropolitan countries only a decade or two ago. These differences in access form part of what has become termed the 'digital divide', that is, the possible tendency of new technologies to exacerbate differences between the rich and the poor. One of the central questions guiding our research revolves around the question of whether the cell phone (as it is manifested in Jamaica) represents a symptom or a solution to the digital divide; that is, does the cell phone reduce or exacerbate differences between the wealthy and the poor of this world? But there are no easy answers to this question and, as technology continues to move forward, new issues emerge. For example, *The Economist* (12–18 March 2005) recently devoted its front cover and editorial to the possibility that the cell phone, rather than the Internet, was the key technology for helping the world's poor move out of poverty. Our own research led to us to further question the degree to which the Internet through the cell phone might also become equally important in the long term, given the relatively low expense of cell phones compared with computers.

As we hope this volume will demonstrate, trying to assess the relative merits of new communication technologies in alleviating conditions of poverty is no simple matter and the answer to these questions is not likely to remain the same across every country or region. Nonetheless, our hope is that this volume will make a considered contribution to an ongoing and essential debate for those of us for whom social science is intended to contribute not just to academic advancement but also to understanding contemporary issues outside the academy which evolve over the course of days and months rather than years and decades, a contribution to debates that take place not only in academic journals but also in newspapers and television as well as the Internet. This is not at all typical of the traditions of anthropology, which is a discipline that aims to contribute to a general comparative study of humankind, through the patient and long-term collection of materials through ethnography, comparison, analysis and theory.[5] We want to build on this tradition, but add another possibility, which is that we can use anthropological methods such as long-term ethnography (Bernard 1995) to tackle something as dynamic and extensive as the astonishing spread of the cell phone while also producing material and conclusions that engage with anthropological debates on new technologies and changes in communication and connectivity, as well as Caribbean anthropology generally. The difference is that we aim to understand the phenomenon as it is occurring.

But the word timely also seems to us appropriate to the emerging academic debate on this topic. Between 2004 and 2005, the first general books that summarize the findings of work on the wealthy societies of the metropolitan world are being published, such as the work of Richard Ling (2004) in Norway and Ito et al. (2005) with respect to Japan. This book is also intended to be timely in the sense of complementing these early works by becoming one of the first volumes to consider the impact of the phone in the developing world. One of the reasons the early emphasis is upon metropolitan regions is that much of the financial backing for research has, in part, come from commercial forces concerned with wealthier consumers and also because these are the regions in which most research was based (see Pertierra et al. 2002; Ling 2004). Our study, in contrast, is funded by development aid and is undertaken under the auspices of anthropology in a place where, as the figures show, the impact on low-income households is likely to be, if any-thing, more dramatic and perhaps more significant in the long run. Above all, we felt a moral commitment to rapidly document, understand and evaluate how this particular communication technology is changing the face of countries such as Jamaica, an evaluation that could in turn be utilized as the basis for an informed response for further research and support of new communication technologies in the developing world generally.

Outline of Contents

The aim of this book is, then, clear-cut and unequivocal – it is the task of evalu-ating the consequences of the cell phone for low-income populations through pre-senting an ethnography of the cell phone in Jamaica. In order to accomplish this aim, the various chapters that comprise this book take up particular and comple-mentary perspectives. Here in the introduction we have briefly summarized the prevailing literature first on the global impact of the cell phone and then the spe-cific nature of communication in Jamaica. These two perspectives frame our enquiry and establish often contrasting expectations of what we might encounter. We can thereby be clear as to the degree to which our findings accord with or enable us to rethink these expectations. But, before we can understand Jamaicans' use of the cell phone and especially why the cell phone has made such an impact upon the landscape of communication in Jamaica, we need to consider how it is they obtained cell phones in the first place. Chapter 2 is therefore a discussion of the dual role of the major commercial companies and the Jamaican government in instituting a situation where today, in a country of 2.7 million people, there are 2 million subscriptions to cell phones. This provides us with an initial consideration of one of the main topics that are central to the kinds of debate that publications such as *The Economist* are keen to foster: that is, the impact of liberalization and the relationship between the state and commerce. The context for the extraordinary and rapid spread of the cell phone is given in the following chapter, where we introduce the basic economic and social parameters of low-income households in contemporary Jamaica. By introducing the results of our survey work in the two locations where fieldwork took place, we are able to convey more precisely what we mean when using this term 'low-income' to describe individuals and house-holds

Chapter 4 is concerned with the issues of possession and usage that have been the mainstay of the commercially driven research that has dominated early studies. It thereby comes closest to the previously established literature on the cell phone. One of the most important aims of this chapter is to provide readers with a sense of how Jamaicans carry themselves in relation to the phone, and the ways in which the phone changes how it feels to be Jamaican. By considering our evidence in relation to this wider literature we can ask ourselves how far it is reasonable to think in terms of a Jamaican cell phone. Certainly there are marked differences in the use made of the varied potentialities of the technology, which lead us a long way from any simple technological determinism.

The heart of our ethnographic description comes in the following three chapters. Chapters 5 and 6 establish the grounds for this volume to be seen more generally as an anthropology of communication. In these chapters we shall argue that, just because our focus is on low-income families, it does not mean that we reduce our anthropology to a simple logic of function and coping. Indeed, we suggest that to account for our evidence we need to turn around the apparent relationship between what are considered economic and other aspects of social relationships. The way people obtain money and resources that enable them to survive is itself seen to be in many ways parasitic upon a more foundational drive towards certain modes of communication. Low-income Jamaicans give, exchange and receive help in a manner that seems designed to maximize communication and connectedness. Our argument is that we need to understand this anthropology of communication in its own terms. Our study of coping strategies is therefore enhanced by not reducing communication to a function of that struggle to survive. In Chapter 6 we demonstrate that coping strategies are fundamentally based on connectivity since, for nearly one-third of the households we surveyed, income is derived through social connections rather than either work or entrepreneurship. But we then also show that this form of connectivity derives from a particular mode of communication, locally called link-up, which we analyse in Chapter 5.

In the final three chapters we recognize that, in addition to trying to contribute to this project of an anthropology of communication, this volume is also intended to contribute to the sorts of evaluations undertaken in development studies and policymaking. We move from our ethnographic examination to a more policy-focused analysis in three stages. In Chapter 7 we remain within our more conventional anthropological perspective on such issues by reflecting upon the very concept of welfare and the salience of understanding welfare in Jamaican terms. The chapter explores the word 'pressure', well known from the lyrics of globally successful Jamaican music, and the insights this term provides for comprehending the ways in which Jamaicans also assess and understand issues of welfare. In Chapter 8 we focus upon the impact of the cell phone in three key sectors of development: education, health and crime. Yet we remain committed to relating these appraisals back to particular Jamaican ideologies, for example, by examining Jamaican relationships to gambling and religion as the backdrop for assessing this idea of welfare.

In our final chapter we bring these themes together under the overall rubric of evaluation. As anthropologists we are committed to a consideration of the way Jamaicans themselves evaluate, not just the phone, but each specific aspect of phone use, from its consequences for social relationships to its effect on entrepreneurship. But we also needed to find a way to relate this evaluation by those who participated in this study to that demanded by powerful bodies responsible for policy, whether the Jamaican government or the World Bank. One of our strategies is to compare our material with the approach of academics, such as Amartya Sen (e.g. 1987, 1992, 1999a, b), who have tried to take rather esoteric economistic models and make them instruments of welfare evaluation that engage with the declared interests and choices of populations. In our conclusion we attempt to highlight the dangers of focusing upon any one particular player in this story, whether commerce, the state or the 'popular voice'. Instead we concentrate on trying to make the relativism of anthropology, whose conclusions are highly specific to time and place, an asset in policy formation, rather than simply a critique of those generalizations required by policymaking.

The Cell Phone

In the remainder of this introduction we define our project in relation to two bodies of literature, both of which create expectations for our findings. In this section we consider writings about the global impact of the cell phone, while in the final section we deal with studies that start from the opposite end, that is local forms of prior communication. It is in the meeting between these two that we hope to establish our study within the wider terms implicated in the subtitle of this book – an anthropology of communication.

While there have been many academic contributions to the study of telephones and their impact upon society, Fischer's (1992) work on landlines and Ling's (2004) early research into cell phones have been particularly influential on this volume. It is important to our project to start with Fischer, who provides a general appraisal of the social impact of the original landline phone in the USA between 1900 and 1940. This is because our approach to the cell phone is that it needs to be considered as a telephone in the first place and only then in terms of its specific quality as a cell phone. Fischer (1992: 5) concludes that 'the telephone did not radically alter American ways of life; rather, Americans used it to more vigorously pursue their characteristic ways of life'. This seems to us to establish a core theoretical foundation. When people adopt new media, we tend to assume that they first seize on all the new possibilities that the media offer in order to achieve previously unprecedented tasks. But this may be a mistaken expectation. When Miller and Slater (2000) studied the impact of the Internet in Trinidad, what became clear was that Trinidadians did not focus on the unprecedented new possibilities. Rather, the technology is used initially with reference to desires that are historically well established, but remain unfulfilled because of the limitations of previous technologies. These pent-up frustrations thus determine the way the new technology is first seen, what Miller and Slater termed 'expansive realisation'. As will become clear in this volume, we see the results of our ethnographic study of the impact of the phone in Jamaica as in many ways complementary to Fischer's historical study of the initial impact of the phone in the USA.

We also seek to build upon the general arguments that have emerged from studies of the adoption of media. Ling (2004), for example, provides one of the most thoughtful texts that attempts to assess the literature concerning the impact of the cell phone to date. Following Silverstone and Haddon (1992) and Silverstone and Hirsch (1992) he argues that the evidence to date supports an approach termed the 'domestication of technologies', which was devised in order to move beyond arguments between various forms of technological determination and social determination. Several of the terms and ideas employed in this approach, such as appropriation and objectification, were adopted and adapted from Miller (1987, 1988)[6] and, in the main, this is the perspective we employ here.

In essence such approaches have their original derivation in dialectical philosophy, here introduced under the term 'objectification'. In effect, this means that we do not imagine ourselves as studying the adoption of objects by subjects, because there is no fixed thing called a cell phone or fixed group called Jamaicans. Rather, this book will seek to find out what Jamaicans have become in the light of their use of the cell phone and what the cell phone has become in the light of its use by Jamaicans. What one has to study are not things or people but processes (Miller 2005). But in turn we also have to accept that there are many types of cell phones and many more differences amongst Jamaicans. We do not apologize for using such terms – everyone in Jamaica uses them constantly, so that the general term 'Jamaican' exists as a constant discourse in the voices and aspirations of its people, irrespective of its relationship to any ideology of nationalism (see Thomas 2004). Indeed, as we shall demonstrate, it has become a thoroughly international term, much less tied to location than in the past, and one of the instruments that has effected this change is, of course, the cell phone itself. This is just one of the ways we argue that it is Jamaicans who are as much subject to change in this new relationship as the cell phone.

While our book has much in common with the other studies that are emerging on the cell phone as a case study of media adoption, there is also a contrast that we hope marks out much of the originality of this volume. Most of the initial work on the cell phone has been published with titles such as *Perpetual Contact* (Katz and Aakhuus 2002) and *Wireless World* (Brown et al. 2001). This reflects the source of these studies in metropolitan regions where the landline was already ubiquitous. As such they seek to highlight the significance of the cell phone as a mobile phone. It is the contrast between the mobility and individuality of this phone as against a landline that makes for the obvious focus of this early work (see Ito 2005).

In contrast, this volume is subtitled *an Anthropology of Communication* because there is no intention of isolating the cell phone's unprecedented attributes of mobility at the expense of its more general integration into Jamaican life as a phone. On the contrary, we would rather use this opportunity to think more generally about the nature of communication as a value and practice. This reflects the position of our book as a kind of 'second-wave' research, which follows the focus upon metropolitan regions with a concern for the billions of low-income households that populate most of the world and who are only in the last year or two gaining access to this technology on a scale that warrants studies of this kind. In most cases landlines were not ubiquitous and the situation is therefore very different.

Fischer (1992) is therefore a useful precursor precisely because he was concerned with the meaning and the use of the telephone per se (see Marvin 1988; Umble 1996). For example, one of his most important observations is that those who marketed the phone were actually quite slow to appreciate that it would be largely used for sociable conversation (Fischer 1992: 85). If anything, the people who 'invented' the telephone were consumers, especially rural consumers, who were the most keen to obtain the phone and appreciate its potential (119). Overall, and in contrast to the car, there was little public debate about its impact, and it did not dramatically affect the localism in small-town life. Fischer discerns no obvious or major social or psychological impact, and 'the best estimate is that, on the whole, telephone calling solidified and deepened social relations' (266), rather than replacing face-to-face relationships. What the telephone appeared to engineer was a general expansion of talk (268). In these conclusions one can see how Fischer comes closer to the kind of ambition one would expect of a more general anthropology of communication itself, rather than just the specific motilities of a cell phone.

Nevertheless, it is the cell phone that is the subject of this book and we also recognize the many valuable contributions that are emerging from the study of this technology per se and the evaluation of its initial impact and specific history (e.g. Galambos and Abrahamson 2002; Agar 2003; Ling 2004). Whereas Burgess (2004) adds a sustained analysis of the various scares, fears and medical dangers that have been associated with the spread of the cell phone, Ling (2004) has stressed the increased sense of personal security and its importance in legitimating the giving of phones by parents to children (35–55). Such justifications are also tied to the 'ability to organise activities "on the fly" as perhaps one of the most central advantages of the mobile telephone' (Ling 2004: 18; see also Ling and Yuri 2002). Ling, in particular, contributes a number of useful terms for analysing such micro-coordination, such as 'midcourse adjustment', 'iterative coordination' and also 'softening of schedules', which illustrate the ways in which the cell phone can be used to increase flexibility (2004: 70–76). More intriguingly he argues that mobile telephony is starting to challenge the status of time itself as the basis of social coordination (78).

One of the most common research priorities, partly given the commercial imperatives underpinning much of this research, surrounds understanding the imperatives behind youth adoption and use of the phone (Weilenmann and Larsson 2001; Kasesniemi and Rautiainen 2002; Taylor and Harper 2003; Ling 2004: 83–121; Ito et al. 2005). Ling takes these further by examining both the general sense of emancipation and the implications of modern life, where children do not expect to follow their parents' practice and the insights of one generation are seen as less useful for the next (2004: 95). This focus on youth also tends to coalesce around topics such as fashion, style and the body (see also Fortunati 2002; Fortunati et al. 2003) and the deep impact of phone costs on pocket money and budgets. Another associated theme is the impact of the phone on the internal relations within the family (Ling and Yuri 2002; Schejter and Cohen 2002), including the dynamics of surveillance and freedom between children and parents (Ling 1998; Green 2001; Ito 2005).

In addition, the intrusive nature of mobile telephony (Ling 2004: 123–143) and the relationship between privacy and the dissolving boundaries between the public and private sphere remain an important contribution (Licoppe and Heurtin 2002), which in turn leads to a consideration of the etiquette that has developed around the use of the phone (Kim 2002). Perhaps most striking to observers has been the rapid rise of texting (Ling 2004: 145–167; Ito et al. 2005). In this case the literature on young people in Scandinavia, which argues that texting is an asynchronous discourse that anxious children can ponder conspicuously in groups as well as inconspicuously in class or under their bedcovers, is matched by a fascinating literature on the Philippines. In the Philippines texting quickly became central to many activities, ranging from flirting and forming relationships to its possible implication in political mobilization and the overthrow of governments (Pertierra et al. 2002).

Most pertinent to the purposes of this volume have been attempts to forge a wider evaluation of the phone, within the terms of a general debate between what has been called social capital on the one hand (e.g. Baron et al. 2000; Fine and Green 2000; Putnam 2002) and the rise of individualization on the other (Beck and Beck-Gernsheim 2001; Ling 2004: 169–195). More specifically, our work weighs in on a vigorous discussion about the degree to which social networking has become increasingly predicated on individual networking (Castells 1996, 1997, 1998; Wellman, 1999, 2002; Harper 2003). We demonstrate that the particular configuration of communication between individual and social networks has a different history in Jamaica, which impacts upon the cell phone's usage today. In order to highlight this distinctive relationship as it pertains to Jamaica, where ego-centred networking is traditional rather than a novel consequence of new technology, we use the Jamaican term 'link-up', which we hope will help academics more generally to rethink the way they see the role of the cell phone in integrating individual and social networking (see Horst and Miller 2005). At the very least our evidence should act as a salutary pointer to the parochialism of many of the assumptions made in these discussions concerning the relationship between new communication technologies and social networking.

The issue of social capital as opposed to individualism leads in turn to the overall evaluation of the phone's impact on the welfare of populations, and thereby to the heart of this volume's concern for the welfare of low-income populations. Here we turn to a quite different literature, which comes under the general category of the 'digital divide', which today includes both divisions of wealth and poverty within metropolitan countries (e.g. Hakken 1993; Mossberger et al. 2003) and more general issues of global inequality (e.g. Hakken 1993; Escobar 1994a, b; Navas-Sabater et al. 2002; World Bank 2002, 2005; Henry 2004; James 2003), and poverty (e.g. Beck 1994; Alcock 1997). This literature raises key issues concerning the degree to which new media technologies are primarily forms that will enable low-income households to leapfrog prior forms of economic inequality and connect to the resources and information that are becoming an integral part of the global system of communication or, in contrast, exacerbate income differentials, thereby condemning the world's disenfranchised to continued poverty. Poverty may now be intensified by the increasing distance between those who have access to such resources and those who do not. Although most of the work on the digital divide has been devoted to the assessment of the Internet, it has clear implications also for the cell phone. In turn the discussion of the digital divide links our work with the much wider literature on development and the problem of low-income households, both in the Caribbean and elsewhere.

The situation that we encountered in Jamaica resonated with certain issues in the development literature more than others. For example, the role of the phone in linking transnational families and populations is critical to several of the chapters that follow, becoming integral to the general evaluation of the 'remittance economy' and the role of communication in the vast spread of transnational migration more generally (e.g. Basch et al. 1994; Smith and Guarnizo 1998; Thompson and Bauer 2001; Vertovec 2004; Riak-Akuei 2005; Horst 2006; Wilding 2006). We have also been influenced by the work of our colleagues on this project, who have developed the concept of the 'communicative ecology' (Slater and Tacchi 2004; Slater 2005). They argue that in order to understand any one particular technology of communication one needs first to appreciate its role as part of communication ecologies, which may be embedded in media such as radio or the bus service. Their stance resonates with our commitment to a wider anthropology of communication. For example, while in metropolitan countries the mobility of a mobile phone is understood as extending and being extended by the mobility of the car or train networks (e.g. Jain 2002; Okabe and Ito 2005), in Jamaica it is the phone's impact on welfare in particular, for example, health, that is mediated by its relationship to the transport system as a system of communication.

Being situated as part of a four-country comparison (and thus privy to some of the current analyses taking place in relation to this endeavour) enabled us to find common ground such as this stress on communicative ecologies, but it has also alerted us to the striking differences in context that make generalizations about the digital divide problematic. For example, the way phones are organized in mini-entrepreneurial schemes, which are in turn closely linked to the initiatives of the state and non-governmental organizations (NGOs) in South Africa (Skuse and Cousins 2005), is strikingly different from anything we encountered in Jamaica. Nor can we match the range of experimental initiatives in community-based media centres that are documented for India (Tacchi 2005) or the fascinating way in which the Internet and cell phones are being used in distinctively different ways to create complementary relations to social networks both within and outside Ghana (Slater and Kwami 2005).

What does emerge from such a four-country study is the sheer dynamism of what we are encountering (Tacchi et al. 2005). A few years ago the entry and impact of the Internet seemed a swift and dramatic incursion of a new technology with significant consequences for everything from the way global business would operate to the rise of transnational marriage (Constable 2003). Yet in 2005 even the Internet looks slow and slight. While most low-income populations (in effect the bulk of the world's population) still experience this as a distant and curious phe-nomenon, the cell phone mushrooms up from inside mud-brick shacks and under corrugated iron sheet roofing to become an insistent and active presence that has us rushing to even acknowledge, let alone appreciate. We are not jumping on a bandwagon, we are desperately trying to simply keep up with the world, which is patently moving on and has little time for our conservatism and inertia. In such cir-cumstances academic work that helps to give us some purchase on these changes seems more important than ever.

Communication in Jamaica

It will be evident in our review of the literature on the cell phone that we see texts that consider the widest possible context for understanding the usage and conse-quences of the telephone as much more effective than those that start too narrowly from a supposed intrinsic quality of the technology itself. This in turn is how we envisage linking the literature on the phone to our more general ethnography of the cell phone in Jamaica. Once again, our starting point is the widest possible con-sideration of communication rather than viewing this as reducible to the tech-nology of its medium. We remain within this concept of communicative ecology

(Slater and Tacchi 2004), meaning the 'the complete range of communication media and information flows within a community' (2). Communication for us includes locations such as the market or church, media and transport, as well as the specific nature of oral discourse. It is the attention to these wider contexts of cell phone use that constitutes the background to much of the ethnography that follows in subsequent chapters.

From the first moment that the people we now refer to as Jamaicans arrived as 'crowds' on the Jamaican shores (see Mintz and Price 1992), a flexible and creative approach to the means and modes of communication emerged. Despite the vast differences among the new arrivals, they created communication networks within the plantation system as well as between different plantations and markets. The communication that was foundational to later development was not that between the slave and the plantation owner, but rather at the margins of the plantation, where African and Creole slaves created social and economic worlds outside the purview of the plantation owners. These were forged in three primary spaces, the market (and related provision grounds), the 'negro village' and the church, which were frequented during the free time of the evenings, weekends and especially the week between Christmas and New Year.

As Burton (1997) observes, whites 'remained largely ignorant of the nighttime and weekend lives they led in their villages, where from the earliest days "plays" and similar rituals became the major focus of *cultural* resistance to slavery' (50, Burton's emphasis). Within the slave villages, rituals, plays and other performances involved singing, dancing and drumming. It was also in the villages where the new Jamaicans forged extensive kinship networks (Smith 1988; Besson 1995b) and residential patterns (Patterson 1967; Mintz and Price 1992; Smith 1996), new institutions, such as family land (Clarke 1966; Besson 1995a, 2002), and cultural forms, such as funerals and celebrations. These sociocultural forms became the basis of most subsequent anthropological analyses of Jamaican Creole social structures. Since slaves were often exchanged or required to work temporarily on other plantations (Burton 1997) and also interacted in the markets, there was also a significant degree of movement between the plantations. Higman (1995: 166), for example, reveals the extent to which families and the relationships between men and women transgressed plantation and parish boundaries by mapping the degree to which kinship patterns reflect the criss-crossing of plantation and village boundaries (Patterson 1967; Burton 1997).[7]

The market (especially the Sunday market) played a prominent role in the exchange and communication of information. During the seventeenth century, plantation owners permitted Jamaican slaves to cultivate their grounds in the unusable soil on the perimeters of the plantation (see Patterson 1967; Higman 1988; Henke 1996). Intended primarily to supplement their meagre diets, the surplus provisions were carried to the market for monetary exchange or barter on Sunday, market day. Citing first-hand accounts by Mathison and Foulks, Patterson (1967) argues that markets were central to the exchange of news and information. As he describes:

> The market itself was all noise and bustle and wild, extravagant gestures which seemed always on the verge of, but never quite, exploding into violence ... brothers, sisters, temporary 'wives' and 'husbands', aged friends and week-end lovers are all intently looking for each other. When they meet, especially the old women with their 'chints pelisses and closely bound handkerchiefs', the gossip ... begins at once. (Patterson 1967: 229–230)

The social pull of the market was so strong that, even when there were opportunities to sell their wares on the journey for a fair price, Patterson notes that they preferred to go to the market and enjoy the socializing that accompanied such economic transactions.

The church was equally important in the forging of the wider communicative ecologies. The impact of Baptist missionaries, with their employment of black preachers (often from the USA), such as George Lisle, Moses Baker and the Reverend William Knibb (Austin-Broos 1997), became evident in their pivotal role in the organization of slave resistance and the formation of an anti-slavery critique. Although other missionaries such as Moravians and Methodists also played important roles (Besson 2002: 98–99), Jamaican slaves saw Baptists as allies since slaves were often given positions as leaders within the church. One of the key figures in the Christmas rebellion of 1831 was Samuel 'Daddy' Sharpe, a Black Baptist missionary who read newspapers aloud to the slaves on his (and others') plantations in Montego Bay. Through these prayer meetings and other church networks, Jamaican slaves learned of the Haitian and American revolutions. Organized through such meetings as well as during weekend and holiday Christmas visits, the Christmas Rebellion of 1831 occurred two days after Christmas and included 20,000 slaves, making it the largest rebellion in the Americas. After emancipation, the alliance between Baptists and ex-slaves was central to the creation of the free villages (Besson 2002).

These three locations, village, market and church, have become the sites through which new forms of media become established. On the one hand, there is the increasing presence of mass media, such as newspapers, radio and television (especially cable television of late), which links them into national and transnational connections. On the other hand, there is the consolidation of internal communication through the appropriation of media such as photocopy machines, printers and loudspeakers. The churches, for example, have intensified their relationship to their congregations through media such as photocopying, but at the same time they have developed national religious mass media, such as the very popular Love FM radio, and in turn a relationship to the enormously powerful

North American evangelical networks (such as the Trinity Broadcasting Network), which are experienced locally as ever-present[8] gospel radio and television programmes, which preach both local and global variants of evangelical Christianity. In her study of Caribbean migration, Thomas-Hope (1992) notes that, while radio use and ownership were widespread throughout Jamaica in the late 1980s (present in over 90 per cent of the households), for a considerable period newspaper readership was more restricted to upper- and middle-class Jamaicans, due in large part to relatively lower literacy rates among the low-income Jamaicans (129). Prior to the introduction of the cell phone, more recent surveys of media indicate that, out of a population of nearly 2.7 million, 1.9 million had access to radio and 0.97 million had access to television, including 0.28 million with access to cable television (Market Research Services 2002). In contrast, in our rural site there was only one shop in the town centre that sold newspapers on a regular basis and most families restricted their usage to perusing the jobs section of the Sunday edition or, as one man phrased it, '*Star* gazing', meaning looking over the shoulder of another reader who purchased one of the more tabloid-like newspapers, The *Star*.

In our ethnography it became evident that the local communication ecology needed to include not only these locations but also the communication between them, since the link between the cell phone and transport was critical to understanding the use of the cell phone.[9] As we shall demonstrate, this includes not only the development of an extensive roadway system organized by the Jamaican government, such as Highway 2000, which is planned to collapse the travel time between Kingston, the capital, and Montego Bay, the second biggest city, but also the extension of air travel. Indeed, the higgler (or Jamaican market woman) beloved in both the academic and fictional literature on Jamaica is now a transnational figure, who is just as likely to be seen in the airports of Miami, New York and Panama as she is peddling clothing, shoes and other goods in the markets of downtown Kingston or small towns such as May Pen (see Freeman 1997). As Chapters 5 and 8 reveal, perhaps the most extensive transformation and linkage between the cell phone and older forms of communication have arisen through the development of the taxi system. Moving between neighbourhoods, districts, villages and towns in their cars and minivans, taxi drivers transport not only people and goods between places; they also 'carry news' (Sobo 1993), money for bets and information about happenings across the island

Orality, Performance, Noise and Other Callings

There is, however, another precedent to understanding the use made of cell phones which looks much more narrowly at the form taken by oral communication itself. In his seminal series of essays that examined expressive culture in St Vincent, Nevis and Trinidad and Tobago, Roger Abrahams (1983) focuses upon the importance of words, wordplay and orality in the West Indies (and Afro-American culture generally). As he notes, 'the ability to contend with words is, then, a social skill and highly valued as such' (55). He distinguishes between two types of wordsmiths: the good talker and the good arguer. The good talker performs (sometimes as the master of ceremonies) at weddings, funerals, tea meetings and other serious events where structured speeches take place and is typically a prominent member of the community with a good command of standard English as well as decorum and elegance. In contrast, the good arguer belongs to the everyday sphere of public spaces such as the 'crossroads' (or 'the road' in Jamaica), the market, the rum shop and the 'corner' (see Wilson 1966). Using Creole variants, the good arguer is valued for their ability to creatively use words and maintain conversations in an impromptu manner, the entertainment value of his conversation as well as the ability to manage verbal sparring.

Whereas good talkers are concerned with family, the home, the church and other aspects of respectability, good arguers 'play' in the peer-based reputation-seeking arena outside the home. As his title *The Man-O-Words in the West Indies* (Abraham 1983) suggests, both forms of expression have often been considered male domains, although Abrahams (perhaps rather more than Wilson 1966) also discusses women who engage in such reputation-seeking forms of expression, such as the higgler, and the verbal agility shown by women in the exchange of cursing.[10] Subsequent work on female spirit possession in Pentecostal churches (Austin-Broos 1997) and gossip (Sobo 1993) as well as reputation-building among women (Besson 1993) has also helped balance this gendered discussion of reputation, respectability and communication.

Although Abrahams's work did not take place in Jamaica, his work resonates with much of the subsequent attention to performance, play and orality. Richard Burton's (1997) historical work on the culture of opposition in slavery focuses upon Jonkonnu performances (see Beckwith 1929) and Christmas celebrations. This stress on mimicking and satire is also noted by Patterson (1967: 253–254) with reference to the content of Jamaican slave songs, and has contributed to the extensive literature on stories about Anancy, the clever spider character known for outwitting 'the system', to borrow a phrase from the Rastafarian worldview (Burton 1997: 61).[11] Communication as resistance was central to the processes of 'opposition' (Burton 1997) and what Jean Besson (2002) calls culture-building, or the way resistance is complemented by forms of engaging, appropriating and transforming the European institutions of communication (see Alleyne 1988; Mintz and Price 1992; Cooper 1996).

It was the earlier account by Abrahams, with his focus upon noise and sound that was probably most prescient in understanding the subtleties of communication in contemporary Jamaica. In his analysis of communication among men liming at the crossroads, he contends that when West Indian men are together having a conversation it is not a conversation in the conventional Euro-American sense whereby one person speaks while others listen. Rather, a conversation involves a group of men who appear to be speaking at once, holding their own often quite separate arguments. Within this group of ever-escalating and overlapping voices, the successful 'man-o-words' makes 'the conglomerate of these individual voices not silent but harmonious' (Abraham 1983: 127). The epitome of this creation of harmony often takes place in church services in the 'call and response' pattern of worship (Abrahams 1983) as well as when congregants receive the spirit. This divine communication is evident not only through the jerking, shaking and dancing resulting from bodily possession, but also through the coveted ability to speak in tongues (Austin-Broos 1997). Other, less dramatic variants may signal communication with the divine during the collective outpouring of individual, personalized prayers to Jesus. In a similar vein, while partaking in their sacrament (ganja), Rastafarians participate in 'reasonings' that often involve consecutive, but individual expositions of their world view in a collective setting (Chevannes 1994, 1995).

In her analysis of orality in poetry as well as in contemporary dancehall lyrics, Carolyn Cooper (1996, 2004) continues this tradition of attention to the rich creativity and understanding of 'sound' and 'noise'. Cooper (2004) argues that the politics of noise is a critical feature of Jamaican communication, conveying and playing with meaning as well as insinuating itself into the social cracks of Jamaican society without words, such as through the spread of 'night noise' (and dancehall culture) into the spaces of middle-class Jamaica (see Austin-Broos 1995; Stanley-Niaah 2004). Indeed, in the form of contemporary dancehall, this quality of noise has become an important element of Jamaica's contribution to global popular culture. But within Jamaica it has distinct roots. For example, drumming and music generally were central to ritual and ceremony and often the form through which communities were alerted and gathered (Austin-Broos 1997; Besson 2002).[12] In reference to the nine-night festivities following a death, Wardle (2000) argues that domino games, food, hymns and the arrival of the guests take on a rhythm of commotion that works together to keep the momentum of the gathering, the successful journey of the spirit to the spirit world being contingent upon the degree to which enough noise and commotion have been created (see Hurston 1990). As we highlight in Chapter 4, the cell phone thus enters into a highly developed soundscape.

Conclusion

Juxtaposing the literature on the global impact of the cell phone and the local precedent of specifically Jamaican communication provides the frame within which our own enquiry can be set. In some cases, what is significant is the considerable difference in expectations that these two literatures create for our study. In examining the history of Jamaican communication from religion to music, the focus is on the contribution of obtrusive noise as central to the creation of community, often in resistance to the establishment. In stark contrast, the literature on the cell phone emphasizes the embarrassment, anxiety and need for restriction created by obtrusive noise and conversations resulting from cell phone usage in public spaces, Not surprisingly, then, Jamaicans tend to hold a more positive view of the cell phone and easily accept the ringing cell phone or subsequent public form of private conversations, even in the hallowed halls of the church. Similarly the communicative ecologies of the church or the taxi system that derive from a consideration of Jamaica differ dramatically from those of commerce or youth culture, arenas that have dominated early cell phone studies.

But in creating this juxtaposition we want to carefully avoid the suppression of one literature by the other. Indeed, there are many expectations that follow from the history of communication in Jamaica that are contradicted by our study of the cell phone. For example, given the importance of communication expressed primarily through forms of oral expression and performativity, many Jamaicans reasoned that the widespread success of the cell phone was best accounted for by a particular sense of Jamaican loquaciousness, or more colloquially that 'Jamaicans luv fi talk'. But we found that, rather than loquaciousness, a surprising number of these calls were extremely short and, in terms of content, seemed to communicate little more than a brief exchange of pleasantries (or in some cases unpleasantries), which seemed to truncate before they began. Most of our analytical efforts in the following chapters are concerned with understanding the brevity rather than the length of phone calls. It is not that this analysis will remove itself from issues of precedent. On the contrary, we have quite a bit to say about the foundations for what comes in our text to be called the 'link-up' mode of communication. But what emerges through our analysis is the necessity of returning to that wider contextualization of social communication and communicative ecologies in order to understand why this mode (rather than some other mode we might equally well have predicted) comes to dominate contemporary use of the cell phone.

As a result, our conclusion with regard to the literature on Jamaican communication is similar to that of the global use of the cell phone. In both cases we shall find evidence that is very different from what might have been predicted from these literatures. For example, the local case makes nonsense of the supposed global transformation from social to individual networking or from intensifying immediate as opposed to extensive relationships that are found in the general literature on the cell phone. Our overall aim is rather to follow a path that we would term dialectical. This will not be a study of the Jamaican appropriation of the cell phone. It is a study of both Jamaicans and the cell phone and the reciprocal process through which the Jamaican cell phone has come into being.

Finally, we want to consider the other term that makes up an anthropology of communication, that is, 'anthropology'. Here our aim is to strike a balance between the various literatures. While we are committed to development concerns, and the generalizations that are imposed by the terms and categories employed both in that literature and that of media studies, we also bring a sensitivity to the perspectives of the Jamaicans we encountered within our ethnography. The very starting point of any anthropological endeavour is the empathetic encounter and the attempt to take on and convey the perspectives of those one is working with.[13] As non-Jamaicans, we remain very conscious of the problematic issues of power and the false goals of pure objectivity or, indeed, subjectivity, that are implicated in one of the most powerful evaluative terms used by Jamaicans, that of 'respect'.

For this reason our account weaves back and forth between an engagement with the two types of literature we have just discussed. Chapter 2's attention to the infrastructure behind the provision of cell phones and the focus upon low-income Jamaicans in Chapter 3 primarily use more generalized and analytical terms. But in subsequent chapters, such as Chapter 5 on 'link-up' and Chapter 7 on 'pressure', we develop our commitment to understanding those ways in which Jamaicans both see and experience communication in specific ways. Furthermore, our interpretation of the Jamaican sensibility represented in the term 'respect' includes a desire to resist simple generalizations about 'Jamaicans'. For this reason, the core ethnographic descriptions come in the form of stories about individuals and small groups. At one level, these people and these events represent no more than themselves, the qualitative encounter with the particular, rather than evidence for the general. But that is the crux of ethnography – that somehow we try to retain the fundamental linkage between academic generalization, or, indeed, policy prescriptions, and a language and style that retain something of the humanity and individuality of the people upon whom those generalizations are based.

It befits an ethnographic study to try to convey these findings through the experience of ordinary low-income Jamaicans at a personal level and through the idioms within which they themselves expressed their experience of these changes. Particularly as we approach the final chapter, we seek to retain something of their own concepts of evaluation and welfare. We have found that, when publishing in this form, some readers are less convinced that such individual stories constitute proper 'evidence' for the generalizations subsequently made. But we feel, in contrast, that this is precisely how ethnographic and qualitative materials more generally start as experiences and then gradually become the confidence with which the author makes generalized statements and claims. It seems to us preferable to retain this openness and honesty about the process of exposition and, indeed, the greater openness to criticism that it entails.

–2–

Infrastructure

Before we can appreciate the ways low-income Jamaicans have integrated the cell phone into their lives, we first need to provide an understanding of how Jamaicans came to have these phones in the first place. We fully intend to contribute to these economic and political debates about trade liberalization, the role of the state and the relationship between monopolies and regulation, with clear conclusions given in our final chapter as to how the Jamaican evidence bears on the general discussion of liberalization in the telecoms sector. But we also want to convey the story of these changes as they were experienced through our ethnography. It was clear from early on that these companies are understood as 'characters'. No one just owns a cell phone – they have a Cable and Wireless phone, a Digicel phone or a Centennial (sometimes called MiPhone). In turn, everyone has strong opinions about these companies, whose advertising, hoardings and sponsorship dominate contemporary Jamaica. These companies are not just tokens of academic debate about capitalism or even telecommunication; they are major figures within the Jamaican landscape.

What could be called the prehistory of telecommunication ended only around 1987, when areas such as Orange Valley, the site of our rural ethnography, possessed one rather dilapidated public phone box and seven business phones within the town proper; this situation did not improve until the mid-1990s, when landlines were installed within many of the households in the main town.

Comparing the telecommunication situation between 1993 and 2003, the area went from an almost complete absence of phones to comprehensive access. In fact, the entire island ended 2004 with 2 million subscribers to cell phone networks. A recent media survey suggested that 86 per cent of Jamaicans over age fifteen own a cell phone, while only 7 per cent of households rely entirely on landlines. In 2003, 75.9 per cent of all phone service was through cell phones (OUR 2004). But five years ago these figures would have been hardly imaginable. There may well be a global transformation going on, with equivalent titanic struggles between companies played out across the world, but for Jamaica no one is concerned with those other battles. It is the sheer grandeur of the gladiatorial contest of the last three years in Jamaica, between the great incumbent Goliath and the young upstart David, which captures the imagination.

Cable and Wireless

Any discussion of telecommunication in the Caribbean must begin with Cable and
Wireless (C&W), a British company that can be credited with the introduction of
the submarine telegraph, which was the first modern telecommunication device in
Jamaica (Maurer 2001). Today, as throughout its 128 years in Jamaica, C&W dom-
inates the supply of communications. It is the provider of almost all fixed lines,
with around 100,000 commercial and 400,000 residential lines, more than half the
households in the country. It is a supplier of Internet services, as the largest
Internet Service Provider (ISP), and it was the original cell phone provider,
although, as we shall see, in that sector it is a rival company, Digicel, that domi-
nates the market.

In 1987 the Jamaican government more or less transferred its moribund
domestic telecom's provision to C&W. This transfer was fairly ambiguous but provided C&W with a guaranteed after-profit return on equity and exclusivity over
most telecommunications for twenty-five years (Wint 1996). As a privatization,
this was hardly vanguard liberalization and produced a chorus of complaints from
those who felt they had been unfairly excluded from this 'market'. Phillip
Paulwell, the Minister of Information and Technology, who has dominated policy
since his appointment in 1993, opted for a more genuine liberalization. Under
attack from ISPs such as Infochan, who originally were excluded from access to
the telephone system as well as new World Trade Organization (WTO) moves
towards liberalizing the telecoms sector,[1] C&W and the Jamaican government
renegotiated their contract in 2000. This too was ambiguous and there has been
almost continual argument in the courts about the precise nature of C&W's
monopoly ever since. A key player has become the Office of Utilities Regulation
(OUR), which is supported by overseas aid[2] and has tended to take on quite a high
public profile,[3] complemented by the Fair Trading Commission and the
Broadcasting Commission. Even compared to the more affluent Caribbean states
of Barbados and Trinidad, 'Jamaica has over a decade achieved a substantial
degree of embedded regulation' (Stirton and Lodge 2002: 4).

As Miller and Slater (2000) observed in Trinidad, C&W have been in some
ways a model of conservative commercial interests, often becoming the bottleneck
for potential development, and a company that is seen by many as taking several
Caribbean countries 'to the cleaners' (Stirton and Lodge 2002), although within
business circles they may be viewed more simply as having followed the obvious
interests of an incumbent company. In practice, much that has transpired is beyond
their control. For example, up to recently the telecommunication system has been
bankrolled by the somewhat arbitrary provision by the USA of money for the local
termination of international calls, a windfall that for some time left C&W with
little incentive to do anything but gratefully accept this significant income. By

1997, when this income amounted to $US6 billion worldwide, the USA decided to radically and unilaterally reduce these payments, an act that completely transformed the local picture in Jamaica. In short, this was not a negotiation or something the local companies controlled. It was simply the local impact of decisions that were being made by the US government as to who should benefit from what part of an international phone call.

This is but one example that indicates the rather arbitrary way in which the concepts of 'costs' and 'fairness' works within telecoms, a point that becomes still more evident on close inspection of local debates between the OUR and the telecommunication companies. As a regulator this body has responsibility to ensure 'fairness'. For example, it needs to make sure that companies receive a reasonable return on costs and investments but not in such a manner as to prevent competition. But the trouble is that one can calculate costs a hundred different ways, depending on what is counted within the frame of evaluation and what is regarded as an externality. For example, if in a system of fibre-optic cable the 'cost' of a call is the same whether it is to the house next door or to China, the question then becomes whether it is reasonable to charge more for long-distance calls on the basis of investments and international payments and, if so, which calls should be included. It is clear on the OUR website that companies make all sorts of claims to costs that often bear little relation to each other or to the calculations of the OUR. In this, the micro-picture reflects the global picture. The $US125 billion gambled worldwide on licences for third-generation phones is generally regarded as the biggest business risk of all time.

To follow through the Jamaican example, C&W argued that the government has neglected to protect what was left of this income stream. Even after the radical reduction, US payments for terminations represented more than the profits on their domestic and mobile phone system combined. But by 2004, while India charged $US0.24 and most Europeans around $US0.10 per termination, in Jamaica full liberalization allowed small companies to undercut C&W and thereby reduce payment to a mere $US0.017 (1.7 cents) per call, barely more than the minimum $US0.01 the regulations grant C&W as owners of the system. This, C&W claims, not only devastated their income in favour of companies that have no commitment to invest in Jamaica, but deprives Jamaica as a whole of desperately needed foreign exchange. C&W (personal communication) used this example to claim that Jamaica represented a failed rather than successful liberalization. It should be clear that this was not the familiar form of liberalization in which the government opened up licences for commercial competition by other cell phone companies. It was in the back-room deals where the government opened up the dissemination of moneys that derived from a unilateral US government decision about termination of calls.

All of this matters a great deal because, from another perspective, this easy money had had unintended negative effects. C&W claimed they had used it to subsidize the local landline system, so that in 2001 monthly rental was a mere $JA280 (then $US5).[4] When it then sought to double the cost of phone rentals in a move towards recouping actual costs, the public assumed that they were suddenly being massively overcharged. The point of this story is that one of the main reasons why this company is seen as having a particular character comes out of a rather fortuitous history. Much of this history is not really the responsibility of the company, but from the perspective of consumers none of this mattered. They simply saw it as symptomatic of what they increasing viewed as the company's complacent and arrogant character. We heard a host of reports during our research of C&W's sluggish provision and response to problems. One of the worst examples involved a primary school in Orange Valley, which told us how it had spent decades trying to obtain a telephone line and had recently had to return a grant for Internet supply because it could not obtain a line despite company promises to the school and the government that it would provide schools with access (see also Chapter 7).

In general, C&W retained the opprobrium associated with the oppressive nature of big corporations and historical relationship with colonialism, such that field-work on C&W was a master lesson in the rich discourse of Jamaican expletives. While official figures gave C&W a presence in the cell phone market of around 17 per cent, in Orange Valley it was virtually non-existent in mid-2004. In Portmore retail phonecard sellers most often gave us the figure of 10 per cent for sale of their cell phone cards. We also heard countless stories about households giving up their landlines, which suggested that the official figures for this practice were rather conservative (for relative prices, see Table 2.1). With respect to the company's claim to have maintained relatively cheap landline rentals, now at $JA500, most people noted that in other countries such rentals cover the cost of most local calls. Given the small quota provided by the company, most households pay monthly bills four or five times this rental rate even when they see themselves as being abstemious in usage. Finally, the policy of charging for every call on top of the flat rate for Internet calls meant that the blame for the lack of Internet development in the country was largely laid at their door. As a result, further price rises in phone rentals in 2004, though keeping these well below the $JA1,400 to $JA1,500 that C&W regards as the true cost of maintenance, were greeted by a cartoon in the *Gleaner* (30 January 2004) stating 'Rahtid [a Jamaican expletive], lookhowah putting myself outa business.'

C&W's profitability locally has been something of a roller coaster in recent years, something more than matched by the recent financial history of its parent company. Nevertheless, in 2004 C&W still looked like a company determined to keep its corner and continued to invest in Jamaica. According to Whitehorne (2003), C&W paid $JA2 billion a year in taxation, another $JA300 million on advertising and promotion and employed 2,000 people in 2003. Having already

Table 2.1 2004 Telephone Charges

Landline		
Business:	Installation	$JA940
	Monthly rental	$JA1,250
Domestic:	Installation	$JA660
	Monthly rental (including 60 minutes of free intra-parish calls)	$JA500*
Calls		
International		$JA15.75/minute
National		$JA1.00/minute†
To C&W cell phone		$JA7.00/minute
To Digicel cell phone		$JA10.00/minute
Cell Phone (C&W)		
International		$JA18.00/minute
To C&W landline		$JA7/minute
To C&W cell phone		$JA7/minute
To Digicel cell phone		$JA17.70/minute
Cell Phone (Digicel)		
International		$JA17.75/minute
To Digicel		$JA8/minute
To C&W (land or cell)		$JA15.80/minute

* Nearly double the 2001 rental of $JA280.

† Lower for intra-parish calls.

invested $JA40 billion in infrastructure, they were committed to spending a further $JA6 billion. They secured $US92 million from Canadian and UK banks for a programme to expand GPRS (General Packet Radio Services) and in 2004 C&W's credit rating allowed the company to borrow on exactly the same terms as the Jamaican government. The background to all this was the continued need to invest in new 'generations' of phone technology (see Appendix).

C&W also hoped that investment in philanthropy would become the explicit and recognized arm of what they felt was an unappreciated investment in the country's infrastructure. In 2003 C&W gave out $JA200 million in sponsorship, which included a C&W foundation that supported various philanthropic activities aimed at education, such as a school website competition, and a wide range of sports and cultural events. The problem was whether philanthropy and sponsorship, which made them one of the most high-profile companies in Jamaica, could compensate for long-standing antipathy. Moreover, many people still felt that C&W remained an unresponsive company; a new housing estate still expected to wait years for a phone system. According to the OUR, only 55.6 per cent of libraries, 21.6 per cent of post offices and 36.9 per cent of health centres have a telephone service (Sullivan 2003). Nonetheless, by late 2004 C&W's reputation received a boost when their phones fared better than their rival Digicel under the ravages of Hurricane Ivan. They developed a popular campaign for a two-for-one handset deal as well as repackaging the appeal of landlines, a campaign called 'Home Fone – your comfort zone', where 'time is always on your side'. As a result, we witnessed slight signs of revival in our fieldwork. In addition, the new president, Jaqueline Holding, arrived in 2004 to take on a workforce that by then had been reduced from 4,700 to 1,600 staff, radically simplifying its fifteen layers of hierarchy. Perhaps most telling was the appointment of Stephen Brewer as the chief executive of their mobile division (*Gleaner* 6 February 2004). Brewer was previously responsible for rescuing another incumbent media service, Eircell in the Republic of Ireland, which developed from 100,000 customers to 1.5 million customers and subsequently prepared its sale to Vodaphone for $US3.4 billion dollars. When we consider the primary cause of C&W's problems, the rise of Digicel, this was a strategic move.

Digicel

While in Ireland, Stephen Brewer would have witnessed the rise of Denis O'Brian, one of the 'Celtic tigers'. O'Brian, at one time personal assistant to Tony Ryan of Ryan Air, made his first fortune through companies formed on the basis of the deregulation of media in Ireland. It was the proceeds from the sale of these Irish media companies that led him to seek investment in other regions that were liberalizing their telecoms markets. The Caribbean, which had remained a virtual monopoly fiefdom of C&W, looked ideal. Trinidad was expected to move first, but when it failed to follow through on deregulation O'Brian turned to Jamaica. In 2000 Jamaica auctioned off two new cellular licences. One of these went to Centennial, but the key new player was Mossel Ltd (trading as 'Digicel'), which was owned by O'Brian.[5]

In contrast to their first choice of Trinidad, Jamaica's economy was in a far more perilous state and had an unenviable reputation for crime and violence. Yet it was evident that C&W was extremely unpopular. Digicel decided to develop a high-quality GSM (Global System for Mobile) roaming service, with Jamaica as the entry point to the rest of the Caribbean. In the end, they placed a bid of $US47.5 million, a good deal more than originally intended for a country that several of the key figures had never even visited at that time. O'Brian financed the entire endeavour. Only after they were established did they manage to persuade the World Bank in March of 2001 to bankroll its commitment to media liberalization by providing an equity loan of $US46 million, although the bank cautioned that growth estimates beyond 100,000 subscribers were too optimistic. Still, in a situation where only 6.5 per cent of the population had mobile and 20 per cent fixed line access, the World Bank (see below) surmised that 'It would also provide a demonstration effect, showing other Governments in the region that the liberalization of their telecommunications sector will benefit their population and could be followed by international capital inflows.'

Not surprisingly, C&W were as obstructive as possible – after all, no one could operate without linking to their fixed line system and they stymied Digicel's original plans for an international roaming system, which was delayed until 2004. In the meantime, Digicel faced the task of establishing everything from efficient call centres, to the importation of special equipment, building robust towers and training all manner of personnel. By dint of almost a 'frontier entrepreneur' attitude of considerable and evidently infectious enthusiasm, 120 towers, forty dealers and twelve stores were in place in record time, at a cost of $US400 million. Digicel started trading in April 2001, achieving their first year's target of 100,000 customers within two months. Just prior to this launch, C&W aggressively marketed their cell phones and hugely expanded their distribution, but without the supportive infrastructure their reception and reliability became notoriously poor, which ultimately helped Digicel achieve its reputation for higher quality. Individuals working in the shops at the time of the launch told us of their shock at being inundated by demand. Digicel lowered international charges by 30 per cent to $JA20 and then both companies settled at $JA17.70 to $JA18.00, which remained the price thereafter. By the end of 2002, Digicel overtook C&W, reaching 600,000 subscribers, and expanded to 245 GSM cell sites, which gave them 70 per cent of the coverage island-wide. Their 400 employees were supplemented by a much more extensive network of independent dealers.

Boyett and Currie (2004) compare the original aims of the company with what actually transpired. The starting principles were summarized as follows:

1. To establish and develop rapidly a highly profitable cell phone company in Jamaica by concentrating on providing a better quality of service than that previously available.
2. To float and sell on the company as soon as its profitability levels were significantly attractive, creating considerable gain for the start-up investors (mainly the Chairman and executive managers).
3. To construct a flat and flexible organization that mirrored the high technology and innovative companies of North American and European experience.
4. To 'Jamaicanize' the company through devolving management responsibility from the Irish middle management to locally recruited middle managers, allowing the Irish to be withdrawn over a fairly short time frame. (Boyett and Currie, 2004: 55)

In practice, Boyett and Currie argue that Digicel's success hinged upon the ability of the Irish executives to ditch these initial principles and appreciate that

'Jamaicanization' would involve very different processes from those originally envisaged. The Irish pushed their new flat management structure, eliminating tired old hierarchies in what they saw as a relaxed and easy-going region. But this type of 'modernity' demands highly developed and self-confident infrastructures with many protective elements, and would have been a disaster in the fragile condition of emergent Jamaican management, with potential for confusion and corruption. Digicel had to compromise, to a degree, and re-establish the more hierarchical system Jamaicans were used to. This compromise worked best when hiring Jamaican managers with experience of working in the USA, who could mediate between their 'modernist' sensibility and traditional Jamaican management and established clear structures of authority.

The other side to this process was the ability of Jamaican entrepreneurs and managers to adapt to 'Irish' Digicel, who hoped to escape from the colonial connotations of the British and be seen as 'Jamaican' despite the vastly longer presence of C&W. The Jamaican Harry Smith, fresh from a highly successful marketing of Red Stripe beer, produced much of the astute image construction Digicel employed, ranging from colours resonant of the Jamaican flag and Rastafarianism, which contrasted with the conservative blue and white of C&W. Digicel also carefully targeted sponsorship of local culture, media and sports. Their drive for island-wide rural coverage was helped by local entrepreneurs who, in one case, liquidated a series of successful grocery stores in order to invest heavily in opening up retail outlets in the countryside. Again, the reasons for their success were not always those anticipated. Over the course of a year we never met a low-income Jamaican consumer who even knew that Digicel was an Irish company (apart from those actually employed by them). What had proved more important were local Jamaicans persuading the company to create longer term local ambitions before expanding to the rest of the Caribbean, and by 2004 Digicel had an extraordinary local presence. A typical example was the massive popularity of the television programme 'Rising Stars', based on the 'pop idol' format, which depended upon the public voting via their cell phones for aspiring musical performers. Digicel also competed with C&W over philanthropy and cultural sponsorship, such that it was very hard in 2004 to find any major musical or sporting event in Jamaica that was not sponsored by one or other company.

One of Digicel's most effective weapons was its pricing structure, although this is the factor that should have favoured the incumbent. When Digicel was launched, the consumer had a choice between a landline call at $JA0.21 per minute and a Digicel phone that would cost $JA10 a minute to that landline and $JA8 to phone another Digicel cell phone. In order to succeed, Digicel needed to turn this around. Digicel's first move was to provide billing by the second rather than the minute. It continued with various astute moves. They offered $JA1,000 phone credit with the purchase of a new phone during the 2003 Christmas season and throughout 2004

Digicel doubled the first prepaid card their customers purchased each month, by far the most talked about promotion during our fieldwork. In addition, they constantly offered new services on a kind of loss-leader basis, such as free texting for a time (before it settled into a fee of $JA3 per text). In 2003 they also introduced free Internet access through the phone. In contrast, C&W launched on a fee-paying basis. Digicel only began charging for Internet access on 12 July 2004, by which time a surprising number of low-income Jamaicans seemed to be aware of and had used this service, even in the rural hinterlands. This may have been helped by Digicel's appropriation of the Internet as a model for cell phone usage, with telephone services advertised as ranging from chat rooms to datelines to downloading ringtones. Usage was reported at 14,000 downloads a day (Digicel, personal communication). By mid-2004 C&W had almost ceased to be a cell phone operator in Orange Valley and had become the smaller network in general. This meant that in 2004 the higher costs of cross-company calls had been transformed from Digicel's main liability into their main asset.

With a customer base of nearly a million and a half achieved in three years, profits that secured further long-term borrowing, coverage of 97 per cent of Jamaica, 200 retail outlets, and most of what was required to launch its attempt to repeat the Jamaican story in the rest of the Caribbean, by 2004 Digicel had surpassed almost all its ambitions. In 2003 they were already in Grenada and Aruba and were trying to secure a place in the more lucrative markets of Barbados and Trinidad, although C&W, presumably somewhat chastened by the Jamaican story, were making much more serious efforts to bolster their advantages as the incumbent prior to Digicel's actual entry. In June the *Gleaner* (2 June 2004) reported that regional subscribers were spending an average of $US23 per month providing a monthly revenue of $US33.35 million. The *Observer* (16 June 2004) estimated that Digicel employed close to 1,000 people throughout its seven operation centres within the Caribbean.

Yet by 2004 there were other straws in the wind, heralded by the OUR's concern that Digicel might be becoming a monopoly. This would have been a travesty. More plausible, however, were claims by smaller companies that the situation in Jamaica was approaching a duopoly. On closer examination, the price structure of the two main companies had settled into near conformity across the board. In several respects Digicel had become an incumbent, and the question was whether it would subsequently start to adopt the conservatism often associated with incumbents as opposed to the radicalism that characterized its launch.

From the perspective of our ethnography, Digicel is the central character in this volume's story because it successfully targeted the remote rural areas such as Orange Valley and the less affluent populations in Marshfield, a low-income settlement within Portmore, which were the two locations of our fieldwork (see Chapter 3). Their sensitivity to low-income conditions was again evident in the hugely successful launch in 2004 of the 'call-me' text (see Chapter 6), which allowed users without credit to try and find users with credit to bear the cost of their call, a facility that quickly came to dominate almost all texting in Jamaica. Perhaps the most extraordinary ethnographic finding was the passion with which these two companies were described. Using idioms taken from the dominant Pentecostalism (Austin-Broos 1997), there was a feeling listening to some people that C&W had reserved itself a special place in hell and damnation. In contrast, in our first week of fieldwork an elderly man in Orange Valley made the rather extreme claim that 'first there is God, then Digicel'. It was also noticeable that the many Digicel employees we met were also rather effusive about the wonders of their company culture, for example their 'fun days'. They tended to wear the Digicel logo and capitalize on their association because of the high regard in which the public held them, although C&W probably retained more affection in higher-income, urban and business circles. This is where the story of company rivalry really did take on the structure of heroes and villains. But one should be careful about reading too much into this. However apparently entrenched, clever cost-cutting has a way of making such deep-seated opinions suddenly less important. People who had used every expletive against C&W were suddenly tempted by a new special offer on handsets, so we are aware that things may yet change again quite radically. The point is rather that these companies were much more than just phone companies. Each had a place in public discourse as objectifications of the values and concerns of the population at large, characters through which people thought about good and evil, fairness and oppression, conservatism and modernity.

Other Players

Oceanic Digital Communications, a holding company backed by New York-based SAC Capital Associates, acquired a cellular licence at the same time as Digicel. Unable to finance operations due to the drying up of capital following the burst of the Internet bubble, it seemed destined to fade away. To the surprise of most operators (including, one suspects, Oceanic itself), the Inter-American Development Bank came up with $US30 million worth of financing. Notwithstanding the remarks just made about impending duopoly, it is hard to see quite why the bank saw this as a key development project. Inspection of the loan documents suggests an impressive lack of understanding of the local situation (IADB 2004). Oceanic had previously garnered only around 85,000 customers, based on metropolitan coverage. With the new finance and a commitment to island-wide coverage, it relaunched as MiPhone with an advertising campaign in 2004 that rivalled those of the the two market leaders, based on undercutting prices for internal calls ($JA4 per minute) and for international calls ($JA14 per minute). It was also trying to develop new initiatives, such as internal networks on new housing estates and a flat-rate unlimited call system for businesses. In the longer term what may matter more is that its licence was for a CDMA (see Appendix) rather than GSM system, which points to a potential advantage in the future since CDMA is the system that is likely to dominate the next generation of phones. The other name to suddenly appear in this field in 2004 is not just big, but the biggest, AT&T. In the absence of competition, the US giant, acquired by Cingular in 2004, snapped up a licence, which the government decided would help push liberalization further, for a mere $US6 million. AT&T claimed that it would focus on networking the tourist resorts prior to looking at Kingston and other possibilities. The name alone certainly gives the two major companies something to worry about. This portrayal can therefore only be a snapshot of a highly dynamic situation.

The Cost of the Cell Phone

Essential to understanding the experience of these phone systems is the quite radical differences in pricing, especially between landlines and cell phones (see Table 2.1). In 2004, a cross-company cell phone call cost around seventeen times that of a landline-to-landline call and nearly as much as an international call. Based on research on behalf of the OUR, Market Research Services (personal communication) carried out interviews with 1,200 Jamaicans between December 2003 and January 2004 and found that 86 per cent of those surveyed used a cell phone, with an average of three phones per household. Even in the fifteen to seventeen age group the figure is 70 per cent. The only lower figure are those aged over fifty-five with 55 per cent. Overall 55 per cent of households have only a cell phone, 38 per cent both landlines and cell phones and only 7 per cent have only landlines. With respect to capabilities 98 per cent are C&W. For those with cell phones 70 per cent have only Digicel, 17 per cent only C&W, 9 per cent both Digicel and C&W and 2 per cent Oceanic phones. Digicel is considered by 77 per cent to be their principal phone. On their phone 91 per cent say they have text and 26 per cent Internet. Text is used daily by 27 per cent, Internet by 10 per cent, 'call-me' texts are sent by 82 per cent (see also Chapter 6). Of cell phone customers, 98 per cent exclusively use prepaid phonecards, and 2 per cent use post-paid bills. Digicel (personal communication) estimates that their cards and vouchers are now available in around 5,000 outlets and that they sell over 2 million phonecards per week, of which 89 per cent cost around $JA125, which is the $JA100 for use on the phone plus government tax and retailers' profits. Cards are sold in denominations of $JA100, $JA200, $JA500, $JA1,000 and $JA5,000.

Put together, these figures add up to something of a conundrum. They may seem less surprising in a place such as Scandinavia or California, but in Jamaica such charges can constitute a significant proportion of an individual's weekly budget.

The same survey confirmed our findings that most Jamaicans claim that their choices are dictated by the desire to save money. Given that claim, it is particularly odd that, despite the vastly greater cost of using a cell phone over a landline, only 7 per cent of households use landlines exclusively and 92 per cent use their cell phone from home. This is especially difficult to explain because the primary cost of a landline is the rent, which includes a local free call quota. How can Jamaicans be making their choices on the basis of cost when an ordinary cross-company cell phone call costs as much as an international call? Indeed, even a standard call from a landline to a Digicel phone, at $JA10 a minute, and a standard Digicel-to-Digicel call, at $JA8, look exorbitant compared with calls between landlines. Landlines also remain a cheaper way to call abroad. The bottom line is that, even as households typically claimed they adopted the cell phone in order to save money, our evidence is that, even when adding in rental charges, an average household with three cell phones is spending a whole lot more than it used to because of its adoption of the cell phone. Clearly, then, the actual reasons behind this pattern of usage were not consistent with the claims made by users and could not be reduced to choices made on price alone. For present purposes, we simply wish to point this out as an example of why we need the wider ethnography of usage to help account for the distribution of phones discussed in this chapter. It is only later in this volume, when we have discussed the way Jamaican households operate, that we shall be able to account for this discrepancy between what people say and what they do.

Other Media

One reason for starting our volume with a description of the companies is that we have to allow for the degree to which current trends are the product of commercial and governmental decisions as opposed to the preferences of users. At present there is a marked contrast between our findings in Jamaica and those of previous research in Trinidad (Miller and Slater 2000). While Trinidad took to the Internet with some alacrity, Jamaica has been relatively slow in its uptake. A recent survey commissioned by the government trade agency JAMPRO suggested that there are only 70,000 Internet connections in Jamaica and only 3 per cent of the population is online (Kirton 2003). This is significantly less than Trinidad in 1999 (Miller and Slater 2000). Indeed, the contrast that emerges from the ethnography is still greater since our qualitative work suggested much greater sharing of Internet connections in Trinidad than in Jamaica (Miller and Horst 2005). The stark contrast is with the cell phone, where Jamaica currently surpasses usage in Trinidad despite much lower income levels in Jamaica, although this in part must reflect the fact that Trinidad is only now opening up to companies such as Digicel.

With regard to the Internet in Jamaica, half the connections are with Cable and Wireless and the rest are with half a dozen smaller companies. Costs for one hour's access at an Internet cafe also linger around US$1.50 while one month's subscription for a dial-up modem service is around US$40. Most of the activity is based around tourism and, indeed, many 'Jamaican' sites are actually hosted in the USA (Allen Consulting Group 2002). While many countries with lower GDP seem to have spawned Internet cafes at every street corner, this is certainly not true of Jamaica. In Portmore, with 200,000 people, there are three commercial and one NGO-based Internet cafe, and it is unlikely that most people in Orange Valley have ever come across one. Much of the blame for this lack of usage is placed with C&W and its pricing scheme. Government officials and informed users assume that a new cable planned for 2006 and the associated competition will make a considerable difference. However, in Portmore even an NGO-backed free-access site had some trouble establishing itself suggesting that there are more fundamental questions about the nature of demand at issue here (Miller and Horst 2005).

This has an important bearing on this volume if in the long term it proves to be the more individualized and private cell phone that becomes the preferred route of data access even when the price of both computers and access radically falls. Our evidence is that, while the Internet through the computer is subject to very slow adoption, the Internet through the phone has been rapidly appropriated. A problem here, as elsewhere, is that most web pages are written in HTML (Hypertext Mark-up Language) and incorporate fancy designs not suited to the small cell phone screens, and resources in WAP (Wireless Application Protocol) written for this purpose remain limited. In Japan the highly successful NTT DoCoMo company with its i-Mode devices uses a compact version of HTML, called CHTML, rather than WAP and has had considerable success with these locally (Ito et al. 2005). The general attraction of data access through the individual cell phone was the subject of perhaps the biggest gamble in business history. With some $US200 billion spent on the development of 3G (third-generation) phones, this, so far, doesn't look like much of a bet, given that, at least in Europe, the main uptake has been by customers looking for cheap but conventional voice calls (*The Economist* 2004b). But then the history of telecommunications has never gone according to plan. Who really predicted the success of texting or that the market leader for texting would be the Philippines (Pertierra et al. 2002)? It is anthropological studies that seem required to account for why by 2004 Internet access by phone was coming to surpass that by computers. Jamaica also seems to be heading in the direction of a clear preference for handsets, but this may be for completely different reasons. Again, our assessment of this will emerge from our ethnographic material on usage of the phone in subsequent chapters, but in brief we shall argue that, as in the Japanese case, there may be quite particular affinities between the cell phone and traditional forms of Jamaican communication. As a result, it may turn out that it is a combination of very high-income countries such as Finland or Japan and quite low-income countries such as Jamaica that turn out to be in the vanguard of Internet access through the phone rather than through the computer.

There are also alternative routes to Internet access, such as satellite and local cable. Given the problem of bypassing C&W, one might have predicted that they would already be rather more important than they are. In practice, taking Internet access from satellite is far more expensive than from cable, and the government decision to parcel out this sector into very small regions, each with two licensees, has made the business model for local cable television supply also uncertain. There is considerable discussion about VoIP (Voice-over Internet Protocol) amongst those involved in the telecoms industry. The assumption is that once people have good Internet access they can use this to obtain free international calls bypassing the phone companies. But this prospect has been true globally for many years without much effect. As we write, the SKYPE phenomenon, which is one such system, seems to be finally turning into a genuine mass movement, but given the lack of computers in Jamaica this will only become significant if it turns out that SKYPE itself stimulates demand for computers rather than piggybacking on prior computer sales.

According to the regular surveys by Market Research Services (2002), the most ubiquitous medium in the country is radio, at 1,920,000 listeners, followed by television at 970,800, which also includes cable television, which is legally supplied to 268,000. For radio the key stations are Irie FM and RJR, each with about 25 per cent of the market. Love FM, a religious station, commands 13 per cent of the listeners, followed by half a dozen others, including the most fashionable station in 2004, ZIP FM. For television there are two main local stations, TVJ and CVM; TVJ has 35.6 per cent of the market and CVM 27.1 per cent. Cable accounts for 36.6 per cent of the viewing public, including several popular US-based evangelical channels. Indeed, it is US evangelical stations rather than reggae or dancehall that one tends to hear emerging from houses as one walks the streets of Orange Valley and, to a lesser extent, Marshfield. Easily the most watched programme is the evening prime-time news, with three times the audience of any other programme. The female television audience is somewhat larger than the male and class does not appear to play a significant role in television viewing.

The figures for newspaper readership based on claimed reading rather than purchases were far larger than our ethnography would suggest. The *Star* has the largest daily readership, and probably the main low-income readership at 512,000 and the *Gleaner* the largest Sunday readership, at 590,000. The *Observer* follows. One reason for being cautious of these figures is that Don Anderson's Market Research Services survey claims a 19,000 readership for the *Portmore Star,* while the paper itself only claims a circulation of 2,100. Our ethnography suggested that the newspaper readership in Orange Valley was limited, and they were sold primarily out of one shop. It is more extensive in Marshfield. All of these figures need to be borne in mind later on in this volume when we consider the cell phone in terms of the larger 'communication ecology' that characterizes Jamaican life.

The Government

Although the focus of this chapter has been on commerce and technology, the state has clearly been a key player in the provision of telecommunications. So much has depended upon when, where and whether the government issued licences for cellular or cable. The fact that Digicel came into Jamaica rather than Trinidad was entirely based on this factor. The OUR, as noted, has been a very public regulatory body, and Minister Paulwell has personally associated himself with ICT development. Contrary to liberal business theory, it is the study of the state and regulation that seems to be at the core of understanding telecommunications as a form of contemporary capitalism, whether this is the impact of the WTO or local regulators such as the OUR. Digicel and C&W are useful exemplars of what companies can do and can fail to do, but much has depended upon the constraints and possibilities given them by the state. For example, just as in the USA companies are reluctant to upgrade expensive networks without a guarantee that regulators won't then ask them to share these at inexpensive rates (*The Economist* 23 April 2005, p. 80), C&W have similar complaints about making sure investments in Jamaica make sense, and the OUR is constantly reminded of the interests of the businesses. But it is also the same regulators who in retrospect could have done much more to ensure that C&W paid more attention to the welfare of the population than to its profits in the longer term. For example, in some other countries the spread of the cell phone has been limited by the decision of local governments to use handsets as a means to earn tax income rather than supporting subsidies by companies intended to achieve rapid adoption of the technology (*Economist* 2005b: 11).

The way the government understands the current situation is probably best reflected in its tentative Universal Access Plan, a plan we discussed at some length with various government officials. In effect, we were told that this plan rested on the government's conviction that the combination of licensing and commerce has solved the problem of phone access, given that just about anyone who wants a phone in Jamaica today can purchase one. Instead, the government has seen its responsibility as now focused upon data access through the Internet, which it feels ought to be regarded as subject to the ambition of universal access. Yet, despite the success of commercially driven phone distribution, the government's plan is based on taxing the successful telecoms companies and using the money to launch a largely state-based series of initiatives for Internet access. Not surprisingly, this prospect is not well received by the commercial bodies concerned. From the government's perspective, however, there are key areas of deep concern that it has prioritized, such as education. Conversations with government officials suggest that there is a desperate hope that somehow telecoms can be turned into at least a funding stream, if not a general panacea, based around virtual teaching (see also Miller and Horst 2005).

In other respects, groups such as the Telecommunication Advisory Council and CITO (Central Information Technology Office) established by Government of Jamaica (2002), have been responsible for trying to move forward on sections such as e-government with some success. By 2004 it was becoming evident that there could not be a strict separation between Internet and phone and there were some early experiments with tax alerts from text messaging. Surprisingly, despite its initial flourishing, the future of the handset as a medium of data access is not being considered seriously at a government level. What is very noticeable compared with the preliminary results coming from our sister projects in places such as South Africa (Skuse and Cousins 2005) is that the state's importance lies in its role at a macro level of issuing licences, regulation and policy. Unlike these other regions, the state is almost completely absent with respect to our participatory ethnography since the level of interaction between ordinary low-income citizens and the state is minimal (see Chapter 8).

Conclusions

There is a temptation to think that what is explored in the rest of this volume by us as anthropologists is the study of 'culture', while what has been presented in this chapter is the study of the functional relationship between institutions and structures. This would be entirely mistaken (Miller and Slater 2005). As Miller (1997) argued on the basis of a study of business in Trinidad, we are dealing here not with capitalism, but capitalisms, and often localized capitalisms to boot. In general, and as one can see in the correspondence published on the OUR website, the claim that there is some kind of science that could, for example, determine the true and proper price for a telecoms service is actually exposed by the almost arbitrary way in which each interest group tries to define objects such as costs or fairness. Similarly, the behaviour of major companies such as C&W and Digicel is constantly being interpreted in terms of cultural generalities, such as Jamaican hierarchy or the entrepreneurship of 'Celtic tigers'. It is only when Boyett and Curie (2004) undertake detailed qualitative work on what has been called the 'culture' of capitalist companies such as Digicel that much of what we can observe at a commercial level makes sense.

On the other hand, there is a good deal here that does, indeed, depend upon structure and understanding the specific interests being served, which is why it is far too simplistic to merely reproduce the popular sense of Digicel as hero and C&W as villain. Digicel has introduced an affordable mass market for cell phones, based on a well-researched sensibility to the Jamaican market and a relatively egalitarian and liberating corporate character. This markedly contrasts with a C&W tradition that was widely regarded as insensitive, arrogant and colonial. But by 2004 informed journalists we interviewed, who had previously formed part of the chorus of praise for Digicel as the radical opponent of an incumbent monopoly, had started to talk in terms of duopoly with the implication that Digicel can now be expected to behave in a manner much closer to that of C&W. This, too, may be simplistic. After all, the implication of Boyett and Curie's (2004) work is rather that Digicel may now feel it has the power to become as egalitarian in its internal structure and innovative in its marketing as it has always wanted to be, but has been unable to achieve as yet because of the conservative traditions that dominated the Jamaica it encountered in 1999. The point is that we need both to appreciate the structural conditions, which continually change – what we should discern as the 'interests' of a firm at a particular time – and to recognize that a firm is not simply a machine for the effective realisation of those interests. It also has a particular character, ideology and tradition.

One argument against reducing recent history to some kind of structural necessity is the very different picture that emerges when one compares states within the Caribbean. Although Jamaica, Trinidad and Barbados shared the same incumbent in the form of C&W, they seem to have very different stories to tell with regard to every aspect of telecommunications, including regulation and the wider role of government, and certainly in terms of outcome (see Maurer 2001). For example, the early rise of the Internet in Trinidad (Miller and Slater 2000) contrasted with the far quicker spread of the cell phone in Jamaica. But, as we shall see, this story can be seen from several alternative angles and we are best served by looking at the picture in the round. The story is not one that is likely to settle into some kind of stasis following the momentum given by liberalization. It would actually be hard to imagine a cosy duopoly left to flourish, given the recent entry of Cingular and the revitalization of MiPhone. Everything is likely to change again with the laying of a new cable. The current degree of subsidy on handsets may not be sustainable, but there is clearly a genuine demand for mid-level sets with camera and Internet access, which, partly thanks to remittances, permeates down into low-income households (see Chapter 4). This is also an industry constantly kept on its toes by technical innovation. SKYPE suggests that voice-over telephony is finally making good on its promise, possibly linked to the advent of very cheap computers intended for the developing world, such as the new PIC (Personal Internet Communicator) recently launched by AMD. But this would bring in still further complications, such as the existence of a substantial Jamaican diaspora with considerable access to and usage of computers in North America and Europe. The only thing we can be sure about is that changes will continue to be rapid and dramatic and often unpredictable. Despite this unpredictability, we shall argue in our concluding chapter that we have a clear responsibility to draw conclusions from the evidence of this very recent past.

But the main argument against reducing the material in this chapter to a simple logic of economic or structural necessity will come with the succeeding chapters, where the focus of attention moves from supply to demand. The study of consumption will reveal many active components to consumption processes that provide equally powerful grounds for accounting for the overall pattern of usage that has emerged over the last few years. These provide further grounds for resisting the obvious conclusion of this chapter, which is that knowledge of government and commerce is sufficient for explaining and accounting for the spread of the cell phone in Jamaica, and that both current surplus and prior dearth are entirely the result of economic factors such as price, technology and availability. The story of provision and consumption are not two separate tales with one starting where the other leaves off (see Miller and Slater 2005). Even those employed in commerce would assume that successful marketing demands careful reading and understanding of the market and that the relationship between production and consumption is dynamic. It would therefore be presumptuous to draw too many conclusions from the material presented in this chapter alone, prior to its integration with other stories that emerge from the ethnography of phone consumption.

–3–

Locations

Jamaica is the third largest island in the Caribbean, with an area of 11,000 square kilometres located just 550 miles south of Miami. It gained independence from Great Britain on 6 August 1962. With its natural resources of beaches, agriculture and bauxite as well as the country's commitment to democracy, at the time of independence Jamaica was viewed as having great promise and potential. Today, however, that perception has changed. Jamaica is now the fourth most heavily indebted emerging economy with debts at 150 per cent of GDP (*Economist* 2004a: 39; World Bank 2004) and its overall economic development is patchy. Between 60 per cent and 70 per cent of the country's revenues go directly towards servicing this debt and the country remains heavily reliant on aid, a series of factors that make it difficult for Jamaica to obtain credit from international sources (Planning Institute of Jamaica 2004; World Bank 2004). Jamaica's predicament reflects a legacy of what many see as the disastrous impact of structural adjustment (Manley 1987; McAfee 1991; Bartilow 1997; Harrison 1997; Lundy 1999; Kirkpatrick and Tennant 2002; Handa and King 2003) and a long-term suspicion of Jamaica by the USA following Jamaica's attempts to develop a more socialist orientation under Michael Manley in the 1970s.

The formation of two rival political parties, the People's National Party and the Jamaica Labour Party, is seen as having contributed in great measure to sustaining crime and gang rivalry, especially in Kingston but also in outlying areas such as Spanish Town and increasingly towards May Pen in the parish of Clarendon. However, in October 2002, the People's National Party (under the leadership of former Prime Minister Percival James Patterson) won an unprecedented fourth term and there is some sense of a stabilization of politics and distancing between formal politics and the gangs. Yet retributions for the killing of key gang members of the One Order gang, which caused a series of closures by business persons and an overall high murder rate of 1,417 persons in 2004, suggested that this has some way to go. Indeed, the recent World Bank report on Jamaica saw crime as one of the principal bottlenecks in preventing a more sustained economic development, with Jamaica having the third highest rate for violent crime in the world. Many of these crimes have been attributed to the 3,940 deportees returned to Jamaica from the USA, UK and Canada after having been convicted of crimes. Task forces, such as Operation Kingfish, a coordinated effort by the Jamaica Constabulary force and their partners in the USA and UK aimed at dismantling crime networks, initiated in November of 2004, reveal the extent to which the crime that originated in the politics of garrison communities have become transnational (Planning Institute of Jamaica 2003).

According to the USAID/J-CAR (2004) Jamaica Country Strategy, unemployment remains around 15 to 17 per cent, but the World Bank (2004) contends that unemployment of fourteen- to nineteen-year-old youths in the poorest sectors of Jamaican society was 47 per cent in 2001 (21).[1] Jamaica ranks seventy-eighth amongst 174 countries in the Human Development Index (7).[2] The *Economic and Social Survey* (PIOJ 2004) reports GDP at $US234.1 billion in 2003, a growth of 2.1 per cent, but also notes consistent decline in sectors such as agriculture – down to 6.3 per cent of GDP. Nonetheless, agriculture still accounted for 21.8 per cent of the labour force in 2003. Jamaica also saw a decline in manufacturing to 13.5 per cent of GDP, with a particular fall in the apparel industry. About the only activities to sustain the economy have been bauxite extraction (for aluminium) and tourism, with visitor figures reaching 2.4 million annually. Significantly, manufacturing only provides 66,000 jobs whereas tourism supplies 387,400 jobs.

The more labour-intensive agriculture is fragile and in decline as prices for its staples, such as sugar and most recently citrus, suffer from the undercutting that follows trade liberalization (Harrison 2001). As a result, the World Bank (2004) reports that poverty in rural areas, at 24.1 per cent, is more than three times higher than in Kingston (9). Despite these difficult economic conditions, the poverty rate appears to be decreasing, quite possibly due to the rate of remittances, which have been estimated to be as high as $US1.7 billion (*Jamaican Business* March 2004, p. 13), or an average of $US1,000 a year for those families that receive them. There are also considerable internal remittances, which the World Bank observes often originate with those working in the tourist areas (2004: 45). As the World Bank notes, however, Jamaica has experienced massive skills outmigration and what is called 'the brain drain' over the past several decades, making Jamaicans one of the highest proportional sources of working immigrants into the USA. In fact, 80 per cent of those who receive a tertiary education in Jamaica emigrate, which makes recruitment of teachers and other trained staff increasingly difficult nationally. This, in turn, leads to the Jamaican government's other overwhelming concern, which is with the mass education sector, which bore the brunt of a series of highly critical internal reports in 2004 (e.g. Minott 2004). Although the World Bank (2004) reports 92 per cent enrolment in primary school, completed by 95 per cent of those enrolled, only 68 per cent of these students complete secondary school (6) and between 30 per cent and 40 per cent of students are functionally illiterate at the end of primary education (21). Not unrelated, the fertility rate among girls fifteen to nineteen years old increased to 112/1,000 in 2000, up from 102/1,000 in 1989 (USAID/J-CAR 2004: 8).

With respect to poverty, the *Economic and Social Survey 2003* (PIOJ 2004) highlights several schemes intended to assist in this area, including the high-profile National Poverty Eradication Programme. Indeed, DFID (2001) declared that 'In recent years Jamaican has probably done more than any other country in the English speaking Caribbean to define a poverty eradication strategy, identify priorities, and set up a detailed poverty monitoring scheme' (5). While there have been a series of youth, food stamp and other programmes, from the perspective of the low-income individuals we worked with only two programmes made inroads, the HEART Trust/National Training Agency (NTA) programme, which provides vocational training for adults, and the Programme of Advancement through Health and Education (PATH), which gives social and financial assistance to families with children under age seventeen, the elderly (over age sixty-five) as well as disabled, pregnant or otherwise disenfranchised persons. The benefits ranged from assistance with tuition and costs associated with schooling to food stamps. But there have also been a series of criticisms of this programme. For example the *Survey of Living Conditions 2002* (PIOJ 2003: Table 5.1) reported that only 10.5 per cent of the population had ever applied to PATH, despite the fact that many of the applications can be processed at local schools. Although we met a number of individuals during our ethnography (especially in Orange Valley) who knew about and had at some point utilized the PATH programme, there was often confusion over benefits as well as recourse in the event that there was an error with attendance or if the student was recorded at the wrong school.

In effect, HEART and PATH were almost the only government programmes that individuals felt were accessible, and our ethnography revealed a situation where the relationship between the population and the state remains highly attenuated (see McDonald 2002). Most Jamaicans receive virtually no welfare benefits of any kind and thereby subsidize their own children's education, particularly after Grade 6. The only free health care is often distant, overcrowded, understaffed and poorly supplied and very few people we encountered had ever received any direct financial aid from the government. Apart from the occasional tax and their use of basic infrastructure, such as roads and education, the state is a dim and distant institution. Similarly (and aside from a few church programmes and connections made through mission visits), very few individuals had encountered any form of NGO or development agency. For this reason, much of the development literature, which focuses almost entirely upon the roles of the state and the NGOs, seemed to have precious little relevance to our ethnographic encounter. We found a quite remarkable difference in this respect between Jamaica and, for example, the ethnographic experience of our colleagues working in South Africa (Skuse and Cousins 2005) or India (Tacchi 2005).

Despite the relatively low involvement of formal sources of support, Jamaica possesses a reasonable standard of living compared with its neighbour Haiti and some of the conditions reported by our colleagues in South Africa, Ghana and India. According to the *Jamaica Survey of Living Conditions* (PIOJ 2003), 87.1 per cent of households had electricity, 50.5 per cent exclusive use of a flush toilet and 64.5 per cent of households could access piped water, although this might be outside at a standpipe rather than inside. In terms of consumer goods, 81.9 per cent of households had a gas stove, 77.3 per cent possessed radios, 76.2 per cent owned a television and 69.5 per cent kept fridge-freezers. Another 16.4 per cent of households owned a car and 8.8 per cent computers. As with computer possession, which ranged from 19.2 per cent in Kingston to 2.7 per cent in rural areas (XVIII), there is a rural–urban divide throughout the country. One final rather revealing statistic is that, of 3,013 arrested for major crimes, only twenty-six were women (PIOJ 2003: 24.5).

This, then, is the Jamaica that comes from statistical analysis and the reports of bodies such as the World Bank and the International Monetary Fund (IMF). In the course of this volume we have reason to challenge much of this presentation. For example, the economic data are collected by questionnaires, where, if you ask people how much they earn and then how much they spend, the two figures almost inevitably differ, sometimes to a startling degree. We felt it essential to briefly provide this formal portrait, but we hope that the more informal portrait that we paint here, which is based on our own intensive research and analysis, in many ways gives a rather more satisfactory sense of the setting of this work. In the following section, we situate our own study by presenting a detailed portrait of the economic and social conditions in our two fieldwork sites.

Low-income Jamaicans: from Folk to Ghetto

Within the social sciences, what today might be considered the study of low-income Jamaicans emerged through the study of 'folk', peasant or proto-peasant cultural formations (Mintz 1985b). Beginning with Martha Beckwith's (1929) detailed description of the homes, festivals and funerary practices and Zora Neale Hurston's (1990 [1938]) account of nine night festivities, anthropologists sought to understand the everyday lives of Jamaican peasants and the cultural patterns associated with Jamaican folk culture. Edith Clarke's (1966) seminal study of three rural communities extended these early analyses by examining in detail marriage, household organization and household composition as well as mating patterns and includes one of the most commonly cited features of folk culture in Jamaica, the prominence of the females as 'heads of household'. Sidney Mintz (1974, 1985a, b) focused upon consumption, construction of markets (Mintz and Hall 1970; Mintz and Price 1985), the house–yard relationship and other aspects of the lifestyles of the land-owning proto-peasantry, including the importance of the yard as a material economic space for procuring provisions, a symbolic space (representing one's world and one's burial ground) and a mediating space between the female-dominated house and the male-dominated street (Mintz 1974; Wilson 1966; Foner 1971; see also Chevannes 2001).[3]

Many of these early anthropological and sociological studies concentrated upon understanding these new world cultures in terms of the degree to which Jamaican social structures and practices reflected African 'survivals' (Henriques 1953; Patterson 1967; Apter 1991) or the process of creolization (Mintz and Price 1992; Yelvington 2001, 2005). The much maligned M.G. Smith[4] (1983, 1984), for example, argued that Jamaica represents a plural society consisting of the 'white' elite ruling group, the 'brown' middle category and the 'black' lower, each group reflecting and retaining its origins and its own distinctive set of values, practices and institutions. Other scholars maintained that, while class position, colour, gender and other categories of difference structure the world view and experiences of different Jamaicans, they still shared the same basic values (see Robotham 1980, 1985; R.T. Smith 1988, 1996).[5] Jean Besson's (1984, 1995a, b, 1997, 2000, 2002) careful examination of family land and creolization demonstrates the complexity of the development of Jamaican society. Through her discussion of migration and transnational connections and the way that the proto-peasantry 'appropriated' and 'overturned' European institutions and created new patterns of kinship based upon the symbolic and economic value of land and property, she illustrates the difficulty of associating rural Jamaica with authentic 'folk' cultural and religious forms (see Besson and Chevannes 1996; Horst 2004a).

With the mass movement of rural Jamaicans into Kingston, looking for work and opportunity, in the 1950s and 1960s, urban communities assumed greater importance, as exemplified in the work of R.T. Smith's students, who focused upon middle- and upper-class urban Jamaicans and the ideologies that reproduce them (Alexander 1977, 1984; Austin 1983; Douglass 1992). For example, Diane Austin's (1984) comparison of working- and middle-class neighbourhoods explores the ideology behind the working class's legitimization of middle-class privilege, where she argues that class is produced and reproduced in local neighbourhoods and is perhaps even more entrenched here than in the European studies of Halsey (1972) and Bourdieu (1984). However, the study of non-elite and (in their terminology) lower-class[6] culture and social structures took on a new and heightened importance as larger proportions of Jamaicans found themselves living in conditions of poverty within a new urban environment, such as the tenement yards of western and central Kingston (Klak 1992; Levy 1996; Moser and Holland 1997; Moser 1998; Gray 2004; Rakodi 2004). New forms of patronage emerged, which were epitomized by housing provided by former Prime Minister Edward Seaga and the Jamaican Labour Party (JLP) in communities such as Tivoli Gardens. The categories of reputation and respectability also changed, particularly for men for whom reputation could not only be garnered by associated friendship networks but also through affiliation with local 'dons', who could provide protection and access to day jobs or other critical resources (Stone 1980, 1986; Eyre 1986; Harrison 1988; Gunst 1995; Harriot 2001; Robotham 2001; Sives 2002). Yet, populated by a large number of unemployed youths, Trenchtown and other (in)famous areas of this new urban formation also became the site of some of the most influential religious practices, such as Rastafarianism (see Yawney 1979; Chevannes 1994) and new forms of Pentecostalism (Austin 1984), as well as emergent reggae and dancehall musicians or 'entertainers' (Stolzhoff 2001; Cooper 2004; Stanley-Niaah 2004,).

As Deborah Thomas (2004) has recently demonstrated, the symbols of Jamaican identity today are associated with the urban ghetto and youth-based consumer culture. As she explains, 'In Jamaica, the multiracial harmony envisioned by mid-twentieth century creole nationalists was upstaged, during the 1990s, by an unapologetic blackness. Urban sound systems have stolen the limelight from rural Jamaicans' "folk" forms as Jamaican bodies – still racialized, still classed, still gendered – keep step with global time' (Thomas 2004: 269). Although Thomas's emphasis is on changing conceptions of race, culture and nation, this dichotomy between the values of youth[7] and urban expressions of 'modern blackness' and the waning salience of Creole nationalism ('out of many, one people') of yore represents an important point of departure for understanding the varying experiences of low-income Jamaicans. As we discuss in greater detail in the following sections, there has always been a rural–urban divide in Jamaica, which has implications for income levels, survival strategies and access to educational and occupational opportunities. For example, the *Jamaica Survey of Living Conditions* (PIOJ 2003) notes a large discrepancy between the income levels and living conditions of rural and urban Jamaicans, with rural Jamaicans representing the largest percentage of individuals in the lowest quintiles. However, factors such as violence, which plague urban areas, to a greater extent than rural areas, also impact access and opportunity and for this reason part of our remit was to understand the nature of low-income life and livelihoods in each context. Because this book is as much about how Jamaicans are changed by the cell phone as it is about what the cell phone becomes in the hands of Jamaicans, we acknowledge that part of this process of becoming in and through the cell phone reflects this fundamental shift in the perception of rural and urban livelihoods, the transformation from 'folk' to 'ghetto', and this is specifically why we chose our urban site, which, as we discuss below, we regard as the future of urban development in Jamaica (see Gordon et al. 1997). By outlining the specificity of cell phone use in rural and urban contexts, we hope that the focus on the cell phone makes a considered contribution to understanding the changing nature of Jamaican society.

An Introduction to the Research Sites

Our rural site, called here Orange Valley, was a place where Horst lived and visited regularly between 1994 and 2004. A central Jamaican community which had dwindled in importance since the decline of the railway which transported local crops to Kingston (*Gleaner* 1913; Jacobs 1923; Taylor 1976), Orange Valley is a farming region well known for the profusion of citrus, cocoa beans, sugar cane and basic provisions such as yams and green bananas. Green and lush, local varieties of mangoes, ackee and lime trees supplement the staple crops and diets of the area's residents and their involvement in the orange, sugar cane and cocoa industries. The area has not, however, been directly affected by either the bauxite or the tourism industry. Although the town consists of a school, police station and market and an estimated population of 500–600, most of our research was conducted in the straggling hamlets and households found in strings along roads and crests in the surrounding hill region. Based upon ethnographic evidence and information from the electoral office, we estimate that around 14,000 people living in the hinterland use Orange Valley as their transport hub and local market.

Our urban site was perhaps a less obvious choice. Typically when one thinks of urban Jamaica, images of zinc fence jungles and the 'Harder they Come' spring to mind. Indeed, central Kingston has been the site of almost all urban ethnographic research (although see Robertson 2002). In contrast, we chose an area that was low-income but not necessarily extreme in terms of violence or poverty. Rather we sought to understand the ordinariness of life as a low-income person trying to make ends meet in an urban context, in an area that potentially reflected the future of Jamaican society. The place we chose, Portmore, is one most anthropologists would have instinctively avoided as the region that most Jamaicans think of as their cultural desert. Recently made into a municipality, Portmore is located in the parish of St Catherine approximately 20 km southwest of Kingston, and is home to around 200,000 residents.[8] Originally inhabited by farmers, fishermen and plantation workers in the early 1900s, Portmore was constructed out of wasteland in order to build low-cost housing in the 1960s as an answer to overcrowding in central and western Kingston. With the help of West Indies Home Construction Ltd, the Jamaican government connected Portmore to the commercial, educational and governmental capital by building a causeway between Portmore and Newport West in Kingston. In 1969 the first housing scheme was developed, followed by eight schemes in the 1970s, six more in the 1980s and around 16,000 additional houses constructed in the 1990s, around 10,000 of which went into a new area called Greater Portmore (WIHCON, personal communication). Today Portmore contains over forty churches (several with over 2,000 members, one of 9,000), twenty-five schools, multiple shopping malls, banks, credit unions, a HEART training institute, numerous supermarkets and six fast-food restaurants. Our primary research site was located in a place we call 'Marshfield', one of Portmore's older schemes built for low-income Jamaicans migrating from Kingston. In what follows, we draw a picture of the social and economic livelihoods of each site, based partly on ethnography and partly on a more systematic questionnaire-based survey of fifty households in each site.

Orange Valley

Orange Valley[9] was once a bustling, if nondescript, market town, known for its citrus and other produce, indistinguishable from many others in the hilly interior of the parish of Clarendon. The town proper, announced only by a sign 'Welcome to Orange Valley', has two churches, which bookend the town, as well as a lane of shops and houses. Its small size hardly seems to justify the presence of the post office, police station, fire station[10] and small market. The only other feature of note is a smoothly paved two-lane bridge constructed in the mid-1990s. This bridge and particularly its walkways are widely appreciated by local residents who can still recall hanging on for dear life to the sides of the rickety wooden bridge as the country buses, trucks and other large vehicles passed. Beyond the bridge lies the town square, marked by a small lamp post in the middle of the road. This doubles as a roundabout and, quite often, a stage for one of Orange Valley's resident 'mad men', who preach, dance and act out martial arts scenes as cars and residents pass them by with apprehension and amusement.

The town mixes wooden buildings reminiscent of old-time Jamaica with modern, concrete buildings boldly painted in the latest styles and colours. Green and yellow have been a favourite combination, as well as shades of pink, purple and blue. Hand-painted signs from local businesses alternate with chains, such as banks, credit unions and the petrol station. Western Union, whose familiar black and yellow sign is viewed as a beacon of hope for many local residents, is also conveniently located adjacent to the local cell phone shop and Paymaster, a location where residents can pay their telephone, cell phone, light and water bills. There are over sixty shops, which include a barber, photographer, restaurant, bar, pharmacy and even a lingerie store, as well as twenty small temporary vending stalls. There are also three private doctors in the town, who also work at the local public clinic.

Alongside being a market and retail centre, the town is a small hub for regional transport. The taxi stand for Bethany is located next to the rum bar and pharmacy, taxis to Mountain View are parked alongside one of the local 'nix nox' (odds and ends) shops and directly in front of the grocery store and cambio are the taxis and minivans heading in the direction of May Pen (and the districts along the route). Many years ago Orange Valley residents utilized a bus route to/from Kingston, which left daily and returned in the evening teeming with people and animals, but these were traded in for the modern Jamaican transport system, which includes route taxis and small passenger vans that operate seven days a week, beginning as early as five or six in the morning and ending around eight at night, except on Sundays. Mondays and Fridays are free clinic days and the road leading up to the health centre can be quite busy as mothers arrive with their children early, often waiting until the late morning or afternoon for treatment. On Tuesdays, the heart of the activity is the police station, where residents attend court and meet with solicitors. Another set of residents place themselves at the shops or rum bars in the area, watching and gossiping about the events surrounding the local courthouse with interest. On Fridays and Saturdays, the town remains congested between the market and the town square, where residents congregate as vendors buy and sell goods.

Perhaps more than any other activity the town ebbs and flows with the arrival and departure of the schoolchildren at Orange Valley Primary School and Orange Valley Comprehensive High School (OVCHS). At the end of the school day, around twenty taxis and vans line up outside the gates as students travel to the overcrowded school from outlying districts of Orange Valley as well as neighbouring parishes. Although some of the students have participated in the nationally televised School Challenge Quiz, OVCHS caters to vocationally oriented students and is best known for its track and field programme and football, with well-supported sports days when the school's various houses compete in both sports and associated activities, such as cheer leading.[11]

In addition to the two schools, the churches in the town represent a variety of denominations, including Anglican, Baptist, Apostolic, Seventh Day Adventist, Methodist, Church of God, New Testament Church of God, Jehovah's Witness and a small revival church located in the hinterlands. There is rarely a week when one of the local churches does not hold (or is planning to host) a special rally, church prayer meeting, baptism, concert, harvest or convention. As elsewhere in Jamaica, the churches are dominated by the children and women especially those over age thirty-five, although males in between these ages can be amongst the most vociferous Christians (Austin-Broos 1997). Many of the area's local power brokers attend the Anglican and Baptist church, as well as the Church of God, a popular local form of Pentecostalism. Although not formally organized, there are also a small number of Rastafarians in the town and surrounding districts. This particular area of Clarendon is also well known for the maintenance of 'obeah', a derivation of Africanized religion, denigrated as 'witchcraft' by many Christians (Taylor 1976; Murphy 1994).

Economic Life in Orange Valley

The river that flows through the middle of Orange Valley divides the townsfolk from people who live 'over the line'. While geographically this refers to those who have to cross the shallow river, 'over the line' sets apart what some people consider to be the poorest group in the area, those without access to electricity, indoor plumbing or latrines. It is also a term that possesses moral overtones. People who live 'over the line' are considered dirty and do not 'live good', and Orange Valley residents often discuss the quarrels and lascivious behaviour of the inhabitants 'over the line'. This sensibility is so ingrained that, even when Hurricane Ivan passed over Jamaica, many individuals who live on the riverside (who are considered one cut above people living over the line) opted to wait it out at their low-lying homes rather than staying at the local primary school, because they did not want to be seen as 'mixing' with 'those type of people'.

Most people, however, live in the straggling settlements off the roads leading into the hills around Orange Valley. Although there has been some small-scale movement to new areas by renters, the districts are dominated by a series of original families who established residence through the purchase of land. These often comprise two to three main families who have intermingled considerably, and many individuals can trace their descent to at least two of the founding families in the districts. Because the districts often coincide with sets of families, a series of conclusions can be drawn about the person merely from the reputation of the family name and district. In some cases, this may be positive, families known for being quiet and peaceful, whereas other districts may signify long-term tensions over land and property. These stigmas are strong enough to affect the employment or residential prospects of individuals, who are assumed to bring with them the 'character' of their families (see Rakodi 2004).

According to our survey[12] the average household in the Orange Valley area was rather large, at 5.2 people, which included an average of 2 children under age fourteen, 2.9 adults between the ages of fifteen and sixty-four and 0.3 individuals older than sixty-five. The range was from thirteen persons to a single man. This can be compared with national figures of 3.58 for rural area (*Jamaica Survey of Living Conditions* (PIOJ 2003)) and may reflect our emphasis on distant, 'more rural' households, which tend to be larger than urban households. Over 80 per cent of homes were concrete and 87 per cent of the houses had some form of electricity, although sometimes through illegal connections, which also meant the presence of televisions and radios. Over half (56 per cent) of the residents cooked in an outside kitchen which was often covered with a tarpaulin or other makeshift structure, which made it possible for many households to cook with a stove and cooking gas. In fact, 67 per cent of the households used cooking gas on a daily basis, 23 per cent used wood and another 8 per cent used coal. In some of the rural areas coal or wood was viewed as 'backup' when the gas drums emptied. Of households surveyed, 62 per cent reported using a standpipe for water (typically located adjacent to or down the road from their house) and 33 per cent of the households piped water into their homes; 5 per cent collected water from a spring or used the river for bathing and laundry.

Alongside being a family-oriented settlement, each district is also a small-scale community and contains at least one small shop, often next to or attached to the owner's home. These small shops sell biscuits, bread or cakes, processed cheese, a variety of juices or soft drinks, washing-up liquid, toilet paper, tinned meats, soups, sweets and 'pampers' (the term for all diapers or nappies), which can be purchased individually or in small portions (such as $JA5 of toothpaste). Some shops supply rice, peas, chicken and other staples, while others double as the local rum shop. Most residents in this region practise small-scale farming, intermittent masonry or domestic work and many individuals supplement their income by selling small items from their homes, ranging from chickens and eggs to drinks, cigarettes and phonecards. Many households also rely upon credit, either formally from shops or from friends and family members (see Table 3.3). For instance, George Stone is a single man in his sixties who lives without electricity and collects water from a nearby pipe. A small-scale farmer, George's survival depends upon the sale of sugar cane, yams or other excess provisions, which results in an income of about $JA500 per week. Another $JA500 or $JA600 is earned by 'begging' friends and acquaintances in the district for a little 'change' (Robertson 2002), typically $JA100 to $JA200 at a time. However, he spends approximately $JA1,380 on food and another $JA550 on household supplies in an average week, buying soap powder, bleach or washing-up liquid in small amounts from the district shop, which are consumed over the course of one or two days. George's survival would be almost impossible without the shop's extension of credit and the receipt of a few extra dollars from acquaintances. On many days George cannot even afford $JA40 of chicken back and resorts to satiating his hunger with a meal of seasoned rice (rice with powder seasoning), yams or green bananas grown on his land.

Although the minimum wage was raised to $JA2,000 per week in September of 2003, 24 per cent of our households earned less than this sum (Table 3.1). However, 42 per cent of households earned between $JA2,000 and $JA4,000 per week. A typical wage for a worker in Orange Valley started at $JA2,000 per week for full-time work and peaked at $JA3,000 per week. This income category also included individuals who completed day labour in masonry and other construction activities, work that was often intermittent by choice as well as by circumstance. The vast majority of households earning over $JA4,000 per week were either professionals, such as teachers, or had more than one source of income or person in the household who earned money. Higher incomes generally translated into more

Table 3.1 Household Income Levels in Orange Valley, Clarendon

Under $2,000	$2,000–$4,000	$4,001–$6,000	$6,001–$8,000	Over $8,000
24%	42%	28%	6%	0%

consumer goods, such as video players, kitchen appliances, refrigerators, stereos and freezers.

The area as a whole is reliant upon remittances (see Chapter 6) from family and friends living abroad, foreign pensions and other earnings resulting from seasonal migration associated with the Farm Worker's Programme. This wide-scale dependence on remittances is evident from the approximately £UK10,000 that circulates through the local cambio and Western Union office on a daily basis.[13] This relationship between remittances and the local economy is not atypical for rural Jamaica due to the lengthy history of migration to and from Britain, Canada, the USA and other Caribbean nations (see Thomas-Hope 1992; Olwig 1993). A deeper consequence is the tendency of many in the area to feel they are somehow left behind and merely waiting their turn to experience the real life in 'foreign'.

Marshfield

Marshfield sits at the intersection of two main thoroughfares in Portmore, located in the parish of St Catherine, and is linked to the centre of Portmore by three main roads. Despite the appearance of mobility, the scheme's design seems to undermine this accessibility as there is only one main road where regular transportation travels. At the beginning of the scheme sits a series of taxi drivers, who carry passengers down the main roads, where buses ply to and from Kingston as well as Spanish Town (the parish capital of St Catherine). Here too a series of vendors take up residence selling biscuits, snacks and cold soft drinks out of igloos (portable iceboxes) and temporary stalls, while other vendors display their sugarcane, naseberries, june plums and other fruits on the sidewalk. In the evenings, many of the day's vendors leave and are replaced by the smoky drums of men cooking jerk chicken and large vats of fish tea (soup), patronized by those returning home from work.

Dressed in fitted skirts and blouses with heeled shoes or pressed trousers and company logo shirts, Marshfield's working population emerges between six and eight in the morning to catch one of the crowded buses to Kingston and Spanish Town (see Freeman 2000 for a comparison with Barbados). The better-paid employees wait for a ride in the local 'executive' buses, which are theoretically less crowded, air-conditioned and travel a non-stop route between Portmore and downtown Kingston and Half Way Tree for $JA60 (one-way). Lesser-paid employees travel in the 'white bus', or the Jamaican Urban Transit Company (JUTC) bus, for

$JA40 (one-way). A journey to 'town', as downtown Kingston is called, and Half Way Tree, or mid-Kingston (Austin-Broos 1995), can take as little as twenty-five minutes but can also last an hour or more, depending upon the traffic. The two-lane causeway is rerouted one-way into Kingston between six and nine o'clock in the morning and one-way back to Portmore between four and seven o'clock in the evening to facilitate the many commuters.[14] After the working population departs, many of the older men and women come out in their yards to sweep the veranda and pavements, chatting with a neighbour or two under the few, cherished, shady trees. Later in the day, young men in the area emerge from their slumber and begin congregating on the corners in their 'crews' while awaiting the dismissal of the students from the local high school, primary school and two basic schools. Groups of men can be perched on the walls until well into the night. As a member of the Marshfield community observes:

> What I see in Marshfield is people unemployed and they don't have anything to do and the only thing them can do is go on the corner. Marshfield is the only community where … go 24-7 and see people on the road, no matter what time a night, morning, day or evening it is. You might go in [another scheme] now you might jus see pure houses, anybody lock and gone. But no matter 2, 3 o'clock [in the morning] in Marshfield people always de pon the road. Sun too hot so them sleep in the day … You always have people everywhere in Marshfield.

In addition to being lively all hours of the night, Marshfield is a peculiar place in that, while there are a police station, fire station, library, post office and clinic, there are theoretically no formal commercial activities. In fact, until the late 1990s, with the building of Portmore Mall and other smaller shopping plazas, Marshfield residents had to travel a considerable distance for the majority of their food needs. However, residents took matters into their own hands, converting front rooms into beauty parlours, pharmacies, small shops, auto part supplies and in-home nurseries. While most of these enterprises operate without licences and within illegal extensions, local residents appreciate the convenience and, with the painting and advertisements, they have transformed what began as a monotonous row of 400 square foot single-storey identical houses into distinctive neighbourhoods with their own corner shop, while at the same time providing a source of income for many of the women, who spend their days caring for children and the house, an occupation that often reflects the lack of other job prospects.

This trend of taking matters into their own hands is a common theme in the area. When WIHCON built the original homes, residents complained about the slow construction of schools and other infrastructure in the area. They also organized a citizen's association and, in some areas, an unofficial neighbourhood watch. Residents have assumed responsibility for the cleaning of the area walls, fences and gardens, a task that is seasonally rewarded ('Christmas money') by the government through the local councillor. These tasks are carried out and organized by a series of what are called 'ends'. Ends are as much a geographic entity as they are a social group. Marshfield has a series of eight ends, beginning with Arsenal and Chelsea in the first phase and ending with Unity. Organized by what they refer to as elders, most of the members of the crews are a series of men, often unemployed or working third-shift jobs, who are visible as they sit on a wall, under a tree or on a stump or concrete slab on the corner to 'cool out'. In addition, the crews and ends come together to compete in their local football league, in dancehall-style parties and in preparing for the Christmas season, pooling together to purchase whitewash and lights with the aid of an illegal electricity connection.

While most of the crews and 'endsmen' contend that the divisions are relatively benign, outsiders to the community (and more middle-class housing schemes in Portmore itself) view Marshfield as a 'ghetto'. They associate these social constructions of 'ends' and 'elders' with garrison communities such as Tivoli Gardens and Arnette Gardens in Kingston which are affiliated with particular political parties and governed by 'dons' (Stone 1980; Sives 2002,). Despite the fact that Marshfield and many of the other housing schemes were created during Michael Manley's reign and the strong relationship between the social democratic People's National Party (PNP) and the Matalon family, who are the founders of WIHCON, who built the scheme (Judith Bruce, personal communication), there is decidedly little political affiliation in Marshfield. Many residents view politics as 'politricks' and are distrustful of any governmental benevolence. There is little to suggest that the 'ends' and 'elders' are the equivalent of dons or reflect any deeply entrenched politicization. Rather, the 'elders' are seen as more equivalent to 'dads' than 'dons', that is, as small-scale leaders of the community who monitor local events and happenings.[15] In Unity, the elders organize and recruit youths for the local soccer league and they are responsible for raising the money from residents and their overseas connections for these events (see Olwig 1985 for a discussion of crews in St John). They also organize 'parties' with DJs on the ends, which last well into the night, and negotiate with police for a 'bligh' so that their party will not be closed down. The male elders also redistribute money in the community sent from former residents of the area who are living in 'foreign' and make sure that members of the community eat a meal, sometimes organizing communally cooked meals, called 'boats', or communal meals organized by men (see Chevannes 1999, 2001). However, the elders also practise vigilante justice, dealing with theft, rape and disruptions to the balance of the community. There are also turf wars between big men in the community who seek more power on the ends; at least two incidents occurred in Chelsea during our research, one of which resulted in a fatality. In addition, and much like the communities where dons rule, the 'endsmen' proudly declare that 'their daughters and girlfriends' can walk 'freely' through the community 'any time of day or night' without fear. Certainly, as anthropologists, we enjoyed this 'protection' and ability to walk through the various ends without incident or harm throughout the day and early hours of the night.

With 1,471 homicides, 2004 was one of the most violent years in Jamaica.[16] Certainly Portmore and Marshfield were not immune, particularly given the close proximity of Portmore to Spanish Town (13 km), where violence ensued after the demise of a key member of the 'One Order' gang. The parish of St Catherine alone experienced 174 homicides, including seventy-one in the Portmore area of St Catherine South (Constabulary Communications Network 2005; Dinham 2005). During our six months residence, Horst and our research assistant witnessed the aftermath of a murder of a taxi driver on one of our well-travelled routes and we became aware of at least eight gun or knife incidents, half of which resulted in fatalities. Nurses at the local clinic discussed shortages in dressing supplies which they used to re-dress gun and knife wounds after the initial treatment at the over-crowded Kingston Public Hospital or Spanish Town Hospital. Marshfield has always been considered one of Portmore's 'hot spots' for crime and violence and, by extension a testament to the failure of the government and the NHT. In fact, many elderly residents regard Marshfield as blessedly peaceful compared with the ghetto areas they often moved to the area to escape. They in turn attribute violence in part to the lack of foresight in bringing individuals from rival communities in Kingston and to outsiders who 'wait it out' or 'cool out' in Marshfield until 'the heat' dies down, but meanwhile bring guns and criminal activity into the area.

Houses in Marshfield are designed in rows of five to seven units that share at least one wall. Aside from the two end units, each 400 square foot home is virtually identical, with two bedrooms and a small bathroom with sink, toilet and shower. In the original units, half of the house contains an open-plan living room, dining room and kitchen. The house itself is built on the WIHCON system of pre-fabricated panels, including the roof, which is fixed to the walls at the corners. There are no foundations, and slat windows only at the front and back, which many liken to a deck of cards. Each house also has a small plot of land, which can be transformed into a yard or laundry area. Unlike later schemes, like Greater Portmore, the NHT did not envisage expansion upwards. While many residents feel they have 'beautified' their homes over the years, they still suffer from the original design flaws of limited size and lack of ventilation, as well as mosquitoes and debris, which are both attracted by the gullies of stagnant water that separate the phases of settlement during the rainy months. Heat, stuffiness and mosquitoes are often mentioned as background to the neighbourhood squabbles.

It is hardly surprising that the endless blocks of what seem to be 'minimal' and repetitive housing have attracted constant criticism from middle-class Jamaicans. Yet the scheme was intended to provide mortgages at no greater cost than the rent charged in the traditional 'yards' of downtown Kingston (Brodber 1975). However flawed in execution, when comparing these solid, owner-occupied houses, with indoor plumbing and kitchen, with the tenement yards, with communal standpipes and outdoor toilet and kitchen facilities, that they left behind, it is hard not to see at least some improvement in their living conditions. One woman described the benefits of her move to Marshfield:

> I was living in a tenement yard, paying rent, and I don't think I could continue to raise my children and pay rent. I had one of the little houses to myself, nothing was happening, but I just wasn't comfortable paying rent cause I didn't like to owe, and I think if I live sometime being a single parent I might not able to pay the rent. And people take liberty a yuh children, people do. At least I can tell you one morning the lady said something to me to cost me to ask God to give me even two zinc on a roadside to put me children them, cause it mek me cry fi days, weeks every time me remember it. The children had a little fuss and she look at them – the owner fi the place – and said when yuh have pickney like them deh yuh should a get a little spy a back to [a slum area of Kingston] and put them. And that pierce me heart, and said to God please give me two zinc on a roadside. I was willing to live on a roadside with me children than live in that situation, cause I didn't want them go thru some of the things them to go through some of the things that I go through. So that's why I wanted a place where I could lock them in, keep them in and grow them for myself. And the Lord did provide this little place for me.

This peace of mind, particularly the peace of mind of having control over the people they interact with as well as the security of keeping one's children safe from molestation, is perhaps the most important contribution of the low-income housing movement by the Jamaican government, and the reason why the people who actually live in the area were overwhelmingly positive and proud of Portmore's development.

Economic Life in Marshfield

Local employment, after being virtually non-existent, is starting to grow in Portmore through formal commerce, such as shopping malls and a new informatics and call centre sector, informal domestic enterprises, such as small shops, workshops, day care and preschools. Nevertheless, most formal employment is in Kingston or Spanish Town and therefore involves at least an hour of travel time on a daily basis. Within our survey, 20 per cent of households contained at least one formally employed individual, who typically earned an average of $JA21,407 per month as teachers, company supervisors or customs agents at the wharves in Kingston. But, given the common family structure of single-headed households, 48 per cent of households benefited significantly from money received from those employed in other households, including baby-fathers, boyfriends and siblings, to the tune of $JA7,671 each month. Such external contributions represented the primary household support in 30 per cent of households. Also 14 per cent of households depended on remittances as their main source of income, with overall average receipts of $JA6,920, or just over $US115, monthly.

Table 3.2 Average Weekly Income in Marshfield Housing Scheme Portmore, St Catherine

Under $2,000	$2,000–$4,000	$4,001–$6,000	$6,001–$8,000	Over $8,000
34 per cent	12 per cent	16 per cent	20 per cent	18 per cent

While individuals in Marshfield enjoy higher salaries and a higher average living standard than Orange Valley, our survey also suggested a greater disparity between those who 'have' and those who do not. While average individual income was just over $JA5,000 per week, a disproportionately high number of households received more than $JA6,000 per week, thanks to supplementary income from non-household sources, such as boyfriends and remittances (Table 3.2). In other words, households with more secure income also tended to be better connected socially and economically. In contrast, those 34 per cent of households earning under $JA2,000 per week had less access to formal employment but also to supportive social networks and remittances. Their very survival depended largely upon patronage and assistance of baby-fathers and other family members, as well as hustling and juggling. Often their baby-fathers and partners had difficulties earning consistent money themselves or had multiple children and families to look after, which meant that they in turn could not afford regular help in childcare or cooking, other than immediate kin.

Rural and Urban Distinctions

Our survey in general supported the evidence found by the *Jamaica Survey of Living Conditions* (PIOJ, 2003) for greater poverty and poorer schooling in rural areas. According to Moser and Holland (1997) and others (Henry-Lee and Le Franc 2002), the perception of poverty is less a question of fixed income, but rather of vulnerability to crisis, which in turn is related to 'asset ownership', including housing, and productive and social capital. Experience of violence also plays an important role in the experience of vulnerability (see Henry-Lee et al. 2001). In Orange Valley, over two-thirds of the households own their own homes and/or lived in family homes, with the remainder renting houses, rooms or a section of a house. Although owner-occupied homes were sometimes quite dilapidated, there were clear advantages in this freedom from rent, which was typically $JA2,000 to

$JA3,000 per month; rent ranged from $JA500 in the poorest districts to $JA7,000 in Orange Valley proper. This difference was greatly exacerbated by the inability of renters to grow food for household consumption or sale to the market or engage in exchange of excess fruits and crops with those growing other provisions. Commonly this combination of self- and mutual provisioning could reduce household costs by $JA1,000, a dramatic difference for the survival of rural households.

Marshfield revealed an even greater discrepancy between high and low incomes, due largely to high rental costs. Of homes surveyed, 18 per cent were rented at a cost ranging around $JA5,000 a month for an unfurnished room with shared kitchen and bathroom, to between $JA8,000 and $JA12,000 for an unfurnished house. Often these are dilapidated. Charmaine, for example, paid $JA8,000 per month (two-thirds of her baby-father's salary) to rent a two-bedroom, one-bathroom rental house with basic kitchen facilities (no counters or other amenities had been added). The house lacked a proper fence and grilling and was surrounded by piles of dirt and broken cement blocks. Most days Charmaine and her children sat in the stuffy room with their door held open by a concrete block and a string. According to long-term residents of Marshfield, the departure of many of their neighbours to 'foreign' (on one short street five houses were rented) and the subsequent movement of renters into the area had contributed to the downturn in the area. This was felt to be true even when homes stayed within the original families and were occupied by their kin, suggesting a typical trajectory of a generation of those supported by this secure housing and more stable livelihoods who subsequently emigrate, leaving the house itself to another generation of kin. But longer-term residents saw all these newcomers as having less interest in their house or the community. Like the renters of Orange Valley, all residents of Marshfield lived with the inability to grow crops and encountered the higher costs of maintaining an urban household.

Tables 3.3 and 3.4 illustrate these basic differences between rural and urban Jamaica. While everyone pays basic utilities, all households in our Marshfield survey owned a television, stove, refrigerators and other appliances. This created average household bills of $JA2,090 per week and food costs of around $JA2,289 per week (despite savings from buying wholesale) and other costs such as the phone bill. Other savings in Orange Valley include backup fuel of coal or wood when gas runs out, the construction of water tanks and the use of standpipes if they could not afford to have the water piped into their house, which costs Marshfield residents an average of $JA1,468 monthly.

Overall this creates contrary results. At one level, it seems to reflect a common belief that urban residence is a harder, harsher way of life. Without proper connections and the support of family members, urban life creates more stress for low-income persons than in rural areas, where you can consume ground provisions rather than rely upon packaged rice and store-bought food. For example, Mr Stone

Table 3.3 Rural Income and Expenditure, Weekly

	Norma	George	Damian	Simone	Peta-Gaye	Totals	Average	Final Average
Expenses	$4,255	$2,580	$3,255	$5,235	$3,390	$18,715	$3,743	$3,983
Shop	$1,230	$1,380	$1,700	$1,515	$990	$6725	$1345	
Lunch Money	$0	$0	$0	$0	$550	$550	$110	
Bills	$2,880	$0	$0	$0	$0	$2880	$556	
Transportation	$25	$240	$90	$700	$500	$1555	$315	
Gambling	$0	$80	$340	$20	$0	$440	$88	
Other	$50	$550	$390	$2,000	$1,350	$2540	$508	
Money to Others	$70	$50	$600	$1,000	$0	$1720	$340	
Credit	$0	$330	$135	$0	$0	$465	$93	
Income	$4,220	$940	$3,000	$7,230	$3,900	$19,290	$3,858	$4,154
Work	$1440	$0	$2,500	$0	$0	$3940	$788	
Sale of Goods	$785	$400	$0	$0	$1,200	$2385	$477	
Remittances	$2000	$0	$0	$7,000	$0	$9000	$1800	
$ from friends Family	$140	$540	$1,420	$230	$0	$2330	$466	
$ from significant others	$90	$0	$500	$0	$2,700	$3290	$658	

	Sharon	Yvonne	Doreen	Dorothy	Andrea	Totals	Average
Expenses	$5,970	$4,640	$4,090	$1,715	$4,700	$21,115	$4,223
Shop	$1,940	$1,330	$2,030	$6,000	$2,570	$8470	$1694
Lunch Money	$1,150	$750	$430	$800	$60	$3190	$638
Bills	$700	$1,600	$0	$440	$1,500	$4240	$848
Transportation	$400	$350	$360	$1,400	$170	$2680	$536
Gambling	$1,310	$0	$20	$180	$0	$1510	$302
Other	$270	$610	$250	$2,000	$0	$3130	$626
Money to Others	$200	$0	$0	$1,000	$200	$1400	$280
Credit	$0	$0	$1000	$0	$0	$1000	$200
Income	$7,370	$5,850	$4,500	$32,160	$2730	$22,250	$4,450
Work	$1,600	$1,000	$3,500	$27,000	$0	$2100	$1500
Sale of Goods	$0	$100	$0	$2,060	$0	$2160	$432
Remittances	$0	$0	$0	$0	$60	$60	$12
Money from friends family	$1,270	$250	$1200	$100	$2,110	$4930	$985
Money from significant others	$4,500	$4,500	$0	$3,000	$0	$12000	$2400

Table 3.4 Marshfield Income and Expenditure, Weekly

	Winsome	Tanya	Charmaine	Carla	Jennifer	Sonia	Yvette	Monique	Tyrone	Merlene	Average
Expenses	$1935	$2,350	$1,490	$22,235	$6,565	$9,225	$9,345	$6,640	$4,925	$1,134	$6,584.4
Shop, etc.	$935	$2,350	$270	$1,630	$375	$605	$8,235	$2,800	$1,110	$795	
Lunch Money	$0	$0	$0	$360	$0	$150	$0	$0	$730	$0	
Bills	$0	$0	$0	$19,500	$1,000	$8,000	$0	$1,000	$0	$0	
Transport	$120	$0	$440	$615	$0	$340	$510	$450	$840	$0	
Gambling	$0	$0	$0	$0	$0	$0	$0	$0	$100	$0	
Clothing	$0	$0	$0	$0	$0	$0	$600	$700	$0	$0	
Household Goods	$20	$0	$150	$130	$260	$0	$0	$0	$0	$17	
Church	$0	$250	$0	$0	$0	$0	$0	$0	$0	$0	
Medicine/Health Care	$0	$0	$0	$0	$0	$0	$0	$0	$0	$0	
Work Supplies	$0	$0	$0	$0	$0	$0	$0	$0	$0	$0	
Phonecards	$260	$0	$130	$0	$130	$130	$0	$1,190	$260	$260	
Money to Others	$500	$100	$500	$0	$0	$0	$0	$500	$230	$62	
Credit	$0	$0	$0	$0	$0	$0	$0	$0	$625	$0	
Food and Drink	$0	$0	$0	$0	$0	$0	$0	$0	$200	$0	
Services	$0	$0	$0	$0	$800	$0	$0	$0	$350	$0	
Other Money	$0	$0	$0	$0	$4,000	$0	$0	$0	$480	$0	
Income	$2,330	$2,440	$1,130	$27,250	$14,130	$9,120	$10,426	$1,000	$2,260	$3,000	$7,308.6
Work	$0	$0	$0	$19,200	$14,000	$0	$0	$0	$0	$0	
Sale of Goods	$0	$0	$0	$0	$0	$120	$0	$0	$0	$0	
Remittances	$0	$0	$0	$0	$0	$8,000	$0	$0	$500	$3,000	
Jamaican Connections	$2,330	$2,000	$130	$1,850	$130	$500	$426	$0	$1,130	$0	
Significant Others	$0	$440	$1,000	$6,000	$0	$0	$9,600	$1,000	$130	$0	
Drink/Eat	$500	$0	$0	$200	$0	$500	$0	$0	$500	$0	
Services	$0	$0	$0	$0	$0	$0	$0	$0	$0	$0	
Savings	$0	$0	$0	$0	$0	$0	$0	$0	$0	$0	

(George), like other individuals we encountered, is still able to rely upon the food and other provisions present on his land. Nevertheless, urban residence has many more opportunities to earn income, at both a formal and an informal level, and a higher standard of living overall. Most importantly, there is that sense that there is simply much more to do that makes life interesting; rural existence can feel like a neglected backwater. The most significant conclusion of this section, however, is that in both cases most low-income households rely to a very significant extent upon resources that come neither from formal employment nor from informal buying and selling. As we shall discuss in greater detail in Chapter 6, over one-third of the population in our research sites were dependent upon income received from other individuals, and in Orange Valley only 16 per cent of households reported that there was one or more individuals formally employed and earning a regular, reliable salary (22 per cent of households included an individual who was formally employed). Instead, we found that the primary source of survival is other people and social networks (see Henry-Lee et al. 2001). This conclusion lies at the very heart of this volume, since it is the backdrop for understanding the cell phone not as a mere addition or luxury item, but as something that dramatically changes the fundamental conditions of survival for low-income Jamaicans, because it is the instrument of their single most important means of survival – communication with other people.

–4–

Possession

Evaluating a consumer good is always a relative process. Being one of the few people to own a possession is very different from owning a nearly ubiquitous possession. Jamaica moved with incredible speed from a situation where possession of a cell phone placed one in the vanguard of consumption, to the current view that the lack of a phone marks an individual as particularly deficient. The only people we met who could sound positive about their non-ownership of cell phones were elites or those with very high educational capital, such as university lecturers. There were also elderly persons, who were neutral, in the sense that they regarded themselves as outside of any such comparative framework, with cell phones seen as something for the next generation. But even amongst the elderly this was not an especially common attitude. Much of the academic literature in Europe and Japan focuses upon the specific association of cell phones with youth (Taylor and Harper 2003; Ito 2004b, 2005). In Jamaica also youth are seen as having an natural expertise in this area, as exemplified by one man's comment, 'Well, the young people are a different kettle of fish, them use the phone like dem born with it or dem and the phone a twin.' But, this association with youth is not so clear-cut. Due, at least in part, to the relative absence of landlines, the cell phone is almost as likely to be the sole phone used by an adult.

The critical failures, the new dispossessed, were those deemed simply too poor, too young or evidently neglected by those relationships that might have provided them with a phone. When reporting their lack of phone ownership, facial expressions often spoke volumes about an individual's sense of denigration and shame. Unlike a landline based in the home and in the family, this is a highly conspicuous and individual deficiency. As a result, whatever the phone's contribution to the alleviation of poverty, its absence is also a new and highly charged medium for the expression of poverty in Jamaica. It is likely to be some time before a balance ensues between the clamouring of the ever-younger child to be included and an age below which a child is seen as too young for cell phone ownership. Given the relatively low cost of entry-level phones at around $US30 to $US50 and the handing down of phones to impoverished relatives when a new, better-appointed phone is purchased, it is likely, however, that soon very few older Jamaicans who desire a phone will lack one. Many Jamaicans report that they have 'run through' several phones over the past few years. Even within this low-income group, it was common to be on one's second or third phone and one individual in Portmore, who had had phones with all three companies, claimed that he was already on his twentieth cell phone. Most new cell phone purchases came as a result of theft, breakage, loss or simple mechanical failure, but there was an emerging drive to purchase in reponse to changing fashion and the desire for new features, although this was generally frustrated by lack of resources. In effect, Jamaica is approaching the point at which the lack of a phone will come to signify not so much poverty as destitution.

For children and low-income households, the phone is often received as a gift, such as for a birthday or Christmas present. Much more rarely, there were cases of children, even schoolchildren, buying a phone for their parents and grandparents, particularly on Valentine's Day and Mother's Day. Often children and low-income individuals received a phone when the owner decided to buy a more up-to-date phone and gifted on their old phone. In many instances, this would now be a rather less desirable C&W phone. Others share a phone. For example, a daughter purchased a phone to use for texting out of school time, but her mother uses it for voice calls during the school day. Her mother is also expected to keep her numbers written down, leaving the internal address book for the daughter. Between being gifted a phone and not having a phone lies the ambiguous position of being able to borrow the phone. This is quite common in rural households where a brother possesses a phone and his sister feels she can beg use of it with some frequency, but it is still not her actual phone. One individual mentioned that he purchased a phonecard on a monthly basis and borrowed a neighbour's phone in order to ring his daughters. Obviously this is open to difficult negotiations and lending can be an act of humiliating the recipient as well as of generosity.

The sense of personal ownership comes across in two ways: the reaction to the loss of a phone and its incorporation as style. The former will be discussed in Chapter 5, because the core loss is associated with the phone list and the social networks it reflects. This can be the cause of major distress and difficulty. Although Jamaicans often talk about and make fun of the status display potential of the cell phone, this is not nearly as common a practice as implied. Jokes revolve around people pretending to use a phone that is actually broken or claiming an up-market model, but being communally busted when their actual phone rings. Such things do happen but they are not common. Most Jamaicans possess a very standard low-cost handset from Sony Ericsson, Nokia, Panasonic or Motorola and maintain their original face plates. Even when young men and women know about and talk about the features on expensive phones, they buy phones from shops on the basis of special offers on the cheapest models. Since these are often subsidized by the companies, the difference in price between the cheapest models and phones with additional features can be considerable.

Despite all the talk about status, if people are asked directly which phones are currently high-status or in fashion, most people are unaware of the specific brands and model of the phones, but instead provide vague answers such as 'the flip phone' or 'the sexy little silver phones'. Many individuals keep their phones out of sight in their purses or pockets and take them out specifically when needed or rung. Another proportion of Jamaicans actually travel with the cell phone in the palm of their hand, almost as an extension of their hand. One can often see several people grouped around a table with cell phones held up or resting on the table, but again these are usually very ordinary models and reflect more the frequency with which they are used and their close identification with the individual. Expensive phones tended to be owned by middle-class executives, who keep these well hidden when not in use, so as not to attract attention. But for the low-income populations we worked amongst, the extra features of non-standard phones were well beyond their means.

There are exceptions, especially among students, young people and others who in other respects are clearly interested in self-display. Although it was primarily associated with men, both men and women may keep their phones on a holster worn on the hip. A more feminine practice involved wearing the phone in the back pocket of tight pants, particularly low hip-hugger jeans. In both field sites, women and men wore phones on ribbons around the neck. This was viewed as safer and more convenient, particularly by working women. However, some women complemented this pragmatism with display, such as coordinating the colour of the string with the face plates, colour of shirts, nails and even hair. But there are other more creative ways to wear a phone, such as a well-endowed assistant who always kept her phone firmly lodged between her very evident breasts.

Indeed, rather than individual style, what were more evident were general trends in fashion. By the end of 2004, the two phones that were considered 'hype' included the miniature Panasonic and the flip phone, which had recently become more affordable due to the arrival of Sagem, a French cell phone company, on the scene. Some saw style as more a women's concern, 'The girls dem, dem waan have a hot phone weh dem can pop up ... yuh find people put themselves out a the way and try have a phone fi say "bwoy [boy] me have a boasty phone".' As another girl phrased it, 'Yuh dress probably to match your phone or yuh dress a certain way to fit the status of your phone itself.' Fashion-conscious women generally preferred to have something like a small pink clamshell design that looked feminine or sexy. Other women make more of changeable fascias.

But plenty of others saw males as the relevant gender, noting that 'Woman not really fussy, just a phone to make and receive calls. A man now, him want the wickedest phone, the blingest phone, the phone with this or that.' Another person noted, 'Recently I saw a guy with a camera phone, when yuh press it, it actually bright up the place when it flash.' Indeed, Heather (co-author) was surprised at the enthusiastic response received when she offered her Sagem C-2 (a basic, low-end flip phone) to her Jamaican 'uncle' since the numbers and silver colour of the phone appeared to be on the feminine side. Although the standard Nokia 3310 and 3330 are seen as having a certain male quality, as practical, well-weighted and sturdy, in that they are said not to break when you drop them and to fit right in the hand, the phones themselves were not considered a 'man's phone'. What could be masculine was the pose and position of the phone. As one Portmore schoolgirl noted about some young men she knew:

> A most of them stick them phone in a them groin, like a gun them have, and a pose pon it, and say 'yow a my gun this'. Yuh nuh. When yuh check it out, a fool fool thing that. Yuh can't have something so. Yuh can't have phone deh so. A them thing, deh mek police shot people. Yuh see. It so me nuh really wear my phone in a my waist.

> [Most of them stick their phone in their groin like they have a gun and pose with and say 'yo, this is my gun'. You know. When you think about it, it's a foolish thing. You can't do that. You can't have a phone there. Those things make the police shoot people. You see. So I really don't wear my phone in my waist.]

Sometimes the phone itself can make a person feel unique and therefore some individuals strive to find features such as unusual screen savers. More commonly, this was achieved by changing the fascia. A Portmore woman alternated between her four fascias every couple of days. Another suggested, 'Phone is like a fashion thing, because you can change phone face to match with everything you carry.' Given Portmore's proximity to Kingston as the place where they were generally employed, there was more concern there with style than in the rural backwater of Orange Valley. While women changed fascias to match appearance, men often adopted a particular fascia, for example one man had a Lara Croft fascia, another used a Beenie Man fascia and a third had the eyes of Mary J. Blige. Schoolchildren often make little additions, which become important in everyday rivalries. Occasionally people will deliberately match. As one person put it, schoolchildren and young people they can 'look girlfriend and boyfriend through their phones'.

Schoolchildren are the most expressive in terms of their devotion to the phone as a possession that expresses their status amongst peers. As one Portmore schoolgirl recalled:

> My phone mashed up one of the time in last year. Before I got it back they had to give me that to carry, I don't know what it is, but this big phone, it was humongous. I was like, I was on a bus and I was getting a call and I was ignoring it, I didn't want nobody to see me with the phone and I just like back it out and say hello, and about three girls turn around and looked at me and was like 'look pon the phone weh she have', 'look

pon the phone'. I felt so shamed, I carry back the phone and say look here when me phone ready just call-me, I don't really want a phone for the moment.

By the same token, an expensive phone was seen to be a girl-magnet:

Our phone is mostly like the dearest phone, like the thirty odd thousand phone. Them phone deh me cousin spar with ... How we get girl with it? Well him just give me fi him phone and me just pose with it a Half Way Tree and yuh see any girl weh we see look down pon we phone, we just go cross and say, 'yuh like weh yuh see' and we start get fi talk to them and so.

[Our phone is the most expensive phone, like the $JA30,000 phone. My cousins and I play with those phones. How do we get girls with it? Well he just gives me his phone and I just pose with it at Half Way Tree and you see any girl we see looking at the phone, we just approach and say 'you like what you see?' and we get to start to talk to them.]

The most specific and important display property of contemporary Jamaican cell phones are ringtones, and most Jamaicans are happy to express an active interest in tones, in some cases changing and updating them several times a week. As one schoolboy from Portmore replied when asked if he had downloaded ringtones, 'Like only a million, like every single new ringtone me buy ... cause me have the connections. We have fren dem with a lot of connections. So we just hook them up and download until me finger dem drop off.' Although many phones have been linked to the latest dancehall or reggae rhythm, there are actually a very wide variety of tones used, and classical music is quite common, even for those who have no idea where the tune originates. Around the time of the 2004 Olympics, the theme from the movie *Chariots of Fire* was heard. Quite a few religious 'Christian' ringtones became prominent amongst those who find the ringtones of dancehall music offensive and immoral. For this reason, some recent handsets that can record music and transform recordings into a ringtone are very popular, as is the feature that facilitates the sharing of these tones. The quite complex feature, which allows individuals to compose their own tunes, is well known and used, given the general facility with all aspects of music in Jamaica. The phone companies had extensive promotions for ringtones and special deals on their sale. The facility to assign ringtones to particular callers also appeals to those whose phone usage is dominated by keeping different relationships apart. Some even try to match the tone to what they see as the character of the caller, such as a 'sour' tune for a persistent ex-boyfriend.

As Fortunati (2002) notes, the phone certainly adds to the relationship between style and the body, although, even for regions such as Italy and Jamaica, which are stereotypically associated with a concern for style, this pertains to only some individuals. Perhaps more significant is the idea of the cell phone as an accessory that adds audio as well as visual elements. In Jamaica, this is not just through ringtones but also through often deliberately loud and expressive conversations in dialect. While much of the literature has focused on the obtrusive nature of this sound and the way it disturbs the boundaries between private and public life (Licoppe and Heurtin 2002), the examples primarily derive from observations in regions such as Scandinavia and Japan (Ito et al. 2005). The situation in Jamaica is very different since so many people see music as critical to their expressive identity. Humming and singing and 'making noise' in public is well established. And, as we noted in Chapter 1, so is expressive and loud conversation. It is true that previously clothing and accessories lacked an audio component, but, if anything, that was unfortunate rather than accepted. The affinity with the audio aspect of the phone as style is evident and comes across not as obtrusive and artificial but in some ways as natural and welcome, an example of what Miller and Slater (2000) called 'expansive realisation' when a new technology allows a previously constituted desire to become realized (the concept is discussed on pp. 11–13). Still, the affinity to music and noise is expressive of only one genre of the public realm. The cell phone, as well as eliding the audio and visual, clearly bridges between appearance and functionality, in some cases standing symbolically for an explicit pragmatism rather than for wealth or fashion consciousness expressed through a blue unadorned Nokia phone.

While people delight in a discourse about the superficial others who are desperately concerned with their phone as an aspect of their appearance, this is probably misleading as a description of most Jamaicans' relationship to the cell phone, which in the main is quite pragmatic. As such, the phone has become much more like most clothing, where again there is discourse about competitive display and 'hype', but the reality is that most Jamaicans dress in a rather homogenized ensemble of jeans and T-shirt, which says more about commonality than competition. A statement by one wealthy Jamaican is suggestive:

> I think it symbolizes maybe in a small way some kind of success, and I think people is just fascinated to know that while they can't afford maybe a big car like the person who is very successful, at least they have the ability to speak whenever they want. It is kind of an equalizer, the great equalizer.

Looked at closely, this statement starts with an expression of status competition but ends with the sentiment more of equality and a general sense of an addition to low-income livelihoods that is shared. Today the cell phone's function is as a system of communication rather than as an accessory. It has been allowed to establish itself and as a result it is a symbol more of inclusion than of exclusion. In short, within a very short time the cell phone has become mundane.

More than a Phone

There is a marked discrepancy between cell phones in London and in Jamaica, and this distinction lies not in any difference in the actual handsets. Rather, the difference lies in a fundamental perception of what a cell phone as a possession signifies. For most Londoners, a phone is almost entirely an instrument to make and receive calls and any other functions are secondary, except perhaps for those younger users who are particularly excited by playing games. For most low-income Jamaicans, however, the possession of a phone is the possession of a small multi-purpose tool that can become tantamount to an individualized communication technology centre. One reason for this is a different attitude to 'free stuff', such that this multitude of secondary features may be disregarded by people in wealthier situations. But low-income Jamaicans feel they possess a special skill in the exploitation of things obtained as 'extra' or largesse and, as such, exploit such facilities for all they are worth. Indeed, a nurse claimed, 'Once you have a phone you don't need a computer. It does everything, it is a calculator a watch, you can type on it, some of them are also tape recorders.' One very clear example of this was the attitude to the phone as a watch or clock. For low-income Jamaicans, the cell phone has become their principal everyday timepiece, and in many cases a watch is now seen as superfluous. As well as telling the time, the cell phone has become the alarm clock that gets people up in the morning, handy calculator, quite often a diary and calendar and certainly the principal means of storing contacts and one's personal social network. Others focus on the hands-free features or the ability of the phone to record short memos for use in work. As an enthusiastic user put it, 'You can store data on it, you can store information, store meetings, store birthdays, store whatever, so it's actually like a little diary and a phone in one. So basically to me the phone change my life ... it help me to be more organized.' This means that, rather like a computer hard disk for many people in metropolitan regions, this is where part of one's social 'memory' is located. One is not just naked without a phone but lost without it, since one forgets where one should be and what one is supposed to be doing.

Often what matters is the way one can micromanage social affairs. For example, a woman explains that 'Mi don't really want talk to him but what I do is sometime I store names and when mi see yuh name come up mi no have to talk.' Another individual gives anillustration, 'For instance in me phone you have this feature that is call "profile alert", where you set up profiles, if they are calling it might turn red, you change up the colour, change up the picture on it, you change the ringtone so you change it altogether. So when that person is calling everything changes.' As in other studies (Ling 2004: 70–76), this is complemented by the cell phone's capacity to help in micromanaging meeting up:

Yuh maybe gone out with your fren or yuh supposed to meet somebody at another place yuh can't find them, yuh just wondering where they are, until you're tired of waiting and yuh can't find the person yuh just go back home. With your cell phone you can maybe describe the place where you're at and they can come get yuh.

Children are particularly attracted to the games, but can equally quickly become bored with them, such that they may lend their own and borrow their friend's phones so that everyone gets a share of the range of games that are available on the common phones. They also have a tendency to turn other features into communal games, such as text messaging or swapping favoured texts. This aspect of the phone as an entertainment centre is by no means restricted to children, since game playing and experimenting with a phone's features are a form of entertainment that travels with each individual. Not surprisingly, it can be observed on long bus journeys. Jamaicans tend to be quite private, and conversations on buses (other than between those who already know each other) are not common unless an event occurs to spark conversation. In many respects, the cell phone is quite unprecedented for its ability to alleviate boredom, both in making calls but also in its much less expensive function as a games centre. There is a clear correlation with age in terms of playing games and using features. In some cases, parents will rely on their children to deal with aspects of their phone, including saving names, numbers and other features they do not feel comfortable learning to use.

There is no feature on a cell phone, however deeply buried, that cannot be made into a useful tool in everyday life. Even a very low-level Nokia can be turned into something quite creative. For example, by composing pictures pixel by pixel on these monochrome screens, they can be populated with handcrafted hard-core pornography that can be sent by phone. Such images impress through their ingenuity rather than their realism. On the other hand, a proportion of users make no use of other facilities, and there were some quite young adults as well as older men and women who said they did not know how to text. Clearly, the potential to become a personal ICT centre increases in relation to the facilities on a particular handset. Phones that double as radios, MP3 players, cameras and data storage of various kinds are exploited accordingly. The ability of one phone to store fifteen seconds of conversation was enough for a man to have kept handy some dramatic 'phone sex'. The key distinction is that, where in London these still tend to be regarded as gimmicks, in Jamaica they are seen as important additional facilities that become integral to the sense of the phone. Since most people cannot afford more than the basic phone, these are generally facilities bundled with low-end handsets, which influence knowledgeable youths, who may choose their phone accordingly, but for others it is more a case of being educated by more experienced phone users in the potential of a handset.

Clearly, these various aspects of phone possession and phone use may go together, especially for slightly wealthier consumers. For example, a woman in Portmore has a special black leather casing for her phone, which she uses to listen to the radio. She has integrated the camera element to the extent that the picture of the person calling appears on the screen as they call. She downloads the latest dancehall tunes as her ringtones and spends at least $JA500 a week on calls. But the phone is also the centrepiece of her wider life. She received the phone as a gift from a friend living on another Caribbean island and much of her work is based on sending him Jamaican goods which he cannot obtain where he is living. She, in turn, earns part of her living helping him and acting as his Jamaican contact. In such cases the stylistic elements of the phone are not really an accessory, they are more an integral part of life, so that caring for the phone's appearance and making it central to one's audio life is expressive of its larger integration into an individual's life. Indeed, it is probably true of Jamaican life more generally that there is a powerful integration of aural and visual adornment. As one man described the situation, 'The woman dem, I see dem mek love on the phone and they carry like the phone is somebody.'

Conversation

So far the material discussed comes from what most people would regard as secondary or peripheral aspects of possession as against the primary use of the phone for communication – that is, conversation and texting. Conversation makes up much of the evidence used in subsequent chapters and its very presence in combating loneliness and isolation will be discussed in Chapter 7. Chapter 5 is concerned with characterizing the most common type of phone call, which tends to be quite terse, with little content. One effect is a general attenuation of the forms of politeness that would otherwise punctuate the start and end of phone calls. Often a call starts with merely a 'Yes' or 'Yes, Heather' and launches straight into the purpose of the call; the termination of a call is often equally abrupt, consisting with merely an 'allright' or 'later' to finish off the call. Price-conscious international calls can also sound excessively laconic – How are you? Allright. Did you see Uncle C? When are you coming to Jamaica? Allright.'

The longer calls tend to be associated with particular kinds of content. One is boyfriend–girlfriend calls, which usually means the individuals involved lower their voices and mumble, since it is hard to be out of reach of public listening in to conversations. The cell phone is seen as a considerable boon over the previous dependence on landlines for such conversations. Another form of extended call is based on individuals talking about their problems, such as 'My husband did not come home again last night and I really don't know what to do … I am thinking of leaving.' Calls that are about getting problems off ones chest tend to be the longest conversations and are generally referred to as 'counselling' (see Chapter 7).

There are many claims and counterclaims about the gendered use of the phone. Probably the most stereotypical would be statements such as that made by a schoolboy: "Boys use the phone for like short, short conversations man, say like you call your girlfriend, is like "hi baby, what's up, are you ok, everything nice, ok bye bye". Females now they call you and they remind you of everything weh them see inna the day.' There are too many of such genres of conversation to treat each individually, but one that tends to have wider ramifications is extended quarrelling by phone. In most cases, as when face to face in the home, this incorporates elaborate performative elements and employs the visual gestures of co-presence: the pout, the throwing up of the hands, the getting ready to leave, the grimace. For example, a taxi driver engages in a protracted argument and final reconciliation with his girlfriend over the course of some two and half hours of intermittent conversation. Many of the gestures become specific to phone use. He can abruptly end a phone call while she is yelling into the phone. She, in turn, can let the phone ring a considerable and considered length of time before deigning to pick it up. In addition, he makes all sorts of gestures for the benefit of his passengers, but also for his own benefit in that he can make them without her seeing and taking umbrage. At various moments, he moves as if to toss the phone through the window, rolls his eyes, throws back his head and hands to express unbelieving astonishment that anyone could really be as unreasonable as her. He also mouths curses and other derogatory remarks that do not travel through the phone line.

In Jamaica conversation has always been seen as having the potential for display. One of the finest anthropological contributions to the region was called *The Man-O-Words in the West Indies* (Abrahams 1983). It was the first serious study of both the necessity of performative language and its accomplishment. This facility for performative language has more recently become better known internationally through the popularity of a number of genres, generally associated with music such as rap and dub. The cell phone incorporates the older tradition of non-musical performative comment and conversation. This is particularly evident on public transport. For example, a young man on a bus sitting with a female companion on either side of him receives a call from yet another woman. He talks as loudly as possible, celebrating the increasing annoyance and jealousy of one of the women sitting with him, who is poking him in the ribs and trying to get him to stop. Schoolchildren also often converse in a manner as clearly directed to their co-present peers as to the converser on the other phone.

The other side to this coin are older people still learning about the potential of the cell phone to make private calls public. Again on a bus, an elderly woman receiving a call starts to talk loudly, but in this case it is because she is not conscious of her surroundings. She animatedly declares, 'Oh no they gone lock him up, lock him up!' and tells of various trials and tribulations. After some time, she looks around and says back to the phone, in a much lower tone, that she really cannot talk about all this now on a bus, where it is not really private. At this point, the entire busload (which has been glued to her conversation) broke out in laughter, much to the embarrassment of the woman, who then quickly terminated the call. Similarly, when a man in the bar receives a call, he may decide to stay in the bar because he wants people to hear the conversation, go outside because he wants them not to hear, or go outside because he wants them to think he has something he does not want them to hear.

The public presence of the phone can also embrace a communal element of cell phone use in various ways. Many people feel an obligation never to let a phone ring without being answered. There is an assumption that any call might be significant, or at the very least you are doing the person who owns the phone a favour by saving them the trouble and cost of having to phone another person back. Occasionally, when visiting a house, the householder may offer to use their current to recharge your phone if you are worried about your charge. During Hurricane Ivan those with generators or car batteries often allowed others to charge their phones, though usually for a fee of around $JA100 in Orange Valley and Portmore.

Much more commonly, the phone is associated with the individual and with privacy. For example, in both field sites, women who live quite close to each other and are not talking about anything in particular may choose to talk by phone. The reason lies in the expectation that, as soon as one goes 'on the road', one has to take some pains as to appearance, both of yourself and often of the young child that has to accompany you. These preparations can take some time. Low-income Jamaicans in general are extremely informal at home, wearing just a nightdress or T-shirt well into the day if they are not going out and, in some instances, talking on the phone may be seen as worth the cost given the effort that is thereby saved in not having to dress to go visiting. Such calls also allow gossip to be maintained without this being evident in public. In turn, this leads to one of the major fears about the phone, which here are less its potential for harming individual health (see Burgess 2004) and more its potential for harming the community (for an extreme example, see Umble (1996) on the Amish). Levy noted that, despite the overwhelming desire for a phone in the most impoverished ghettos of downtown Kingston, areas torn apart by gang war and dons, they could also appear as a threat associated with accusations of being an informer: 'A woman was run out of Zinc City and her possessions including her bed and brand new fridge, thrown from an upper floor, because the small radio in her hand was mistaken for a cellular' (Levy 1996: 46).

Texting and Internet through the Phone

While many older people still did not text, the general awareness of texting grew considerably during 2004. Most participants in our surveys sent and received fewer than six a day, but a few sent and received more than twenty. This is apart from very concentrated texting in chat rooms, and the rapid and vast spread of 'call-me', which, for some low-income individuals, became almost synonymous with texting itself (see Chapter 6). A number of people we interviewed suggested that texting was last year's fashion and has thus dwindled with the introduction of new features. Texting did seem significantly less popular in Jamaica than in many other countries and bore little relation to the situation in the Philippines or Japan (Pertierra et al. 2002,; Ito et al. 2005). Remarkably few people seemed to use or even know about predictive text, even though this would have been available on most of the handsets at the time. Apart from 'call-me', texting was also more associated with the young and especially schoolchildren. People said they disliked the effort that had to be put into texting as opposed to calling, as well as the fact that they had to wait for a reply, which contrasted with the instant response available when calling. While it probably takes considerably less time, the manual nature of texting meant that it was often referred to as more time-consuming than calling. There were exceptions, including those who embraced non-predictive text both because they enjoyed being creative with the task of trying to be concise in the way they spelt out words such as 'ur' for 'your'. Most importantly, non-predictive text was also seen as saving people with limited education from embarrassment since any inability to spell correctly would be disguised by this kind of texting. Indeed, this may well be the reason why predictive text had not become the norm.

Texting could become the core of the daily interactions between boyfriends and girlfriends. One of the most positive responses was that of young women who claimed that they could express themselves through text messages in a way they couldn't with voice, implying that they were too shy to say these more intimate or poetic and romantic communications in person or over the phone. Certainly a number of schoolboys and girls built up a library of romantic texts that could be sent to boy- and girlfriends as part of courtship. These can be mundane, such as 'Good morning sweets. How was ur night? I think about u endlessly through the night', or more poetic, such as 'If I could be anything in the world I would be a tear so I could be born in your eyes, live on your cheek and die on your lips.' Texts can also be the basis for circulating jokes and obscenities of various kinds. Secondly, although apparently dyadic, school-based relations are often actually a more communal activity, with a group centred around the individual exhorting and advising them as to the best next move in relationships that are to a large extent experiments in learning about relationships as a genre.

As Harper (2001) notes, to understand the different genres of communication one has to compare the forms of social interface they represent, including the modality of temporality they lend themselves to. Miller and Slater (2000: 182–183) provide the example of Internet communication being seen as ideal for deeply spiritual communication, because of the time it gives to assimilate a message and compose a reply: significantly greater than face to face and significantly less than a letter. Harper cites one study as suggesting that texting is seen as the ideal form in which to dump a boy/girlfriend since it is much harder to respond with a 'Why?' These schoolchildren do seem to be experimenting with different relations of the private to public, co-present to distant, instantaneous against considered response through the use of texting. As a sixteen-year-old girl put it, 'Like when mi a go break up with him, mi can write and sey the relationship is over and all a that, but mi can't call him and seh the relationship is over. That so hard. But it is better when him not seeing me and me not seeing him. So mi can just write it down and just send it.'

All of these reasons for preferring text are complemented by practical issues, the most important of which, cost, is of particular importance to schoolchildren. Additionally, a student can usually get away with sending a text during a lesson but not with speaking on the phone (see Chapter 8). Schoolchildren also send multiple texts. For example, an enthusiastic Pentecostal schoolboy sometimes sends around religious messages to encourage his peers, such as 'May the joys of the Season fill your life with love and righteousness.' A facility that chimes with the romantic use of the phone is the ability to store texts. Several schoolgirls in particular, talked of saving a number of texts received from boyfriends and going back to read these from time to time as a means of keeping the sender present. Another man composed a poem to his sweetheart and took advantage of the cheap rates for text messaging to send her one pair of rhyming sentences a day until the poem was done.

The other phone usage that more or less grows out of school culture concerns sending and sharing of pictures and data. This forms part of the schoolchildren's internal competition over status based on obtaining the latest phones with the most advanced facilities. As such, these new facilities need public demonstration. Picture messaging, which is generally taken as a fun activity, is an example of this. A few people followed the guidance of the mass advertising campaigns for picture messaging by bringing phones to parties and events. For example, at the Reggae Sunsplash Festival in Montego Bay, some members of the audience sent pictures of the international performers, such as Ludicris and Kanye West, but, given the high ticket price ($JA2,500), this excluded any of the low-income Jamaicans we knew. Overall, picture messaging seemed quite rare and the facility to store pictures is more likely to be used to retain one or two images of one's family or lover, rather than to actually send pictures from one phone to another. This extends a previous practice, which involved laminating pictures that would be used to decorate (and often identify the owner of) the phone fascia.

Far more important than picture messaging was Internet access through the phone, which, much to our surprise, had already become a significant aspiration for low-income Jamaicans. This was notwithstanding the general antipathy to Internet access through the computer for this income group and the cost of Internet-enabled phones (Miller and Horst 2005). Internet access was relatively new at the time of fieldwork, but because it remained free with Digicel through the summer of 2004 some of the individuals we talked with had already accumulated considerable experience in using it. Most of the individuals with such phones did not possess a computer with an Internet connection, which made the phone much more like a personal computer, a situation that mirrors the trend for young people in Japan (Ito et al. 2005). We never met a low-income Jamaican who used a personal digital assistant (PDA), such as a Palm Pilot, but the phone could become the centre of various Internet-related activities. People who are brought up on computer keyboards find texting with a phone clunky and awkward and those with broadband find WAP a joke. Yet people whose first experience of Internet access is through the phone see it as the vanguard of modernity. Chat rooms, which seem to computer users to be inconceivable as a phone-mediated operation, are enthralling to cell phone users, who may enter chat rooms several times a day. As one young woman noted, 'You could be getting forty texts at once, the phone just never stopped vibrating!' Many of the experiences associated with the Internet, like making friends from Lithuania and chatting about their customs and their private lives or swapping pictures and anxieties about boyfriends (see Miller and Slater 2000), were becoming seen as phone-based possibilities.

As with early Internet use everywhere, it was hard to escape a certain hardcore topic of conversation: sex and pornography. As a sixteen-year-old girl described the situation:

> You use this nickname to go in because you don't want anyone to know who you are. It was ok but it was a lot of rude thing. You have different kind of chat room, you have Christian chat room, one we yuh just want talk bout sex, one we yuh just want talk bout love. All a them a the same thing because everybody just want call in bout mi just want have sex now so yuh can contact mi at this number and meet mi where and where.

Many of Digicel's advertisements that encouraged Jamaicans to use these facilities were clearly modelled on the parallel development of MSN and email through the computer, such as: 'Chatta Style, check out the new style of chat, an Internet chat room from your Digicel phone, you can chat with friends and meet new friends, text to join 555–Chat (2428) and you're in and now you can share the vibes, sound, colour picture.' Downloading hardcore pornography was central to the demand for

Internet access through the phone for many young men. Staunch Christians and others who feared such developments would inevitably talk at rather considerable length about how users wanted to move from downloading pictures to what was always described as watching live sex shows on their screens. The fear was that these activities would be extended into 'real life'. This was probably a combination of fantasy and hysteria, in more ways than one, given how slow most Internet access proved to be in practice. Downloading porn was not particularly furtive for adults, unlike the more easily embarrassed schoolchildren, and was also probably more equal in gender usage than in most countries. Moreover, it was not an activity that a person necessarily sought to hide and many women seemed happy to display their growing collections of phone porn to just about anyone who was prepared to stand around and take an interest.

Pornography is, however, by no means the only use made of Internet phones. Individuals were also found who surfed online through the phone for sports and information and also went on chat rooms, laboriously typing in their chat using non-predictive texting on their phones. Much of this seemed not simply a question of cheaper phones as against more expensive computers. It was part of the wider evidence for the preference of one medium over the other due to private, individually owned access and, in turn, a more personal identification with the technology. There were more people in Portmore who looked down on slow cell phone access because of their greater experience of computers, but most people simply did not see their Internet phones in these relative terms. For them it was the excitement of entering their first chat room or downloading the first song, or suddenly finding themselves in possession of obscure information about subjects they never knew they wanted to be informed about. The weather forecast in Jamaica, New York, has surely never before been quite so exciting.

The Contrast with Landlines

Most of the published literature on the cell phone concentrates on the specific contrast with landlines since in affluent countries the telephone itself was taken for granted for generations. As a result, the emphasis in this literature is on issues of perpetual access and mobility (e.g. Katz and Aakhus 2002). In Jamaica the emphasis is often very different. A major factor was whether the area or household in question had possession of a landline. In the small districts around Orange Valley where we concentrated our ethnography, these remained rare. Even where landlines had been made available, there were several consistent discussions about the history and experience of landlines that culminated in an unusually negative relationship to them. This seemed to continue from an even more negative relationship to the public phone. This included the amount of times these were out of order and unavailable, something more usually blamed on vandalism than the company. Another problem was precisely that they were public, and people in small communities often feel there is little privacy in general and resent the degree to which they were unable to escape the public gaze. There were many tales about having to walk long distances, then queue for hours and, when one did have use of the phone, the people next in the queue would 'be in yu ears, telling yu hurry up and get off the phone, me waan use it.' For all of these reasons, several of the phones in shops were effectively used as public phone boxes through paying the appropriate fee to the shopkeepers. Some shopkeepers used a facility to see what each call cost and charge precise amounts, while others used it as a business to make a profit. These became an important facility in that when relatives abroad wanted to make contact they had to leave a message in such shops and hope this would be passed on to the relevant person.

Perhaps most telling with respect to negative attitudes to the landline were the recurrent discussions over the relative cost and the different systems of billing. In part, this reflected the absurd complexity of traditional landline bills. In particular, making calls abroad was restricted to those who qualified for a special code, which was in and of itself unnecessarily cumbersome, especially once the cell phone revealed how unproblematic calling abroad could be. In addition, and because these bills were monthly, there was a constant suspicion that the bill was inflated by the company and that C&W must be 'thieves' or 'fooling poor people' by billing them for conversations they had never had. Upon finding us an audience willing to listen, people would become quite forceful in these condemnations. As one otherwise calm older woman argued, 'Cable and Wireless is a thief, I hope yuh have it, they are thieves, because they make a lot of mistakes and they charge yuh for the mistakes they make.' People talked constantly of the shock they felt at bills that they had not anticipated and suddenly felt they could not pay, and the pressure put on them and lack of concern for their problems (see Chapter 7).

The situation was rather different in Portmore, where the landline was a standard facility in Marshfield houses long before the cell phone became available. Nevertheless, the negative comments made about the bills and about C&W were only slightly more muted. According to those statistics we were able gain access to, the cell phone had resulted in a decline in landline usage by around a tenth. But these figures did not tally with our ethnographic data, which suggested that more like a third of low-income households had chosen to rely entirely upon the cell phone. The most common way for this to happen is for the household to face an unexpectedly high bill and opt to not pay the bill and thus be cut off by C&W. The suspicion, however, was that this was in effect simply a way to move from a dual system to reliance upon the cell phone. This ending of a landline by default may also account for the discrepancy between official giving up on landlines and our sense of what was actually happening. As one householder put it, 'Yea, and it give you problem, cause when them use the phone them don't want to pay the bill, mi haffi quarrel. So mi glad when everybody did get, but nuff somebody chop off. For majority a di people dem phone chop off.'

Underlying this giving up of landlines were various deeper concerns. The arrival of the monthly house phone bill was a bone of contention in many of the households we were familiar with simply because of the number of people with access to the phone. Indeed, when we went to live in Portmore, the matron of our house had recently decided to abandon the house phone (with the bill unpaid) to teach her children a lesson about abuse of the phone. At our request, the phone was reconnected, but accompanied by stern warnings to the children. The first month appeared to go smoothly, a sign of frugal use, but then the bill began to rise again. Despite chiding individuals for expensively calling Digicel phones from a C&W landline, it was clear that her collection of 'contributions' was falling well short of the actual bill. Where neighbours and friends also have access. the problem is exacerbated. The cell phone is seen as something whose individualized billing permits an extended household to 'live good' together.

While difficult to demonstrate analytically, it may well be that one of the main reasons there was such violent criticism and almost visceral dislike of C&W and the whole system of landlines is precisely these tensions that arise from a landline being shared around a family. In general terms, Jamaica is unusual for the degree to which relations between members of the same household are monetarized, and a sense of fairness is rendered most explicit in the monetary exchanges that go on within a household (Robertson 2002). Along with this can be a fear of being cheated or unfairly treated within the household and sometimes a suspicion that one member is either hiding or failing to share their resources with other members of the household. With respect to the phone, it may well be that the persons responsible for paying the bills were often deeply suspicious that either other members of the household or individuals with access to the phone were using it without fully owning up to this usage, and it was for this reason that the phone bills were higher than they ought to have been. But, rather than making this claim of deceit and, in some sense, betrayal public, they preferred to vent their anger on the company that provided the phone. Yet individuals interviewed who had worked for C&W also made similar accusations against their own company to those of consumers. Householders could never tell themselves whether they were blaming the company for the faults of their family or, indeed, falsely becoming suspicious of their family because of the bad practice of the company. In either case, these are important factors in trying to understand and appreciate the subsequent response to the development of the cell phone.

On the other hand, the fact that the group most likely to talk positively about landlines are older women, who are in effect the matriarchs of their household, is also instructive. A landline, especially one where private conversation is impossible, can become an important element in the control over the household. As the centre of domestic life, the matriarchs are the ones identified with the landline and people who use it are to some degree beholden to them. They can, for example, go through the bill in detail and work out who is making phone calls and where. While in theory the cell phone may cure the matriarch of the headache of family members abusing their access to the landline and force each individual to be responsible for their own bills, it severs the way in which these intra-family economic relations traditionally affirmed the central role and control by the senior female figure.

These same elderly women also tend to pride themselves on their pragmatism in talking about such issues. They will recognize the advantages of a cell phone when going to church at night for security purposes, and that occasionally it is useful when out on the road or to keep in touch with children and other relatives who are out on the road. They also affirm its importance in keeping in touch with relatives living abroad. In terms of actual usage they may not differ much from the rest of the household but it is more their attitude to the phone that is the distinguishing factor. They are clear and explicit about their rejection of anything they see as mere fad or gimmick, including texts, and often feel they are 'too old' for these sorts of things. But the way they respond suggests that there is a positive intent behind their rejection, that they are using their discrimination of what they see as useful and useless elements of the technology to affirm their own status as experienced pragmatists.

All of this helps to explain the way in which phone costs were discussed. The cost per minute of each phone call on a landline is a mere fraction of that by a cell phone (see Chapter 2). As most cell phones are now Digicel and a high proportion of calls from landlines must now be to cell phones, to spend nearly thirty times as much to make calls (as was the case when one had been largely calling landline to landline) seems an extraordinary premium to pay for the privilege of using a cell phone. What was even more extraordinary is how little this came up within an ethnography basically devoted to the subject of phone use and poverty. It seems not unreasonable to suggest that most Jamaicans are 'in denial' in the sense of being unwilling to recognize just how much more expensive the cell phone is for them to use. Occasionally we met someone who talked positively about and swore by their landline, making incontestable points about its advantages for engaging in long conversations and once again we began to question why such things were hardly ever mentioned by anyone else.

There are some caveats here. A landline may be extremely inexpensive on a minute by minute basis but when rental of the line is included there is a major cost that does not exist for cell phones, although, once this bill is paid, it makes even less sense to use a cell phone when a landline is available. Also, and as more and more people obtain Digicel cell phones, it actually becomes cheaper to call people Digicel to Digicel than to use landlines to call a Digicel. Similarly, even if the ultimate bill is greater for the cell phone, the actual experience of having one's credit constantly run out provides the sense of having much more discipline to one's conversations on a cell phone than on a landline and much less cause to regret loquaciousness. In short, the actual experience of using the phone is one of appearing to be in greater control of the cost. Both of these are major factors in the current tendency to abandon the landline altogether. Nevertheless, there has been a two-year process of transition where people have given themselves very considerable additional costs, largely because of an overwhelming desire to move to the cell phone in general and the Digicel cell phone in particular. It is here where both push factors, such as this legacy of antipathy to C&W, and pull factors, related to the way cell phones are used and the degree of individual control, have to be taken into account. To some degree the argument depends on social networking (see Chapter 5), but, to pre-empt this discussion, much of the reason has to do with the precise way in which phones are used and the way the genres of conversation have a bearing on how expensive each type of communication is, as well as the relationship to the billing process and economics of phone use itself.

Nonetheless, most people told us they had moved to the cell phone in order to save money and our evidence suggests that the reverse was true. It is difficult to compare actual figures, which are extremely diverse and involve in almost every instance different complicating factors. As an aggregate generalization, a bill of around $JA2,750 a month seemed common for a landline. Although a typical bill would be around $JA400 per week for such a household, there are many who spend money on fewer than two cards a week, or under $JA260, and many who spend more than $JA1,000 a week. On this basis even a household with two phones in operation would be outspending their monthly landline bill. However, the actual average was three phones per household.

It is difficult to compare actual figures. Some householders could be quite precise, such as the household that said, 'We keep it to under $JA1,500 unless my mother is visiting, in which case to $JA 2,700,' which suggests that it is possible to control the bill in a way most people claim cannot be done. With respect to the cell phone, around 15 per cent claimed to spend more than $JA1,000 per week on their cell phone(s). The rest split evenly between those who spent either over or under $JA260 (the equivalent of two cards per week). Although incomes are generally lower, the expenditure on cell phones is often higher in Orange Valley due to the lack of landlines as well as the relative isolation.

Yet, even if the cell phone cost more, there were economic incentives to use them. As we shall see in Chapter 6, for low-income individuals the problem is often the temporalities of credit and a monthly bill could constitute a crisis compared with an on-going cost. As a young man explained, 'When you hook it up straight yuh can call anybody yuh want and then the bill come to you and then them kill yuh off wid the bill.' Most users of cell phones saw the great advantage of the prepaid card system in the possibilities it offered for disciplining one's usage. People spoke constantly about their ability to control costs. For example, a taxi driver noted that:

> When I had a house phone I use to call my family one a month and the bill so high because we talk long. But now I put a $JA200 card on my phone and I can call and talk and when it done it done. So I call more because I don't have to worry about the bill to come, because I use a card.

This micro-control is of considerable importance, such that Digicel felt that their main selling point when they first launched was their offer to bill per second as opposed to per minute. Nevertheless, people do seem to have reasons for refusing to 'see' the additional costs of cell phones and it is reasonable to suggest that this denial relates more to the internal dynamics of the family and the Jamaican sense of how money within families ought to work than with simply the decontextualized economics of the phone.

Conclusions

In this chapter a series of examples of possession have been discussed, ranging from individualized billing to personal fascias. As an experience of the cell phone, these have also to be viewed as a whole. In London, for example, facility with texting has for some time become part of urban cool. A confident young adult is someone who is speaking to you and at the very same time with one hand texting a message to someone else. The drama of this new faculty can be imagined if one thinks of this as the first time one person has been able to simultaneously speak with two voices. But this has to be done with a certain nonchalance not to appear clumsy. So the cell phone becomes integrated as a kind of intelligent clothing that communicates between the outside and the inside as all clothing does, but rather more explicitly. In Jamaica, flashing a colour screen, opening up the flip phone, or laughing loudly at a private joke told over the phone exploit this ambiguity between overhearing what is unintended for public consumption and making the private deliberately available for public consumption. All of these can be stylistic and performative conceits, which work precisely because there is another generation or another cadre of less confident and accomplished peers who fumble with text, who appear awkward finding themselves engaged in private conversation in public and whose handsets are dull and backward. In the tradition of material culture studies, what we have tried to document in this chapter is therefore not just a new technology but new kinds of Jamaicanness, including Jamaicans whose new identity emerges from a new dimension of social exclusion.

This conclusion would be true of any region where the cell phone has become present, but this chapter also speaks to the specificity of Jamaican usage. Of course, in Jamaica, as elsewhere, the reasons people take up cell phones will to some degree include its most evident features such as constancy of communication, mobility, individual control, privacy or opportunities for micro-management (e.g. Brown et al. 2001; Katz and Aakhus 2002; Ling 2004). Some of these, such as security and social networking, will be the topic of subsequent chapters. But in this chapter the primary issue has been the particular nature of Jamaican individualism. Much of the next chapter is concerned with the specific nature of individualism in Jamaica, which makes it an entirely different animal from that of other regions. It does not have any necessary consequence of isolationism, is nothing like Simmel's individual in a crowd and is not particularly related to Western liberalism or ideology (Strathern 1992). There are many instances in this chapter of behaviour that is much more communal than in many regions, and here is seen as entirely compatible with this particular form of individualism. Its roots may have more to do with issues of freedom and repudiation of oppression as in slavery, as well as the necessarily individualistic coping that came from that same historical foundation (Besson and Momsen 1987; Besson 1992; Thomas-Hope 1995).

What this volume does offer, however, is a sense of how such a general term as individualism works with respect to this particular medium. We have seen how important this individualism has become as an expression of intra-family autonomy expressed through separate billing. In turn, this is connected to the individualism of public performative expression, which takes place in Jamaica less through the personalized phone preferred in some countries and more through expressive talk and conversation that is meant to be overheard. Here the sense of self becomes evident through performative individualism whereby the true person is not seen so much as an 'inner' deep persona but rather emerges through others' response to them. This process is characteristic of egalitarian societies without strong institutional hierarchy (Miller 1994). This performative aspect of the self is also brought out by a cell phone whose aural quality emerges not only in conversation but also through a concern with ringtones and the phone as a 'sound system'. The topic of possession therefore begins a conversation not just about individualism but about the very specific nature of Jamaican individualism, a topic that takes centre stage in the next chapter.

–5–

Link-up

One of the dominant themes within the recent literature on new communication technologies has been that of the increasing tendency towards ego-centred networks, often seen as part of the larger creation of the network society (Castells 1996, 1997, 1998). This phenomenon is often taken to be itself a response to both technological changes, such as the advent of the cell phone, which makes it possible, and social changes, such as the decline of community, which make it desirable. Wellman (1999, 2002) in particular has seen the technological innovations represented by the Internet and the cell phone as instrumental in creating such 'networked individualism', while loosening the social bonds that are the basis of what in one recent literature have come to be termed 'social capital' (Wellman and Wellman 1992; Baron et al. 2000). Harper (2003), who sees these arguments as part of a fairly unreconstructed Durkheimian lament, has rejected this conclusion, claiming that the early results of research on actual usage of the phone lend no support to this general argument. As Harper suggests, if anything, 'the evidence would seem to suggest that what is being done with the mobile is a kind of invigorating of social relations' (2003: 194).

It is certainly possible that there are parts of the world where the spread of the cell phone leads to the rise of individually centred networks, becoming the dominant form of sociality in the modern world, and that this replaces more communal forms of networking. But for the anthropologist perhaps the most serious problem with this debate is the level of generalization, which makes the world as a whole the site of this movement from society to individualism (e.g. Beck and Beck-Gernsheim 2001). For anthropologists, both society and individualism are constituted in myriad ways and what is needed are detailed case studies that show how much more subtle the relationship between individuals and wider networks can be today and how much more complex their relationship has been in the past. This is precisely the point we want to make for Jamaica.

Intensifying Relationships

The view from Everest almost justifies the rather impressive name of the settlement. High up above Orange Valley there may not be snow but there is a wonderful carpet laid out of citrus and small valleys. As in many classic studies of village life (Clarke 1966), almost everyone is connected to each other through the three founding families in the area. The use of the phone can therefore never be something that is easily extracted from this web of connections. The Levy family, which consists of a mother, father, son, daughter and, most recently, a grandson, is tied to one of the founding families through Mrs Levy. The cell phone quickly became central to their family since this is an area that never had landlines, and the arrival of the cell phone conveniently corresponded with their son's move away to school and Victor Levy's work as a taxi driver, keeping each member of the family connected. Prior to the cell phone, Victor would be away for the entire day without contacting his family and his son Max called sporadically, either at prearranged times or, in the event of an emergency, through the Levys' family friend living in the neighbouring district. Now Mr and Mrs Levy speak several times a day, Mrs Levy contacts Max almost daily and Max calls his father at least once a week.

When we first met Tracy Levy in 2004, she was attending a local community college doing preliminary coursework for a business degree. Shortly afterwards, we learned that she mysteriously decided to drop out of the programme. The gossip on the road was that she had fallen pregnant from her boyfriend of the past six months. None of this seemed to come as a shock to her family, friends and neighbours in the district. In fact, many of her neighbours and relatives had to a degree conspired with Tracy and her boyfriend Ricardo to facilitate this and to hide their relationship from Tracy's father, who sometimes gave Ricardo work driving his taxi for the day. Their friend Ziggy allowed the couple to use his place when he was away during the day, as did one of Tracy's older male cousins.

Once the couple had secured places to meet, the issue became coordinating a time since they lived in two separate districts. For this they employed the cell phones of various neighbours and friends. Speaking on or through these phones daily, they would agree upon a day and when the day came Ricardo sent Tracy a text message saying that he was on his way. When he arrived at Ziggy's house, Ricardo then called one of her neighbours, also an extended family member, and asked them to pass by Tracy's house to tell her that he had arrived. She would then go to meet him wearing her school uniform, sometimes calling a friend to see if there was anyone else who might reveal their secret tryst. Tracy had skipped enough school in this fashion that, when she realized she was pregnant, she decided to drop out altogether, even though her late-summer due date would have allowed her to complete the year. The phone was also instrumental in helping Ricardo keep his relationship with Tracy (his main girl) separate from the several other girlfriends he had at the time.

When Tracy's father discovered that his daughter was pregnant, he felt hurt and betrayed. The pain and anger did not subside when he came to realize that

$JA75,000 (or $US1,250) of school fees had gone to complete waste. He felt that everyone was 'in' on their little secret, which made him look like a fool, and he began spending more and more time on the road and with his own girlfriend and less time at home with his wife and daughter. Indeed, his main contact with his wife was now by phone through brief messages, and for a long time he did not speak to Tracy. The events came to a climax the day that Tracy's son fell ill, three days after coming home from the hospital. After trying to call her mother, who was visiting a friend, she resorted to phoning her father, who picked her up and made a very annoyed phone call to his wife to report that they were returning to the hospital in Mandeville. Ricardo first saw his son a week later, when Tracy's father was out on the road. Since she now had to stay home to care for their child, their meetings dwindled to around once a month, and even their phone conversations started to trail off. Ricardo's gradual withdrawal from the picture was no surprise to Tracy's father, given Ricardo's reputation as a womanizer. But this was no comfort to Mr Levy. In part, he blamed the cell phone itself and its ability to facilitate such deceits, but at the same time he was well aware that it was the cell phone that had allowed him to expand his taxi work, earn the money that went into her school fees and supply her with everything he believed she needed.

Such a story, which could be repeated with endless variations, highlights the way the cell phone has become an instrument for creating networks, but also how the phone itself becomes entangled within the individual's and group's connections and relationships. Much of the literature cited in the introduction emphasizes the capacity of the cell phone to assist in the micro-coordination of activities and networking of relationships (e.g. Ling 2004), but this assumes greater significance when, as in Jamaica, one starts to appreciate that what we call a 'network' is such a complex, multi-stranded, overlapping, contradictory formation. In Jamaica relationships between relatives, friends and lovers reflect a dynamism that is fostered by deep generosity and concern for distant others. At the same time, these relationships are mediated by subterfuge and plurality that can transform the phone from a device that connects into a device whose importance lies in its capacity to keep multiple strands separate. We shall argue in this chapter that the cell phone's integration within contemporary Jamaican life is evident in the way it has become not just an 'agent' but also a moral force that for individuals such as Mr Levy shares the blame or credit for developments in one's social life.

The phone's role in coordination is most evident in intra-household communication, where it is used to track house keys, lend money or organize picking up a child from school. One family, which runs a small restaurant in Orange Valley, probably communicates more readily and frequently by phone even within the house than they do face to face. A close family, this constant exchange reveals the constancy of their care for each other (see also Ito et al. 2005). By making the phone rather than the presence of the person the mode of their care, the result is that, when a member of the household is out on the road, the cell phone is used to make it seem as though they were just as accessible. The constant flurry of calls are mainly trivial in content, such as remembering to buy bread or bring home a *Gleaner* or relaying something funny that just happened at the restaurant. It also communicates where they are, how much progress they have made and the time when they should reach a given destination safely. A recent event that more than justified this constant usage occurred when gunmen took up position to waylay and rob passing traffic. When rumour of this plan hit town, the wife at the restaurant immediately called to make sure her husband took a different route. This blurring of proximity extends to their relationship to key shop workers. The head cook also supervises the upkeep of this essential instrument of communication by entering the pass code on the phonecards into their individual phones, as well as any new names and numbers in their phone, which keeps their phone number lists up to date. For such a family a division into the instrumental and the caring or between the material object and the person makes no sense. The phone has effectively usurped co-presence as the very experience of sociability simply because they could sense that by utilizing it they could extend their feelings of closeness and care.

In a similar manner, the phone also becomes part of the extended household. Bijei, who commands a large household, describes two of her entries in her cell phone book:

Racey, one little boy that mi know, one nice little send out boy. Send him to shop ... if him don't do it mi a go beat him up. Everyday when mi can't bother him over him house, mi call him on the phone, him must answer ... Scott is my little friend. [mi call im] only when mi want sumpen mi call him though [for] money, buy sumpen for me a town or sumpen ... call seh is a month.

Racey is one little boy that I know, a nice little send out boy. I send him to the shop and if he doesn't do it I will go beat him up. Everyday when I cannot bother to go over to his house, I call him on the cell phone and he must answer ... Scott is my little friend. I call him only when I want something. I call him for money, to buy something for me in Kingston or something ... I call him once a month.]

This practice of sending out a boy or a child to do little tasks (picking up a loaf of bread or ice or delivering a message to a person down the road) has been prevalent for years. Although in Bijei's case these are older boys, children as young as age three or four regularly run errands, paying for food, alcohol or even cigarettes at a local shop. Similarly, surrounding neighbours and family members can use the phone to check if a child has arrived home or to collect a package for someone if they cannot make it home. The cell phone is a particular boon to the elderly or to housewives with babies, who can now summon a neighbour or child to pick up the cooking oil or a packet of soup or arrange for a new gas drum.

This use of the phone to organize favours extends to voluntary associations and blends easily into the networks involved in small-scale entrepreneurial work. For example, Peter Sharpe's phone contains 171 numbers, which can be divided into those he knows as individual friends and relatives he keeps in touch with and who may do each other favours. These friends and relatives represent his social and economic networks, such as the church band, the church, the partners group, his business, and a large group of back-up numbers saved in the event that he should need them, though some are rarely, if ever, called, or as he phrased it, 'from mi get this number, mi neva punch it!' The two categories of people that are most frequently called are musicians that play in his church band and individuals who also help in organizing church activities. Some of these are family, such as his brother, who plays in the band, some are neighbours in his close-knit district who have become like family and others are church brothers and sisters. There is no clear boundary between these and his business-related calls, since these may be electricians, taxi drivers, customers, his 'partners' saving scheme, and those who make up his egg business (see Chapter 6), simply because his customers and those he needs for services are almost always also friends, relatives and neighbours. The economy of favours leads both to the economy of commerce and to the social networking of family, neighbourhood and church.

These networks are also used to create and maintain friendships. It is, after all, a neighbour who might be visiting a pharmacy and can save you a visit if you call while they are there, or a neighbour who is most keenly interested in what you saw another neighbour doing the night before. The cell phone can circulate information and gossip almost instantly. For example, as Heather (co-author) moved between field sites, she was often amazed by the ability of her own movements to be discussed and shared through the cell phone. With some regularity, Heather would be spotted on a bus or taxi heading towards Orange Valley and would receive a call en route or almost the instant she arrived from individuals who were keen to see her. Even if she was dropped off in a private vehicle at the gate of a friend's house, she often received a call from other friends who had heard about her arrival.

Perhaps the most extreme example of this instrumental and affective networking across distance emerges through the use of the phone in childcare. It was quite unusual in our fieldwork to come across a mother with a young child where the biological father was living in the same household (Clarke 1966; Massiah 1983; Black 1995; Safa 1995; R.T. Smith 1996). Children were sometimes sent to live with relatives of their biological mother or father rather than residing with either, an example of what has been called child-shifting in the Caribbean literature (Soto 1987; Senior 1991: 12–18; Barrow 1996; Olwig 1999b). As a result, one of the single most important uses of the phone comes from its ability to help ameliorate the negative consequences of these separations. The biological mother may see the phone as an opportunity to be in daily contact with the woman looking after her child. Relationships with baby-fathers vary considerably, but once again there are many cases where they are in daily contact. In other cases, contact is mainly restricted to issues of economic responsibility. In the past when baby-fathers were reluctant to give support, baby-mothers had to make long treks as supplicants but the phone now saves them considerable, inconvenient and costly travelling. In effect, the cell phone has become central to this particular form of child-rearing and helps overcome some of the contradictions experienced by the separation between childcare and a continued identification with biological parentage. Yvette, for example, looks after one of her four children but the child's baby-father is in constant phone contact with them.[1] In addition, she employs her cell phone to keep in touch with one of her other baby-fathers and his family, who care for her two older children. While the children are not yet able to own a phone, Yvette imagines an ideal future when the phone will allow her to remain in direct contact with them. What she may not be envisaging (but is quite clear to the children themselves) is that they will soon become proactive in these relationships. Many children spoke of using the phone as their means to cajole or obtain money from both parents in order to, among other things, pay for their own phone bills. All of these cases seem to fit what Harper (2003) describes as the invigorating or intensification of close relationships. However, we want to be clear that in many cases ethnography reveals possible ambivalence and contradictory effects of such intensification, which vanish with any appraisal that simply seems to want to evaluate the phone as either socially good or evil.

The Transnational Family

Migration has been a pervasive feature of Jamaican society and almost all Jamaicans we encountered could list a range of relations who live 'in foreign', a category that typically refers to the main migration destinations of the USA, Canada, the UK and, to a lesser extent, other Caribbean countries (Foner 1978, 1983, 2001; Bolles 1981; Colen 1990; Thomas-Hope 1992; Henry 1994, Horst 2004b). In the past, however, telephone communication has been sporadic due to the expense or inconvenience associated with telephone calls. Mail communication and even telegrams were also far from ubiquitous. Thomas-Hope (1992: 131–132) shows that, in the late 1980s, 37.52 per cent of the populations she surveyed never or rarely received letters from people abroad, 28.57 per cent received letters occasionally and 33.91 per cent received letters frequently, with rural areas receiving the lowest levels of correspondence, and 6.7 per cent had no foreign contacts at all. When Horst first travelled to Jamaica in 1994, relatives living abroad were almost exclusively responsible for maintaining telephone contact with 'home', often through prearranged calls since most rural Jamaicans were without their own phones. One Portmore family recalled how everyone used to bathe and dress for their bimonthly trek to the call box. While they noted that there was one box located about ten minutes' walk away, it was often too congested to make their call. Instead, they walked for about thirty minutes to another call box and waited in line for an hour to place a five- to ten-minute call to their husband and father working in the Cayman Islands.

As phones became more established in urban and rural Jamaica, residents were given three options for making international contacts. Those with phones could apply for an ICAS code, a ten-digit code required for approval of outgoing overseas calls. Not only was there a fee for this code, but it could be used from multiple telephones and, if discovered, one could end up being responsible for another person's calls. In addition, the calls were prohibitively expensive for low-income Jamaicans. In lieu of an ICAS code, Jamaicans were also able to purchase a 'World Talk' card from Cable and Wireless in certain denominations (e.g. $JA50, $JA100, $JA200, $JA500 and, most recently, $JA1,000).These, too, worked out to be extremely expensive and could easily be misplaced. They also had to be used up within a limited time frame (thirty days). Most Jamaicans chose the third option, which was to place a collect call to get in contact with family and friends living abroad, at least until 2001 (see Horst 2006).

All of this changed radically with the arrival of Digicel. One no longer needed a special ICAS code or an operator to mediate the call. In addition, the receipt of the call did not depend upon whether a relative was prepared to accept an expensive collect call or the relative or friends felt compelled to return a call. Most importantly, the price of the calls came down with competition to a mere $JA17 a minute, almost the same price as a local call across different companies. All one needed was a phone, phonecard and phone number and a call could be made to anyone at any time. The only thing that was now required was the discipline to stop oneself from buying more phonecards than one could really afford.

In the case of Jamaica this was not just a huge boon to communication within the often extended and transnational family (Thomas-Hope 1988; Olwig 1999c, 2001; Goulbourne and Chamberlain 2001; Thompson and Bauer 2001; Vertovec 2004); it also marked a fundamental change in the relationship between parents and children. Not only could parents who lived in the Cayman Islands, USA, Canada, England or elsewhere make calls to their children living with relatives in the more dispersed rural areas of Jamaica but their children (and children's care-takers) could also initiate calls to the parents. Many of the schoolchildren we interviewed waited with great anticipation for the weekly call from their father or mother, noting how they sometimes saved their lunch money just to hear their parent's voice. This allowed for much more involvement of parents in their children's intellectual and emotional development. One schoolgirl talked about how she called her mother for encouragement before her upcoming examinations and later updated her on the results. A teenaged young man found the phone to be critical to building up his estranged relationship with his father outside of the watchful eye of his mother's family; the relationship had changed so much as a result of their phone contact that his father was helping him to apply for and to financially support him while he attended community college in Miami.

In many respects, the relationship that could now develop between Jamaica and 'foreign', including the remittance system discussed in the next chapter, echoes structures created over centuries in the relationship between urban centres and rural peripheries. Traditionally the larger extended family had seen clear advantages to retaining both a rural and an urban base. A family in an urban centre whose male teenager looks as if he is heading for disaster can arrange for him to live out his more turbulent years in the relative safety of a rural family. A rural family with a child accepted by a prestigious school in Kingston can organize a stay with relatives in town in order to lower the cost. In all such arrangements, the phone simplifies the logistics of negotiation and coordination that are involved. Prior to the phone, rural families made journeys at considerable cost with respect to both time and money just to discuss some such possible arrangement for their children.

The ways these new transnational relationships are discussed often sound remarkably similar to this older rural–urban linkage. Although some Jamaicans seek to move abroad permanently, most envision working abroad for a period of time in order to take advantage of opportunities or to raise the capital for particular projects at home, such as buying or fixing up a house and most recently, purchasing a car or taxi. Those individuals who manage to go abroad receive significant help with letters, interviews and visas, as well as financial backing and support. Family abroad may also locate possible jobs. With low-cost international calls, families can work out and negotiate the logistics of petitioning for an individual to take a holiday or migrate more permanently. While the work involved in uniting a family for a holiday or a wedding involves layers of bureaucracy not found in the visits to town by family from the country, there are certainly parallels.

The reverse can also be true. Having helped their less sophisticated relatives deal with tax forms and insurance schemes, an urban scion might pay a visit to their rural cousins and return laden with country produce in a manner that remains reminiscent of Ovid's beloved town mouse and country mouse. Today the visits of relatives to Jamaica from abroad during the Christmas season and the efforts made to make sure that their visitors 'enjoy themselves' at the rum bar and eat 'real' Jamaican food such as curry goat or ackee and salt fish, become part of a wider performance of authenticity, although it may not be realized quite to the extent that Olwig has reported for Nevis and St Kitts (1993, 1999a). In addition, the cell phone has become central to making specific requests for items to be included in the famous 'barrels' that are typically sent annually and filled with shoes and clothing, appliances, soap and detergent as well as basic foodstuffs such as rice and cooking oil. While cell phones are relatively cheap in Jamaica, it is also not unusual for visiting family members to bring more sophisticated phones as gifts so that a particular nephew or cousin can keep in touch.

Extending Relationships

However important, neither intensifying relationships nor renewing relationships with those abroad constitutes the heart of Jamaican use of the cell phone. Rather, what is already emerging as the single most important characteristic form of cell phone use, and one that manages to also incorporate both of these other uses, represents a quite specific understanding of the nature and possibilities of communication itself, one where communication no longer appears as a means to some other end, but where we can start to engage in an anthropological analysis of communication itself. This phenomenon, what we call 'link-up', is becoming a central value and imperative in its own right. To be clear, however, we are not suggesting that it is itself a result of the introduction of the cell phone. Quite the contrary. We found that this is one of the most significant arenas in which the cell phone has become appropriated to fit within a well-established feature of Caribbean communication. Indeed, Abrahams (1983) comes remarkably close to precisely the same point almost three decades before the cell phone arrived when he observed, 'Rather than looking on communication as calling for the passing on of a message within a clearly defined presentational unit, the Vincentian seeks to emphasize interpersonal relationships established through talk, and information-passing is subordinated to a sense of celebration in coming together for the purposes of simply pursuing friendships' (123). Whereas Abrahams was focusing upon friendship networks, we came to the same conclusion through wrestling with the problem of understanding the ways low-income Jamaicans used the phone.

Our own understanding of this phenomenon came vicariously when we realized that our attempts to engage with cell phone use through the analysis of conversation were achieving very limited results, partly because the conversations themselves seemed so limited in informational or even affective content. At the same time we were following the brief given by our research project and collecting core questionnaire-based data with 100 households for later comparison with the other three countries included within this programme. One thing that struck us was how many individuals seemed to know, without looking, exactly how many numbers they had stored on their phone's address book. Technically most phones had the capacity to store 200 names both within the phone and on the SIM card, but most people only seemed to know of one or other and, to our surprise, quite a few seemed concerned by what they experienced as a limited capacity of only 200 numbers.

In response, we decided to focus on this material and ask twenty-five individuals, most of whom were part of our general ethnography, to actually sit down with us and scroll through these numbers, establishing the nature of the connection, when they had last spoken and what they had spoken about for each entry (usually saved as either a name or phone number). Obviously there are clear limitations in regarding such a list as a proper reflection of an individual's network. Alongside the recognition that not every person in an individual's personal network may own a cell phone, there are also limits as to how many names can be stored on the phone as well as the fact that cell phones are often lost or stolen, in which case neither the SIM cards nor the phones are safe repositories. We heard many a person cursing their failure to provide written backup when the patiently accumulated contacts were lost, such as when a phone fell down the toilet or was stolen on a bus.

When we first began to appreciate the extensive nature of these lists, we saw an obvious analogy in an influential publication by R.T. Smith. Smith's classic analysis, *Kinship and Class in the West Indies* (1988),[2] summarized a research study involving the collaboration of a number of anthropologists working in the Caribbean.[3] With the intention of moving beyond narrowly defined kinship categories, Smith sought to gain a better sense of people's own perception of kinship by collecting comprehensive listings of all those considered to be relatives from fifty-one principal participants, who were mainly from Jamaica (with an additional component from Guyana). Amongst other findings, what was most striking was the sheer size of these lists of kin, an overall mean of 284, or more than twice the number of kin reported by Schneider (1968) for white Americans (Smith 1988: 49). It was also found that a baby-father's kin[4] became incorporated into a mother and child's network, even if the baby-father himself took no responsibility for the child's emotional, financial, educational or social upbringing. In short, Smith's book appeared to conclude decades of study by suggesting that, in Jamaica, there may be little concern with the precise definition of kin and little interest in the kind of normative and jural rules of kinship and descent that had dominated much of the early history of anthropology. Instead, kinship was more important as an extensive network of potential connections as expressed through the awareness of individuals recognized as relatives.

Given this tradition of scholarship from Smith and others, one might surmise that the cell phone would be a crucial tool in intensifying kinship networks. Both of our earlier discussions, the situation found in 'Everest' as well as the maintenance of the transnational family, might seem to support this conclusion. Yet looking at this material as a whole, what is striking is that, while the importance of kin varied greatly, on the whole it was much less significant than might have been expected. While the average of all our phone address books contained ninety-five names, only thirteen of these were kin. Kin were most prominent among the women, who led relatively sheltered lives and tended to have smaller address books overall. For a surprising number of the larger address books, especially men's, kin were almost entirely absent, although it should be said that in our household survey over half of the 100 individuals interviewed said that their last calls were made to family. For many individuals kin clearly dominate in terms of intensive relationships. The problem was that, unlike in Smith's research, kin were less important in relation to extensive networks.

It would be hard to overestimate the importance of networking or the establishment of connections and 'links' in Jamaica. Certainly, walking down the street, it is quite common to see people meet very briefly and exchange phone numbers for possible future contact. This is not to suggest that everyone freely gives out their cell phone number. Women noted that they often gave men a false number, transposing the digits or making up numbers so that they would finally leave them alone. Others preferred to take numbers rather than give them out to avoid difficult circumstances such as a girlfriend answering a phone. Indeed, almost everyone had a few people in their phone that they had just met but never called because it was too recent.

Yet these chance encounters could also lead to more substantial relationships. Sheryl, for example, found her recent boyfriend visiting a friend in the country. Her boyfriend was a brother of one of the friend's co-workers, who happened to be in the shop the day that they met. Michael kept the name of a man who repaired cars and could obtain cheap car parts. Lisa took down the name of a security guard at the farm workers' programme office in the event that she wanted to apply to the programme in the near future. The guard took her phone number to call when he was visiting his family, who lived in the neighbouring district. Most people's phone lists include numbers that represent potential services, such as someone working at Western Union or a person who can braid hair, but also others that represented possible liaisons that might or might not include sexual partners. In practice, many of these initial contacts were vague and ill-defined.

A basic description of the twenty-five phone lists is provided in Table 5.1, the smallest list containing only eleven names and the largest 209 names (with an average of ninety-five). Three of the individuals we interviewed had more than one phone. Typically the largest phone lists were contained on Digicel phones. Since a few numbers were not disclosed and others were recent purchases, it may well be that our sample underestimates the typical phone list. But it was never intended that this group should be taken as a strict sample of a population. Rather, it reflects the predominantly low-income individuals who participated in this aspect of the research. The lack of elderly individuals in these lists reflects their relative paucity of cell phone possession and some of the smaller phone lists

Table 5.1 Phone Lists

Name	Number of Names	Kin	Non-kin	Gender	Age Range	Location	Current Economic Situation
Allison	16	6	10	F	30s	Urban	supported by baby-father
Bijei	209	17	192	F	10s	Urban	employed full-time retail
Bridgette	34	11	21	F	10s	Urban	former student, sells phonecards
Camille	95	18	77	F	20s	Rural	helps out in family business
Charmaine	12	6	6	F	40s	Urban	supported by baby-father
Damian	126	13	113	M	10s	Rural	student, street vending
Donnovan	39	16	23	M	10s	Urban	student, supported by mother
Dorothy	42	19	23	F	40s	Rural	runs small shop
Grace	154	26	128	F	20s	Urban	student/teacher
Joydene	11	5	6	F	20s	Urban	supported by father and baby-father
Junior	176	16	160	M	20s	Urban	employed full-time retail
Keisha	102	21	81	F	30s	Rural	supported by baby-father, sells phonecards
Lisa	90	15	75	F	30s	Rural	unemployed, supported by boyfriend(s)
Marlon	183	8	175	M	20s	Urban	student, supported by mother and father
Michael	13	0	13	M	30s	Rural	drives taxi
Michelle	45	10	35	F	10s	Urban	former student, supported by mother and boyfriend
Monique	166	11	155	F	30s	Urban	supervisor at shop
Peter	171	22	149	M	30s	Rural	supervisor at shop, farming
Robert	195	7	188	M	20s	Urban	unemployed, supported by uncle
Romeo	193	31	162	M	10s	Rural	student, supported by mother and girlfriends
Sonia	85	5	80	F	30s	Urban	works part-time, domestic help
Tameka	30	8	22	F	10s	Rural	helps out at family shop, supported by father
Tyrone	98	11	87	M	30s	Urban	employed full-time, shift work
Winston	51	16	35	M	40s	Rural	works part-time in construction
Yvette	33	9	24	F	30s	Urban	supported by baby-father/boyfriend
Average number of names	**95**	**13**	**82**				

represent recently purchased phones rather than the actual size of individuals' networks.

The basic figures disguise a number of quite different concerns, each of which may lead to the accumulation of an extensive network. For example, there are many individuals whose lives are consumed by their service to their religious beliefs or their jobs as taxi drivers or involvement in sporting activities. Nevertheless, if there were a single most common form of extensive networking in Jamaica, it revolves around the potential of sexual liaisons. For example, Robert's phone book contains 195 names and numbers. Most of these names belong to women he hopes to have, is having or has had some kind of relationship with in the past. As with many men, Robert possesses various categories into which these are divided. In his case, there are no baby-mothers yet, but there are a series of current relationships, a designated principal relationship and then second and third principal relationship that are ongoing. Far more extensive are the links with women he describes as 'less good looking', who constantly call him though he rarely calls back, and those women he designates as particularly attractive, whom he calls quite often but who only rarely call him back.

In addition to sexual relationships, this kind of networking may also have an explicit additional agenda. Lisa, for example, has always seen her primary aim as finding a man sufficiently solvent and reliable to support her.[5] Now a thirty-year-old mother, she has this mode of survival down to an art, or at least some sort of system. Over the past decade, Lisa has been cultivating relationships with men of various ages and marital status, on the constant lookout for someone with whom she might be able to settle down to support herself and her son, whose baby-father, now living 'in foreign', has been absent almost since conception. Over the years Lisa has had numerous boyfriends, many of whose number are still saved in her phone and she calls on a regular basis just to 'check them' and keep the relationship viable. Those whom she may have loved but who 'could do nothing for her' were often dispensed with for more transient relationships, such as a local big man who could provide her with a few thousand dollars every few months but for whom she would never settle entirely. While some of these relationships involved sexual encounters, others simply involved flirtation.

In addition, Lisa is keen to cultivate relationships with men who travel or live permanently abroad. In fact, Lisa stopped working after she had a falling-out with her mother, who was looking after her son. Since then, her survival has been primarily dependent upon her relationships with two men, her Jamaican boyfriend, who sends her $JA5,000 monthly, often via Western Union, and her German boyfriend, who sends $JA5,000 for her expenses and an extra $JA3,000 for her son, also through Western Union. In fact, she only met with her Jamaican boyfriend every month or two and had not seen her German boyfriend since his visit to the island over a year ago. Lisa's financial stability came to a halt when her

German boyfriend asked her to link him up with another Jamaican woman for a friend. Unfortunately, the woman decided to write to Lisa's boyfriend to tell him that Lisa was sleeping with other men. Lisa's boyfriend started to call her a couple of times a day, harassing her about her whereabouts, what she was doing and how she was raising her son. Shortly thereafter, he stopped sending the $JA5,000 for her upkeep and he also phoned to say that the application for her to join him in Germany was denied. Her relationship with her Jamaican boyfriend also ended shortly afterwards when Lisa learned about the pregnancy of one of his other girl-friends.

Wondering how she was going to manage without these two main sources of support, Lisa began to go through the ninety names saved in her phone, one by one, calling men who she knew 'have it' (i.e. those with regular pay cheques, such as civil servants), old boyfriends and other potential 'friends' to revitalize those links which might help her meet her expenses. About one-third of the way through her list, she asked a friend to send her a phonecard (a request he granted) so that she could continue to reinvigorate her links. In each case, she did not ask for money but was calling to ask 'whagwaan' (what's going on) and see they were 'alright'. While there were a few names that Lisa skipped over, she noted that she should call Owen, despite the fact he probably did not have any money because he is supportive. She now has a standing marriage proposal from another man she met while visiting another Caribbean island a few years ago, one that might help her to secure a job and a viable financial future for herself and her son in that country.

The list of names on Lisa's phone is complemented by a much larger collection of names she keeps in a handwritten list stuck in a file attached to her wall, which remains there for safe keeping. There are seven or eight people she claims to speak to by phone every day, including her present boyfriend but also two (out of nine) males she describes as ex-boyfriends from her list. It is noticeable that such men tend to be defined also in terms of having regular employment, such as firemen or policemen. Others relate to different kinds of help she may require, such as two local politicians who might help in obtaining employment. There are some ten rel-atives, but these are primarily cousins and again blend easily into the general cat-egories of friend or those who might help her in the future. Several of the men are also described as flirtatious or always pursuing her by phone and others include girlfriends she likes to go out with in the evening, and those living in the country-side that sometimes provide her with vegetables or sugar cane.

Another case of the importance of creating extensive networks through the cell phone was Romeo, an eighteen-year-old secondary school student. Romeo received his most recent phone, with features such as a colour screen, voice recorder and the Internet, from one of his girlfriends. Socially active, he kept a range of phone numbers, of which only about twenty were family, another per-centage school friends as well as friends from extra-curricular sports and music activities. He kept names of his 'crew', taxi drivers, teachers (overwhelmingly female), girlfriends and other friends as well as a significant number of his mother's friends and the mothers of his own girlfriends.

What emerged through our analysis of Romeo's phone book was the fluidity of his categories. Female teachers could give him advice with schooling, financial assistance and emotional encouragement, but they were also potential lovers. Schoolmates who were consulted for assignments could be potential contacts for jobs, such as a friend of his who recommended him for a summer job in tourism along the north coast. With almost all of Romeo's contacts who were not currently active (with the notable exception of those in certain extra-curricular activities), he tried to call every two weeks 'just to keep in touch'. Romeo called another set at least once or twice per week. To illustrate, when we first met Romeo, he had six girlfriends. However, he admitted that between calls and visits he was starting to feel overwhelmed and wanted to pare down his list to three girlfriends. Rather than breaking these off, however, he kept in contact with a range of 'potential girl-friends'. Like Robert, he had a series of girls and women whom he called with interest, those who called him and then another set of past girlfriends with whom he might reignite a relationship. A few months later, Romeo had successfully achieved his aim of only three girlfriends, one who was pursuing him, and the remaining two in the category of former girlfriends. He also maintains an extended relationship with his baby-mother, who lives in Florida with their two-year-old son.

While many of these extensive relationships are sexual in nature or overtone, it became clear that this practice of extending one's social network goes well beyond trying to 'get more gyal', as former Prime Minister P.J. Patterson is reported to have described a principal benefit of the cell phone in his last election campaign. Moreover, if these were merely the accumulation of lists of names akin to the infa-mous 'little black book', the phone lists and the extensive forms of networking would be of limited interest. We have highlighted this use of the phone for creating potential liaisons because it is one of the most common uses, but this should be considered in the context of the rest of this volume. In other chapters, we shall con-centrate on the accumulation of names and scrolling through the phones to find names for quite different reasons, such as the way these names are used to help people in coping strategies or dealing with issues such as health care or personal security. There are many Jamaicans who are completely opposed to these kinds of plural sexual relationships we have just documented and use their phones to develop extensive networks of church brothers and sisters, whom they can then summon for particular church events such as evangelical 'tents' and 'crusades'. Others use these networks to develop business contacts, which may range from informal trading in marijuana to selling clothes on a house-to-house basis, as well as quite formal entrepreneurship, such as finding the best price for agricultural products. And there is no clear boundary between these social and economic networks.

In Horst and Miller (2005) we argue that it is important that link-up is not then reduced to any particular genre. It is a form of extensive networking of the kind described by Smith for kin, but in our study we find that it is in no way particular to kin. Networking may develop through the friends of one's kin or the kin of one's friends. It is extensively used for economic development and coping but it is not particular to times of need. It is central to sexual liaisons but is just as prominent in church development. What is more significant is to see this as a characteristic of Jamaican communication, in which the desire to forge links becomes important in its own right. This point is strengthened when we consider the particular form taken by link-up in relation to the cell phone, because it is not just extensive lists of numbers that characterize it, but also the kinds of phone calls that it leads to.

Link-up calls dominate most of the phone usage by low-income individuals. Calls often consist of a question such as 'Hi how is everything?' and a reply such as 'Oh, I'm OK, I'm just enjoying the summer.' There are many strategies for maintaining such connections, even if there is little to them at that particular time. For example, a young woman summarizes the content of a recent call from a male friend: 'I haven't called him for a while and him ask if mi "get rich an switch." That's what he call mi an' ask mi.' Just as Abrahams (1983) argues that men must use their voice (and noise) to articulate their presence in large groups, her friend implied that to fail to keep in touch, even in touch about nothing in particular, would be like saying she is too good for him now. A primary characteristic of this link-up usage of the phone was the effort and expense put into keeping these lists constantly active; in some cases a high proportion of names were called every couple of weeks. These were often very short calls. According to Digicel (personal communication), the average length of a cell phone call in Jamaica is a mere nineteen seconds. It is no wonder, then, that our initial attempt to concentrate upon the content of conversations as a research tool was largely ineffective. Although our own work was limited to the study of low-income populations, some recent work on middle-class Jamaican university students' use of email reveals an almost identical pattern, wherein students sent emails simply to keep in touch (Hinrichs 2004, personal communication). As with link-up calls, these emails had very little content. As Hinrichs (personal communication) notes, 'It is especially frequent and strikingly common to the European researcher, for Jamaican students to write email messages that contain nothing but a reproach to the addressee for not keeping in touch.' Hinrichs's study suggests that link-up may be present for other socio-economic sectors of Jamaican society and in other technologies than those we studied.

In conclusion, the characteristic of link-up is that it consists of making a large number of very short calls, by which an individual not only accumulates a list of numbers but keeps these lists constantly active, with a high proportion of names called every couple of weeks. Most of these calls are just brief communication, nothing more. But these relationships can also be activated in relation to monetary, emotional or sexual needs, as well as what would be considered good-natured friendship, such as a call to stop by an old friend's house when you are in the area. A person you knew from school or you met through a mutual friend can be activated when need arises. In the case of Lisa and Romeo, many of these extensive relationships came with financial benefits, such as when Romeo's baby-mother paid his A-level examination fees. In fact, Lisa herself was keen to help others when she could. When Lisa's cousin decided he wanted to continue his studies, she used her personal networks and resources to help him find money. When we asked her why she was willing to help him at the same time she admitted to struggling to make it herself, she noted that her education was over and done and could not be altered. Her cousin, however, was smart and had his future ahead of him so she felt compelled to help. Lisa and Romeo also continued to keep in touch with individuals whom they called specifically for encourage-ment. Indeed, many of Romeo's teachers and sports coaches had become mentors to him and, when he was just about ready to give up his quest for university funding, he sometimes called them. In other words, these extended links often pick up where local and perhaps more intensive connections fall short. Moreover, while link-up is characterized by very short calls, it can also lead to other genres such as the 'counselling' calls discussed in Chapter 7.

The evidence that link-up may lead to more extensive usage of a relationship when the need arises does not mean that this is simply a functional response to need. As we shall argue in the next chapter, there is another side to this coin, which involves the giving of money that seems to have no necessity or hidden agenda. Indeed, our overall conclusion was that often the asking for resources and the giving of resources were as much directed by the desire to have and maintain the communication as the communication was a means to direct resources.

The Problem of 'Talk'

Link-up has become the foundation to communication as a form of networking. While often without content, it can be built upon to create relationships, realize projects and gain support. It can also become the basis for another kind of com-munication that does have content. Not surprisingly, the phone becomes employed as a means of extending and, indeed, creating 'talk'. A common criticism of the impact of the cell phone by elderly women and staunch Christians revolved around the general concern that the cell phone could be used to spread gossip or encourage other antisocial behaviour. Yet men were just as critical of the causes and consequences of gossip as moral Christians were. Almost as though they had learnt from the same script, men from both Orange Valley and Portmore would explain how easy it was for mistakes to be made by women when overhearing conversations held by men on the phone. As Winston put it:

> The bad side is people who use it to inform on you. You might be doing something here and Harry or Tom can tell on you and spread rumours. My lady friend tells me 'shut the phone off'. I don't like to shut the phone off because I want to know who is calling me. If I get a call she wants to know who it is and I have to explain to her. Sometime when I explain she don't know who it is. For me to get a call from someone I don't know and then say they dial the wrong number asking for a woman or a man. I don't know who they are talking, so I try to explain to my woman that it is a false call. It might look like I am lying. It appears that I know the person when I don't. Every numbers are close and some person can dial the wrong number and ends up calling your number. They might say 364 and it is 346 and you get the numbers mixed up.

The majority of men found some reason to include in their general conversations about the cell phone a similar patient explanation of how easy it is to get a mistaken call. Taken alongside the evidence for how they use their phone lists, it is reasonable to conclude that many men find themselves in situations where the phone juxtaposes women who they would rather did not know of each other's existence. Rows over unexplained phone calls at inappropriate moments were common. Men also expected that their female partners would routinely inspect the address list on their phones to check for the presence of other women, and vice versa, and many women likened themselves to detectives on the popular American television shows *CSI (Crime Scene Investigation)* and *Law and Order*. Several men took down Danny's (co-author) name for their phone lists, not in order to actually keep a record of his number, but to have a plausible additional name, so that 'Danny' actually stood for the number of some female whose presence they were keen to hide.

This in turn led to another negative discourse, which came close to implying that the phone is in and of itself an instrument of duplicity. When you speak to a person face to face, you know where they are. When they are on a landline, a person's location can also be confirmed by phoning the person back to see if they (or someone else) answer the telephone. But with a cell phone, even when the person you speak to is being completely honest about their whereabouts, the instrument itself speaks to a potential lie. In Jamaica, where there is a constant climate of suspicion even among persons who are entirely honest about their relationships, a suspicion that a person almost cannot be merely what they appear to be, then this becomes an important aspect of the mobility that comes with the cell phone. In cross-gender relationships in particular, there is such a presumption of deceit that one can reach a point where people see a lie as a kind of higher 'truth' because as an exposure of deceit it brings a person closer to reality, while a mere truth is seen as the continuation of what must really be deceit. Indeed, Sobo (1993) notes that 'Men ... often have "confederates" spy on their women. Women know that mercenaries often carry back lies just to keep jealous mates' money running to them or to break unions apart' (211). While obviously not the case for all, many of the generic conversations women have about men in general or men have about women in general are based on this kind of association of appearance with deceit. The propensities of the cell phone came to be understood as reinforcing this discourse, which ends up with the common claim that the cell phone has itself made Jamaicans more deceitful.

This can become part of general sense that, far from maintaining or enhancing relationships, cell phone communication leads to their break-up. Michael, for example, talked about his scepticism of the cell phone and its ability to maintain long-distance relationship with his girlfriend living in the USA. His main concern was that he could easily be taken advantage of or made into a fool. Over the cell phone, he could not tell from her voice or words what she was really thinking. What if he is talking and she is rolling her eyes or motioning to someone that she wished he would stop talking and end the call? What if someone was there with her, maybe even sleeping with her? Phone communication simply could not be trusted. Similarly, the phone could create suspicions about the activities of children with their peers as well as with their parents. Certainly, Michelle was not thrilled when her son Chadwick gave his cell phone number to his father living in Fort Lauderdale, Florida. He had not seen his father in over five years and the last conversation between Chadwick's mother and father involved a row over whether or not Chadwick should visit and then perhaps join his father in the States. Since learning of Chadwick's disclosure, Michelle started to dread each ring and, when his phone broke, Michelle admitted to feeling a sense of relief. Although the phone helped to keep Michelle and Chadwick connected on a day-to-day basis – she could call and ask where he was on the road, if he remembered his key or had enough lunch money – she was in no hurry to replace it. In effect, what we see here represents a dramatic contrast to the metanarrative of ICTs affording freedom through multiple identity production.

Conclusion

Interpreting not only what Jamaicans do with the phone but also the prevalent discourses about the phone rests on an appreciation of the fact that communication itself is seen in quite specific and distinct ways. One theme that continues throughout the chapter relates to an oft-cited aspect of Jamaican life, which could be translated as 'pragmatism' and is associated with the stereotype of the 'strong Jamaican woman' (Clarke 1966; Senior 1991; Safa 1995; Cooper 2004). This has always been a problematic characterization inasmuch as 'strong' here could mean powerful or it could mean an ability to cope with adversity caused by lack of power. In practice, this pragmatism has a deeper meaning. The first three examples given in this chapter bear on this. The coordination of liaisons, the place of the phone both within households and in extended households and the use of the phone in childcare may all be related to the way women talk about their needs and their uses of the phone in quite a brusque fashion. But the term pragmatism is misleading if it sounds as though affection is being supplanted by instrumentalism. Rather, in all of these examples it should be clear that pragmatism, in the Jamaican case, is more a recognition that care and affection are most often expressed in what people do for each other. Money is not abstracted from this general economy of favours, but rather seen as just as expressive as looking after someone or saying nice things about them.

This is important in understanding the central phenomenon of this chapter, link-up. At first glance, link-up looks like a kind of minimal form of sociality, the very opposite of childcare or long-term relationships based on a dense web of connectivity. What they have in common is that neither implicates the kind of fear of instrumentality as a neglect of social affectivity that would be felt in the UK or the USA if a phone call seemed to be just about asking for money or speaking to someone for a mere ten seconds. Within this general Jamaican pragmatism, short phone calls designed to use as little credit as possible or calls that go straight to the point of asking for money are not experienced as demonstrating a lack of affectivity. They are rather seen as a kind of Jamaican common sense mutually recognized by both participants in the communication.

This is not to suggest that the cell phone is excused from evaluation and judgement, but clearly these are different evaluations from the norms and values they would be subject to in other countries. There is still plenty of ambivalence about what are seen as positive and negative consequences of the role the cell phone plays in extending relationships. Extended families and boyfriends and girlfriends generally like the ways that the cell phone can bring them together. But Lisa, for instance, did not appreciate her German boyfriend's inclination to use the phone to monitor her activities from afar and Victor Levy did not enjoy the fact that the phone was involved in the subversion that underwrote his new grandson's arrival. Similarly, many Jamaicans appreciate the cell phone's ability to extend their social, financial and emotional support systems but dislike the ways in which the cell phone enabled their other activities, both innocent and illicit, to travel beyond their immediate contexts. Even among family members there was a constant awareness of this tension, particularly when family news arrived, such as an aunt or uncle falling ill with cancer. The pressure of having to keep 'the secret' was seen as now so difficult given the impact of the phone that some people longed for the days of intermittent rather than regular communication. As in the final section of this chapter, it is even possible for the phone to be seen as intrinsically dishonest and destructive of relationships.

On the one hand, we see how individuals develop highly extensive but shallow networks of relationships based on the genre of link-up. On the other hand, at different times some of these can become realized as intensive relationships based around need, desire or friendship. As a relationship achieves more content, there is also more room for contradiction, ambivalence and suspicion, which may lead to a retreat back to content-free communications. A parent kept away in the USA is now back in contact; a girlfriend seems devoted but it is so easy for her to make liaisons with others. Perhaps it should be no surprise, then, that one of the most powerful results of the spread of the cell phone is that people are once again discovering the advantages of intimacy and also of distance.

–6–

Coping

The original abstraction of an economic dimension to our project was predicated upon its funding as an aid project that was intended to specifically consider the consequences of ICTs for low-income families.[1] In the light of the well-established sense of entrepreneurship associated with small-scale vending, higgling and what is called 'hustling and juggling' in Jamaica and the rest of the Caribbean (Mintz and Hall 1970; Levy 1996; Bailey et al. 1998; Freeman 2000; Chevannes 2001), we initially presumed that we would be studying, at least in part, the use of the cell phone to extend and create businesses. It seemed likely that those unable to afford office space or obtain landlines would take advantage of the cell phone's attributes, particularly its relative affordability and accessibility, its mobility and the facility to store and maintain a wider customer base. These would enable a small-scale entrepreneur to sell goods or services to friends, family and acquaintances at a greater distance. In addition, we expected to find individuals using the phone to locate jobs and widen their search for employment.

Although this aspect was not entirely absent, the cell phone did not appear to radically transform employment and entrepreneurial opportunities. Particularly noticeable was the relative absence of evidence that the cell phone is used to find employment, especially in Marshfield. The majority of urban Jamaicans we worked with dismissed the idea that they could ever expect the cell phone to give them direct access to employment. As a group of men in Marshfield argued:

Yuh can't call someone on a job ting. Dat is hopeless, hopeless ... Yuh av fi go in an someone seh 'see my fren here, do some ting for im' ... majority of dem piple work at de same job dem fada did, same job their mother did. They jus bring dem back in de system behin dem. [Using the phone] dats a waste of credit.

[You can't call someone on a job thing. That is hopeless, hopeless ... you have to go in and some will say 'see my friend here, do something for him' ... the majority of people work at the same job their father did, same job their mother did. They just bring them back into the system behind them. Using the phone, that's a waste of credit.]

This statement is less surprising when one considers that only 22 per cent of the households surveyed in Marshfield included a member who was formally employed. Coveted access to work opportunities remains limited by a bureaucracy where it is always assumed that job applicants have to 'wait long' or be on hold. In Orange Valley, there was a bit more credence given to the idea of the cell phone providing greater access to employment opportunities. As in Marshfield, formal employment is low, with only 16 per cent of households in receipt of monthly salaries. Another 8 per cent of the households surveyed in Orange Valley reported regular earnings from jobs as barmaids, domestic helpers and shop help, but such jobs are tenuous and the income unreliable, as exemplified by the fact that, even within the course of 2004, half of the individuals with jobs as domestic workers and barmaids had either quit or lost their jobs and others had changed their employer. The difference in attitude in Orange Valley reflected both the lack of any significant telecommunications before 2001 and differences in expectations surrounding formal employment. In Orange Valley 76 per cent of the population rely upon small, intermittent earnings from masonry, picking oranges, cutting grass in yards, cleaning chicken coops and selling fruits from their small plot of land. Because these jobs are occasional and are spread through word of mouth, the cell phone plays a more central role in the economic possibilities of Orange Valley residents. Barry, an unemployed father, explains his current situation in January 2004:

> Because true the year just start up now, so mi no suppose to work cause the work no start up as yet ... But I normally like, mi would a go pon di street and hear about some work and then enquire about it. So them always like, mi would a leave a cell phone number, so they would contact anytime. Soon as the work [start], they would contact my cell phone. [Before the cell phone] it would be difficult cause sometime [mi] nuh have a house phone ... cell phone out now so it more easier now because [mi] can just leave a number or get a number fi contact the person.

The point is that in Orange Valley people generally have no expectation of formal employment. With so little by way of schools, banks, shops and services, opportunities for formal employment in rural areas are few and far between. Compared with many countries of similar income levels, there is a noticeable absence of state employees, apart from police. In Marshfield, in contrast, residents possess no opportunities for work on the land, although the cell phone may be used to organize intermittent labour in the continual work of house extensions and gully work on the ends.

Occupational Multiplicity

While our vision of a whole raft of new or extended entrepreneurial activities based around the cell phone appeared misguided, there were certainly some individuals who utilize the phone in this way. The purchase of his cell phone was rather transformational for Peter Sharpe, a 32-year-old man who has worked his way from a part-time stock boy to a supervisor at one of Orange Valley's local groceries. Although his employers have gradually increased his salary to $JA4,000 per week, over the past three years Peter consistently earns more money from the sale of eggs. He currently sells an average of 225 eggs per day, supplying the groceries in Orange Valley as well as one of the large chains in the parish capital. From this business alone, Peter earns $JA1,388 per day ($JA700 profit) and employs two workers to look after his chickens, yams, bananas, cocoa and pigs. As he explains it, 'Alright, say for instance I am here. Somebody need 10 dozen egg, 30 dozen egg. I can just call home and say "bring down some eggs for me" and it's there in a minute." Peter admits that without the cell phone he never would have tried to develop such a large business, which involved the purchase and upkeep of 300 chickens.

Like Peter, Junior possesses a full-time job working in sales at a furniture company in Kingston and earns an average of $JA18,000 per month with commissions. However, for Junior this was clearly not his true calling in life. Junior's true ambition, in common with a high proportion of Jamaican men, is to become involved in the music business. As an 'entertainer', Junior arranged for venues, DJs, vendors and dancers, as well as undertaking all the advertising and promotions for the various shows he organized every three months in and around Portmore. In his phone he kept the names of his close DJ friends, as well as a list of 'party girls' and others whose presence might make the party 'happen'. There were also those critical numbers of better-known disc jockeys, radio personalities and music company executives, whom he does not feel ready to call now but envisions calling a few years down the road when his entertainment business takes off. However, Junior still needs his job at the company to pay his expenses, on the back of which he can earn an extra $JA20,000 from each of the shows. As was common throughout Jamaica, he was allowed to use his cell phone during work hours, which is precisely when he made his plans and organized the shows, often spreading the word about through contacts he maintains as part of his regular employment.

Horace, a taxi driver who is affiliated with a large taxi company in Portmore, explained his dependence upon the cell phone in the following manner:

> For example now if my phone battery dead I going to run up and down to get it charged, especially if someone had called and said later I going to call you to make a pickup ... the other phone before this one when I check it and I see it blank out I am so [distressed] ... wondering how many people called me, and when I check it if I see a missed call I'm just anxious to call to find out who called because you know, you may just lose a work ... so you don't want to lose a work. It's important right, you understand, knowing your phone is in tip-top shape.

Horace pays $JA800 per week for a radio connection to the company, which supplies at least half of his business, and he uses the cell phone to build up his own network of customers outside the company. Sometimes, when he cannot afford the radio charge, the cell phone accounts for all his work. This is why Horace makes sure to give each new customer he picks up his personal cell phone number. In addition to expanding his own contact base, he uses the phone as a safety measure against wasted time, money and petrol by confirming an individual is still waiting or that he has the right pickup point. Like Junior and Peter, Horace's use of the phone piggybacks upon his formal contract as a means to expand his contacts, but in his case the cell phone does not merely supplement his income but also enables him to meet his obligations to his wife and children.

In the case of Peter and Junior, these ventures depended not just upon the security of their regular job but also their domestic circumstance. Peter's wife works as a teacher and earns about $JA25,000 monthly, although 40 per cent of her income goes towards travel expenses to and from work. Peter therefore has the basic capital to take a risk in a business that involved hiring two other men part-time. He also works in a prime location within Orange Valley, which helps his business and often saves him 'credit'. His central work location is also key to the $JA1,000 Peter earns each week as a banker for the shop's 'partners' scheme.[2] Junior, in contrast, is single and childless and lives at home with his mother. He therefore has few household expenses. In other words, the reason they appear as exceptions to our general observation about the lack of use of the phone for entrepreneurial work is that, while as individuals their salary might constitute them as 'low-income', their participation in and contribution to a wider household provide them with a sense of economic security or insurance. But not all individuals who live in larger households share this luxury. Furthermore, while Junior and Peter have dreams of making it 'big' or being more independent, they are hesitant to give up their reliable income. In fact, we only met one individual who found it possible to quit his 'respectable' job to start his own business and, like Peter and Junior, he relied considerably upon his ability to save while he worked at a bank as well as the free room and board at his uncle's house. Horace, on the other hand, struggles in this side business because he has been unable to garner the capital to purchase his own vehicle and therefore spends much of his weekly earnings on the rental of the car. Unlike Junior and Peter, this 'side business' of collecting contacts is in fact Horace's only business and the cell phone simply enhances his chances of making ends meet at the end of the day.

Women, despite being burdened with the majority of childcare and domestic responsibilities, also develop side businesses, such as the sale of food, fruit and chickens and a range of services including braiding hair, manicures and pedicures (Massiah 1983; Safa 1986, 1995; Black 1995; Barrow 1996; Rakodi 2004). As one individual described the importance of a cell phone to these house-based businesses, 'I think the cell phone helps some of them, like some people say they have a little business, they put up the number at the gate and someone need some yam. If they sell yam they can call and ask how much a pound and they can get some to buy and in that case it helps them.' For example, every six weeks Dorothy slaughters, plucks and cleans a set of chickens, which she then sells from her shop. When ready to kill her current stock, she calls down to the local chicken distributor and reserves about fifty new chicks. Until she has sold her chickens, she often cannot pay for all this new stock and sends money as she earns it to the distributor with her local taxi driver. As a result, the chicks are ready when she requires them and she also saves the taxi fare. Keeping these expenses down, and thereby keeping her markup low, makes a dramatic difference to Dorothy's customers, often the poorest members of the community, who sometimes purchase one-quarter lb of chicken back at a time and cannot afford $JA100 taxi fare, let alone a weekly trip to the grocery or market to buy in bulk at wholesale prices. In Dorothy's case, she had the backing of her shop and thereby secure credit. With the exception of the sale of Digicel cards, which will be discussed in the following sections, most women we met were simply too tied to the regular crisis of income for any such entrepreneurial activities to become possible. Even more than men, they required secure capital. The degree to which household members, including husbands and wives, may consider themselves separate and individual economic units also mitigates against the accumulation of sufficient capital for entrepreneurship (Sobo 1993; Robertson 2002).

Not surprisingly, cell phones could also be seen operating in almost any kind of business, including those considered to be on the other side of the law (see Levy 1996). For example, Crete explained that he had 'no choice' other than to pursue his side business in the ganja (marijuana) trade, as he only made $JA2,500 per week working third shift at a factory in Kingston. How could he possibly be expected to support his six children, multiple baby-mothers, other girlfriends, mother and himself on a mere $JA2,500 per week? The way 'de system work', it forced him to do a 'likl ting pon di side' and he could not conceive of another way of getting by, despite the potentially dangerous consequences. Indeed, one evening as we were making our way to a taxi in Marshfield, Crete appeared on the main road dressed in a shirt and tie. Crete's appearance was a shock given that he was best known as a character who during the daytime never seemed to wear anything but shorts, tall navy blue socks and a large gold necklace which spread across his bulging stomach. The formal attire was explained by a court appearance, which followed a day in jail and the receipt of a $JA20,000 fine for his activities. Now that he had paid his fines, the day became just like any other and he was back to work at his 'respectable' job. For him, the fine was just the equivalent of the tax he might have paid in a legitimate business. While most of the trade was local, cell phones were increasingly important in organizing the supply of ganja through his country connections.

Another 'back-door' operation that took advantage of the cell phone was placing bets on hundreds of small-scale unofficial lottery schemes, which used the results of the national lottery but without paying tax. The cell phone aided the efforts of organizers to conceal their identity and, along with taxi drivers, were used to create untraceable third-party routes for placing bets. Equally, individuals selling music CDs, DVDs and photograph calendars made particular use of computers to copy and remix music and images. The illegal sale of stolen phones and their parts, such as SIM cards, faceplates and services to break codes, was also considered part of the entrepreneurial activities associated with the cell phone. In Marshfield in particular, it was assumed that people could supply almost any phone to order; given the number of phones that had been stolen during one of the periods we worked in Marshfield, we could testify to a rather healthy business based on the theft of popular phones, such as the Nokia 3310, whose faceplate could easily be changed.[3]

Although these were clearly fascinating cases of creative entrepreneurialism, we need to conclude this section with a reminder that the cases described above are still relatively unusual. Men could see the potential of the cell phone to expand their earnings[4] and women could see the potential for escaping from home-based work. Both were clear about the need for such development, given the mediocre pay for most reliable formal employment, and therefore sought out jobs associated with contracted labour, such as service work. Nonetheless, in almost all of these instances, the individuals depended upon the security represented by prior stable work or income. It is the lack of this foundation that explains in large measure why this new entrepreneurialism based on the cell phone is actually so rare.

Social Networking and Individual Survival

Whereas many individuals do not possess the basic capital to create small-scale businesses, it is clear they do use the cell phone within their day-to-day survival strategies. As one goes deeper and deeper into the daily budgets of low-income individuals and households and considers the way they simply get by from day to day, one starts to see why the phone, far from being peripheral or an additional expense, is actually the new heart of economic survival. For low-income individuals, what finally matters are not earnings that come from employment or the incomes resulting from entrepreneurial activity and sales, but rather support that comes from other people – people who 'have it'. Of the households in Marshfield, 70 per cent received money from others, including other family members, boyfriends and partners, baby-fathers and friends in Jamaica and abroad; 48 per cent received over one-third of their income from others and 38 per cent of the households surveyed in Marshfield survived exclusively through social networks and the patronage of others. In contrast to Marshfield, small-scale farming plays a significant role in the economy of Orange Valley, where 64 per cent of the households we surveyed supplement their income through small-scale farming. In many cases, small-scale farming produces surplus food and fruit, which can be sold, traded or exchanged for acts of goodwill. Nonetheless, 34 per cent also meet their day-to-day needs exclusively through their social networks, which include immediate family, extended family, boyfriends, girlfriends, neighbours, acquaintances and a host of friends. The bottom line in both sites is that over a third of households have no 'income' in the sense of anything they earn through capitalized labour. They exist only through their ability to obtain money from others.

In a recent research project carried out by academics at the University of the West Indies, Mona examined the working conditions and strategies of domestic workers, security guards and workers in export-processing zones and came to similar conclusions concerning coping and economic survival in Jamaica (Henry-Lee et al. 2001). Among the many strategies (skipping meals, recycling food, pilfering, occupational multiplicity and 'throwing partners' (see note 2) to save money) utilized by the three groups studied, Henry-Lee et al. emphasize social networks as one of the critical features of low-income or poor individuals (see Senior 1991: 129–147; Bailey 1998; Clarke 2002; Henry-Lee 2002). Even for people who, from the perspective of the unemployed population, possess regular income, the authors note that 'Every category of worker reported having to borrow money, a practice that was possible only if one had friends or people with confidence in them. Though a small point, it speaks to the importance of having and maintaining good social relationships, which can be called upon in time of need' (Henry-Lee et al. 2001: 30).

In the context of our own project, Keisha perhaps best illustrates the ways in which social connections and social capital operate in Jamaica. A 33-year-old woman who lives in a shared rental flat in Marshfield after growing up in Orange Valley, Keisha has always been considered 'bright'. Over the past decade, she has worked as a secretary at a factory in Kingston as well as in telesales at a Portmore company. When she became pregnant with her daughter, she decided to quit her job to care for her new baby. With the support of her married baby-father ($JA10,000 per month) and the small profits from the sale of an average of twenty-five Digicel phonecards each week, Keisha was able to meet her basic monthly rent payment and food expenses, which totalled $JA8,400 per month, as well as her hefty phonecard habit of $JA2,400 monthly. However, she often had to source money and cards from one of her boyfriends or skim a little off the top of the money that Keisha's sister Carmen sends monthly to support her three children whom Keisha looked after during the day.

After over a year at home with her daughter, niece and nephews, Keisha decided that she wanted to go back to school and further her studies. When Keisha announced her plan to attend teacher's college, she called and met with her baby-father, boyfriend and sister, who offered their support. While Keisha had some savings from her previous job, they said they would try to help her with her school fees of $JA60,000. Because she had to board at school as a student (no children allowed), her sister, who was not working at the time, also agreed to take on the full responsibility for their sister Carmen's three children as well as Keisha's daughter Aaliyah. Aaliyah's father's sister also said that she would look after Aaliyah from time to time. A local grocer offered Keisha a short-term position crunching numbers in their books and, to help with her school fees, he gave her an advance on her salary to help her pay the remaining part of her school fees. However, books, uniforms, shoes and other incidental expenses had not been purchased. Two weeks before the start of term, Keisha turned to her cell phone and scrolled through the numbers. After passing by Adrian, Alston, Andrea, Bups and Cuzzi, Keisha saw the name of a local businessman who always encouraged her to continue with her education. She called him and explained that she had been accepted for school and paid her fees but needed money for books and supplies. However, he told her to come by later in the year since he had recently extended himself helping others. After she hung up, Keisha scrolled through her phone again, calling Doreen, an old co-worker from her telesales days, 'Miss D', her office procedures teacher, Shernette, a friend whom she used to go out with, and another friend from school days, Tomoya. Over the weekend, she also tried her niece, who had a good job in Spanish Town, another former co-worker, a former teacher, a friend and her daughter's godmother.

In all, Keisha phoned fourteen different people. She asked some individuals for money for her school books and other individuals for uniforms. She asked Tomoya for help with school shoes and requested money for towels from her daughter's godmother since her tattered 'yard' towels were too embarrassing to bring to school. In the end, she received $JA1,000 for the towels from her daughter's god-mother and another $JA2,500 from a combination of her teacher, a former co-worker and her friend working in Spanish Town. These three people managed to 'have it' at the time and were willing to share their money with Keisha. In addition, Keisha's sister living and working in Florida sent her $JA6,000 ($US100) to help her out. Although Keisha had helped out a number of the people that she called when she was still working at the bank, it was not necessarily these same people who helped her set herself up in her new course. Some of the people Keisha helped out had their own situations to deal with. Others simply said they could not help her. It all just depended upon who had the money to help her then and if they felt prepared to give at that moment. Moreover, when she originally took down the numbers of the people she called in her phone book, Keisha had no idea at that time that she would be attending school or that she might be one day asking for their help. Rather, she just knew that it was 'good to have friends'.

Low-income Jamaicans may not articulate the importance of connections in terms of social capital, but they are quite aware of the way that Jamaicans use friendship, kinship and other ties as a coping strategy. Andrea describes the way Jamaicans 'operate':

> ... Sometimes mi watch the TV and see some likl piple a foreign now like Africa an so forth like that, Delhi, this an. Jamaica is like, you can see a fren and seh 'beg yuh a hundred dolla' and dem gi yu. But dem places I doan think they can, maybe dem neighbour they can beg an sumting like that.

> [Sometimes I watch the TV and see some little people 'in foreign' like in Africa and Delhi. In Jamaica you can see a friend and say 'beg you $JA100' and they will give it to you. But in those places I don't think they can, maybe they can ask their neighbour.]

What Andrea makes clear is that, in Jamaica (and perhaps elsewhere), the difference between being poor and not being poor is having friends or family that you can call upon in a time of need, even if it is $JA100 for transport to visit a friend who may have no visible financial prospects. What the poorest individuals really lack is not so much food, but these critical social networks. The cell phone, and its ability to record and recall up to 400 numbers, is therefore the ideal tool for a Jamaican trying to create the ever-changing social networks that Jamaicans feel are ultimately more reliable than a company, employer or even a parent or spouse alone. This feature, perhaps more than any other, represents the critical economic impact of the cell phone in Jamaica.

Begging and Giving

To properly appreciate this economy of networking, we need to separate it off from what might be seen as a culture of begging. At first glance, this use of the phone seems of a piece with the ubiquity of everyday asking of money, not only in public of both strangers and acquaintances but also in the internal life of families, penetrating the intimate exchanges within families (see Safa 1986; Sobo 1993; Bailey 1998; Chevannes 1999; Robertson 2002). For example, a husband who catches fish expects to sell this fish to his wife, who sells it in the market. This contrasts with many societies where money is seen as appropriate for non-intimate exchange but not as the basis of internal family or friendship relationships. In fact, begging as it is understood in Jamaica hinges upon a prior relationship between two individuals. In a recent thesis on agency in a low-income fishing community, Lucy Robertson (2002) argues that most low-income Jamaicans practise opportunistic begging, which she contrasts with occupational begging (begging for a living). This is a public act where a person 'begs' someone a small amount of money (less than $JA100) or favour, such as the purchase of a drink. Since people when they are 'on the road' are expected to have money, this is perceived as an opportune moment to ask someone for money. Moreover, people beg not just when they are in need, but even if they have money. In other words, someone might beg you a drink or a $JA40 patty even though they have the money and were indeed prepared to pay for it themselves. In a reversal of the biblical axiom preached in many of the churches, one woman in Marshfield explained to us that 'You can't receive if you don't ask.' Robertson further argues that begging in Jamaica is not easily collapsed into traditional anthropological models of exchange and reciprocity. As she summarizes:

> Begging lies somewhere between exchange and reciprocity. The beggar has freedom to make a return if they wish, or at some point feel themselves obligated to give to someone else, but these donations are not given through indebtedness, or through the compelling 'spirit' of the gift. Money is certainly not given out of self-interest by the giver. The small interest givers may have is to keep some respect from a particular person and also not to receive a negative response from the beggar and be shamed as being mean in front of others. But it is quite clear that this interest is not the compelling force in opportunist begging as the donor never offers to give and may even avoid doing so. (Robertson 2002: 202)

Not surprisingly, this can give rise to a discourse about begging, and within this economy of requesting there are certainly people who are seen as too 'beggy-beggy', such as the individual who always asks for money and seems to never give in return or to remember that they already asked you last week for money; but this relates to exceptional levels of requesting. Newspapers that reflect the more middle-class sensibility of New Kingston also often publish articles about the pubic face of begging. But, from the perspective of our ethnography, all of this misses a vital point. What is striking in Jamaica, in contrast to some countries, is not really why people ask, but why people give. This constant requesting would probably not last very long if it was rarely, if ever, successful. What became clear to us is that it is very successful because most low-income Jamaicans give money on occasions that at first glance seem inexplicable.

An example stems from the discussion in the last chapter of childcare. It is not simply that most children live separately from their biological fathers and often also mothers. When one starts to examine in detail who is involved in both taking care of and providing for a child, the answer in some cases is incredibly complex. Other relatives are the most common carers, but neighbours and friends may take it upon themselves to help with lunch money or pocket money. On some occasions people help provide for a child simply because they take a 'fancy' to them, find something in their looks or character that appeals to them. Indeed, in our surveys with schoolchildren, we found that there were often over five people who had contributed to an individual child's education, including the payment of school fees, lunch money, uniforms, shoes, supplies and transport and many of the contributors could be considered non-kin. This is but one example of a tendency to give money and other forms of support that sometimes seem just a whim, because they do not fit any pattern of generalized reciprocity where that person is likely to obtain some recompense for their generosity over the long term, which is the way anthropologists usually conceive of the immediate present-oriented reciprocity of low-income egalitarian populations (Stack 1974; Stewart 1997; Day et al. 1998). Certainly there are discourses of immediate and of long-term reciprocity, such as the ubiquitous stories of an individual returning from 'foreign' to track down a woman who used to give them food or other 'kindness' and the man who gave a taxi driver $US100 because the driver used to give him free rides. Similarly, more Christian-oriented individuals note that they will receive their blessings in heaven and that there are acts that are considered the Christian thing to do. But, even in these instances, the emphasis is on the act of giving, creating and activating the relationships rather than receiving in return, which is almost always viewed as uncertain.

This culture of unexpected giving is important in relating together the evidence of this chapter and the last. As we have argued in Horst and Miller (2005), it would be very easy to conclude this section by claiming that the vital role played by the cell phone in the coping strategies of the poorest segment of the population is quite sufficient to explain the phenomenon of link-up itself. It is a legacy of poverty and survival that has roots back in the conditions of slavery. No doubt there is some truth to this, and Smith (1988) has some convincing arguments that relate extensive kin networking to the history of the Jamaican people. But our evidence suggests that one should avoid seeing this as simply a one-way explanation of cause and effect. What was clear in the last chapter was that link-up seemed to possess its own imperative. Individuals viewed communication and networking as a value, or even a project, in its own right. Similarly, giving was itself often seen as a means of creating a link to other persons and was in a sense parasitic on the desire to expand networks of acquaintances. While networking is vital in understanding coping strategies, the implications of cause and effect could also be reversed – people give and take not because they need to do so but also in order to facilitate connectedness.

Finally, this consideration of coping strategies also demolishes a common Jamaican stereotype about cell phones. Middle-class Jamaicans often remarked disparagingly about the amount of money low-income Jamaicans appeared to spend on the phone. They told us that, even when people came to plead poverty or ask for state relief or other forms of assistance, they made no attempt to hide their constant usage of the phone, let alone its possession. What came across again and again in such conversations is the degree to which middle-class Jamaicans had become completely isolated from the experience of those they were discussing. They simply had no idea why the phone, so far from being seen as a luxury that added to one's expense, had come to be seen as the necessity that was vital to mere survival. To other low-income Jamaicans, the possession of the phone was mute testimony to the need for keeping open communication with others, the very opposite to being a symptom of extravagance. Overall, the cell phone is about as effective an instrument as can be imagined for assisting in low level redistribution of money from those who have little to those who have least.

The Remittance Economy

In addition to extending local Jamaican social networks, the cell phone has been particularly important for facilitating increased access and communication between relatives, partners and families living abroad. As we noted in the previous chapter, Jamaica possesses an extensive transnational diaspora, which is reflected in almost every cell phone; most phones contain at least one or two numbers that are identified as family and friends living 'in foreign'. Many of these numbers consist of parents and siblings, as well as more extended family, such as cousins, aunts and uncles. They often also include foreign friends and those Jamaicans who visit family and friends in Jamaica for short term holidays and return back to the USA, Canada, Britain or wherever they reside permanently. These are often the most coveted numbers saved within an individual's cell phone, and we witnessed the distress when a number was disconnected, had changed or did not reach their intended recipient. As with internal networks, relatives may be cherished but are also a vital aspect of coping strategies for those with tenuous economic circumstances. It was stated by 56 per cent of households surveyed in Orange Valley and 36 per cent of those in Marshfield that they had received remittances during the past year. Many also recalled the arrival of barrels, typically sent annually, containing clothing, food and other consumer items, which points to the degree to which remittances are not paying for extras but are part of many residents' basic survival strategies.

There are three basic categories of remittances received in Marshfield and Orange Valley. The first are those who receive money for specific purposes, such as the payment of annual school fees. A common ad hoc request is for help with school fees, for both children and adults. For example, Joydene is a young mother of two who relies upon her father's small vending business as the main source of income for her children; her baby-fathers' incomes are often intermittent and unreliable. Joydene wants something better for herself and her children and yearns to be less reliant upon the men in her life for income. A friend told her about a HEART programme in Spanish Town that gives courses in tourism (food and beverage management and domestic help). She decided to submit an application for the domestic worker programme and was accepted to begin the following term. While Joydene had managed to save some money on her own (from frugal spending as well as one of her baby-fathers), she needed about $JA5,000 more for training and transportation while she was in the programme so she decided to call one of her aunts who lived in Baltimore (USA) to see if she might be able to help her out. Her initial statement that 'she was trying to put something together' was brief due to her attempt to save herself credit, but her aunt wanted more information. She ultimately agreed to send Joydene $US50 this week and another $US50 in another month. Joydene hoped to finish in six months and then acquire a job on the north coast at one of the all-inclusive resorts. In the past, one had to plan well in advance, since letters sent in one month might result in money three to six months down the line. Today it is possible to respond to opportunities as they arise with the hope of matching them to funding coming from 'foreign'. The phone has also radically improved the possibility of finding help abroad in dealing with unforeseen emergencies – the auntie in New Jersey who had always been kind in providing help for a daughter's school fees can now be contacted instantly to help cope with a mother's school fees or a sudden illness.

A second category revolves around remittances received on an occasional basis, such as around Christmas or birthdays and in small amounts, usually increments of $US20, $US30 or $US50. In most instances, this money was not sent 'out of the blue' but rather after a phone call made on the cell phone. Tyrone, a 38-year old man living in Marshfield, describes one of his recent calls to a friend in the States:

Yuh just can pick up your phone an seh 'wah gwaan ray ray, yuh see me inna likl position out yah, right yah now weh yuh can do fi help me, ru ru' 'Bwoy, mi can send a $US30 fi yuh or a $US40.'

[You can just pick up your phone and say 'what's happening, etc. I'm in a little situation here in Jamaica right now, what can you do to help me, etc.' 'Boy, I can send you $US30 for you or $US40.]

While some regard remittances as a kind of windfall, others view this use of the phone as a way to meet day-to-day expenses. As Mas Harry, a 65-year-old man in Orange Valley, described it:

I can remember, I needed some money, and it was about eleven o'clock in the day that day. And I just took up a phone and phoned my people abroad. So I get it. Mi get it, in one hour. Send for it at Western Union before one hour … so those are the things people call up … an seh 'beg yu a dinner money, no' an' go and pick it up.

Mas Harry and others like him feel that their friends and family have a genuine desire to 'know de situation out here'. 'Indian', a twenty-year-old man with a child and girlfriend he cannot support from his meagre earnings hustling on the roadside, admitted that he calls relatives living abroad about every two weeks for money for food, rent and other basic living expenses. Stressing the difficulties of life for young men in Jamaica (see Chevannes 1999, 2001), he talked about how impossible it was to make it and why Jamaicans in foreign have an obligation to take advantage of their opportunities to support their kin who have not been so fortunate.[5] Previously, most of his relatives abroad sent money to his grandmother and he only received money if she felt like sharing it. Indian resented his lowly position within the extended family as well as the attitude that, as a young man, he must be able to find work. Armed with his cell phone, however, he can now make his own links with his relatives living in Brooklyn and New Jersey and be sent $US20 or $US30 every few weeks. In his case, the money may well go towards food since he does not farm or live with his mother and therefore has no easy access to the staples that constitute the main (if not the only in very poor households) meal.

The third and perhaps most significant category for many households is remittances received in regular monthly payments. Sandra, for example, relies upon her husband living and working in England to support her and their three children, two of whom are attending school. Although it took him a while to establish himself, for the past two and a half years he has been sending Sandra £UK100 every two weeks, the equivalent of $JA20,000 per month which helps Sandra meet her regularly monthly expenses of $JA17,000 (for food, transport, lunch money, utilities, gas, rent and church offering). However, in some months when the situation gets a little rough Sandra's husband calls to tell her that the money is not coming or that he can only manage £UK50 this fortnight. Sandra has to adapt accordingly, often cutting down on the food consumption, sending her children to school with less money, waiting to pay a bill and relying upon her other personal networks to make up the difference. In Marshfield 26 per cent of households and in Orange Valley 22 per cent of households received these regular monthly or bi-monthly remittances from partners, husbands, relatives and friends living abroad.

From the perspective of the person abroad, the phone also makes the micro-coordination involved in the regular transfer of money home to Jamaica more reliable. For instance, Tonya and her three children lived in a 3-bedroom cement house in the district of Bethesda with her aunt, two cousins and younger sister. Because Tonya is not working and stays at home to care for her two-year-old daughter, the household is largely reliant upon her auntie's weekly income of about $JA1,500 for sewing and seamstress work, the biannual sale of citrus (which earned the household about $JA14,000 in 2003) and regular remittances from her baby-father, mother and sisters. Tonya's baby-father sends $US200 (or approximately $JA12,000) each month from Atlanta and Tonya's sister typically sends about $US100 (or $JA6,000) every three months. Tonya's mother and sisters living in the USA also send a barrel once per year, either in the summer before school begins or around Christmas, which is filled with clothing, food and shoes. Her baby-father typically sends his monthly money to support Tonya and their three children on the 5th of the month and Tonya takes a taxi into Orange Valley that afternoon to collect the money. With the money, Tonya then purchases a $JA200 phonecard and calls her baby-father to tell him 'thanks' and that the money arrived; her phonecard purchase for calling her baby-father constitutes two-thirds of her phonecard expenditure each week.

While Jamaicans have always sent regular and irregular money back home for as long as they have been migrating,[6] money was sent through the post or an international money transfer at the bank. Both of these routes were particularly time-consuming and, while transferring money via a bank was more reliable, it was also costly. As a result, most Jamaicans relied upon the mail service or sending money down with family who were visiting the island. However, this could easily lead to disputes, with either the generally unreliable postal service or relatives blamed for letters failing to arrive or being opened and their contents emptied.

Western Union and Money Gram, in conjunction with the cell phone, have changed all this by facilitating the regular receipt of money that Sandra and Tonya so clearly rely upon. Once money is sent, a confirmation number is received, which can be shared between the sender and the recipient by cell phone. After the money has been picked up, the recipient can then call the sender back thanking them and confirming the money arrived safely. In 2004 the cost of such a transaction was $US11 to send money between the USA and Jamaica and £UK14 between the UK and Jamaica. According to the local Western Union operator in Orange Valley (who also owns the local cambio), an average of $JA1,000,000 is processed through the two organizations daily, or a total of £UK3,650,000 annually. Taking into consideration the 14,000 individuals who we calculated lived in the hinterland of these two offices, this amounted to an average of £UK260 ($JA26,000) annually. This is equivalent to around two months of income for many low-income Jamaicans. The significance of these figures is best considered in relation to the larger place of remittances in the contemporary Jamaican economy,[7] which are generally regarded as the single largest source of foreign currency, more important even than tourism (PIOJ 2004). It can only be speculation on our part, but we would hazard the conclusion that, without this particular source of income, the population of the districts surrounding Orange Valley would be markedly reduced since many families would simply not have been able to remain there.[8] Since, of course, an averaged figure does not reflect actual practice, it is probably also one of the major factors that differentiate what can be observed as those living in a well-appointed home with modern features and those who struggle to maintain even basic facilities.

The Cell Phone as Micro-economy

Many of the points that have been developed in this chapter can be illustrated by moving away from the contribution of the cell phone to economic activities and coping to actually seeing the phone itself as an exemplification of both of these endeavours. In several ways the cell phone has become the ideal case study for understanding the articulation between formal and informal economies. The companies discussed in Chapter 2 represent the formal economy. From their perspective, it is preferable to push post-paid package deals, which have become the main form of cell phone payment in developed capitalist countries and which give them considerable control over and information about customers. In practice, these have come to represent only 2 per cent of Digicel subscriptions in Jamaica. As detailed in Chapter 2, cell phone calls are paid for by prepaid phonecards with a face value of between $JA100 and $JA5,000. With taxes and markup, a $JA100 phonecard costs the user between $JA115 and $JA135. Of the cards sold by Digicel, 89 per cent are in the $JA100 denomination.

These cards may be sold at official Digicel outlets and retailers, but they are also sold at thousands of 'parlour'-style micro-retailers. Digicel reckons there are around 5,000 retail outlets for their cards. As such, they have permeated into the pores of Jamaican society in a manner that is probably only matched by the local informal trade in marijuana. Jamaicans talk constantly about these cards and the ways to obtain them. The signs offering them for sale are a ubiquitous presence on the Jamaican landscape, adorning every bar and small shop. For women, more than for men, the critical determinant in the development of entrepreneurial work employing the cell phone is the degree to which it can be integrated into more general household and domestic labour. Women would obtain capital to buy twenty-five cards wholesale at around $JA115 and then sell them at more convenient locations for around $JA125 to $JA135. Some individuals thereby earned the equivalent of a salary at $JA2,000. For example, Bridgette started selling phonecards in her last year of secondary school to assist the household as well as fund her own phone habit. Since Digicel arrived on the scene, Bridgette has purchased five phones, most recently a new silver Panasonic Internet phone with colour screen. Bridgette started out small, selling to a few friends and neighbours, but she also took advantage of the fact that her mother runs a hairdressing salon from their house, which became an extended customer base. Women bought phonecards from Bridgette while they were chatting and having their hair done and even if Bridgette was away from home her mother would sell them on her behalf. Some days, such as Fridays and Saturdays when her mother earned anywhere from $JA3,000 to $JA5,000 for the day, Bridgette sold at least ten phonecards to neighbours, friends and other customers. Eventually Bridgette felt she could earn enough money with sufficient regularity to contribute to a local 'partners' scheme run by her mother. But Bridgette's ability to fund her own phones from this endeavour reflects the fact that she is living rent-free with her mother. Most women made more like $JA300 to $JA500 per week, which at least paid for their own phone use, a few days' lunch money for their children or a friend to wash or cream one's hair. As we have already noted, it is much easier to start this kind of entrepreneurial activity when one has prior protection from everyday economic vicissitudes.

This activity penetrates still deeper into the micro-exchanges within families or between friends. It is common, for example, to beg a card, often while on the phone by asking for a card number. Alternatively individuals beg the remaining credit on a phone. Many people will check after every call to see how much credit remains. In other words, gifting, trading and begging phone credit can represent a micro-exchange down to just a few Jamaican dollars. This activity dovetails with the formal economy in both directions, because other factors involve the sensitivity of companies such as Digicel to the way their products have been appropriated. In response to this complex micro-economy of phone credit they introduced in the spring of 2004 an additional facility, called 'call-me'. This allowed a person with less than $JA3 dollars on their phone to contact up to twenty-one other persons a week in the hope that they would take the cost of the call on their credit. Within a few short months, 'call-me' accounted for over 80 per cent of all text messaging. Indeed, by the end of the fieldwork, when many people referred to texts they most often meant 'call-me' texts. This in turn reinforced the kind of quasi-kinship link many people felt they had with Digicel, as a company that sympathetically cared for the poor, since this was seen, not as a form of exploitation, but as a form of respect for the ways low-income Jamaicans behaved. Digicel also helped foster this identification by being lenient in not cutting off phones that remained unused or were without credit. It also followed from the integration of relatively low-cost subsidized handsets as a common gift between friends and relatives on birthdays and at Christmas and also between Jamaicans living abroad and in Jamaica itself. 'Call-me' was viewed as ensuring that even those with no credit could still find a way to use their phones for important conversations and emergencies. In this the integration of the micro-economy is also experienced as a kind of emotional economy of identification between the formal and informal economic sectors.

There is, however, another way in which the phone represents an integration rather than a separation between the moral, emotional and economic aspects of experience, because, unlike a landline with a monthly bill, every single phone call could be assessed as an immediate expense. But in this case what is being measured in monetary terms is the relationship. How much credit is it worth spending in talking to this other person? As Zelizer (1987) has pointed out, in many established economies a great deal of institutional and personal work is done to try and separate the moral and intimate from the economic as incommensurate forms of value. Yet somewhere an insurance company, for example, must actually take a decision as to how much money is given out for the death of a child. In Jamaica, in contrast, micro-monetary exchanges have remained part of the intimate economy within families and not relegated to commodity exchange between strangers. It is expected, rather than rejected, that relationships are seen as having value that is commensurate with monetary value, and as such the cell phone fits well within, rather than disrupting, the bringing together of these two concepts of value, the measured and the intimate. In listening to conversations, it is very common indeed for this expense of the call to be part of the conversation. For example, many people see international calls as based today on a $JA200 card, with conversation continuing until the credit ends. Individuals can often be heard being considerate in offering to keep the conversation short, offering to speak again when there is access to landlines or to speak in person. There is often a quite nuanced sense of who can better afford the cost and the burden of making the call.

We spent considerable time and effort examining the consequences of 'call-me', which we assumed would result in some sense of reciprocity and fairness akin to traditional anthropological treatments of the gift and reciprocity (Mauss 1954; Strathern 1988; Godelier 1999), but the evidence did not support our original premise. Again, the evidence with respect to phone use reiterates the conclusions we came to regarding giving and begging more generally. Certainly we could find quotes that suggested a negative attitude towards the use of 'call-me', particularly in terms of men's attempts to use this with women they might be interested in. As an attractive young woman comments one of the men saved in her phone who recently sent her a 'call-me' text: "I think it was really cheap of him, if you want to talk to me, buy some credit simple as that. Basically I just don't like the idea, and sometimes it's not even important when you do call them back, "me just a call fi see if you alright" Cho! [expression of disgust].'

At the extremes, people could get a reputation for abusing this system, but, compared with other places where we live or have worked, we were surprised how rare this calculative sense of reciprocity appeared to be. More common were sentiments such as 'because me do it too, a cheap me cheap why mi do it a jus true di funds lows' or 'everybody hav it ruff'. As such, this analysis replicated our earlier discussion of begging being better seen as the other side of the coin to giving. The significant conclusion is that low-income Jamaicans are quite prepared to give on a small scale, giving that depends not on expectations of reciprocity but on a general sense that giving is a further opportunity to link-up. While in this chapter link-up seems to be a powerful aspect of coping for those with the lowest incomes, it can also be viewed as part of a more general sentiment in favour of extensive networks, where giving and, indeed, begging help extend social connectedness. What we find with the cell phone and link-up parallels what Abrahams (1983) found in his analysis of conversation (see Chapter 5), that is, the subordination of information passing to the larger project of creating communicative links.

The analogy is perhaps better understood in relation to Munn's (1986) work on fame within the Melanesian Kula ring, rather than something designated as economic anthropology. Certainly, in Jamaica one finds an unusual degree of individualism expressed often in monetary terms, including an antipathy to shared budgeting, which could not be more different from the Kula. But this is matched by extensive networking devoted to the practices and process of enlarging and maintaining link-up. It is the expansion of the 'name' of the person in Jamaica that seems parallel with the expansion of the 'fame' of the island in Kula networking. By, as it were, sending out one's 'name' to be retained on the address books of perhaps hundreds of other individuals, the result is a kind of demonstrable expansion of the self, distributed and confirmed by one's presence in the lives of others. This may contribute to coping, but we are misunderstanding the phenomenon if we see coping as cause and networking as effect. In essence, the evidence from this and the previous chapter indicates that to understand prevalent forms of cell phone use, including paying for the calls, requires an appreciation of the very particular configuration of individualism, social networking and pragmatism and, above all, the centrality of particular forms of communication, such as link-up, as the form by which certain kinds of relationship are constituted (Horst and Miller 2005). These are so distinct from the assumptions made in general sociological characterizations of individualism and social capital that they provide a case study in rethinking the very terms of such debates.

–7–

Pressure

Although this fieldwork was funded as part of a programme to investigate the impact of new communication technologies upon low-income households, we felt from the outset that it also represented an opportunity to think more broadly about what we mean by poverty, because conventional approaches to poverty give little acknowledgement to the contribution of communication in its own right and to the possibility that poverty with respect to communication could be a major contribution to the experience of poverty more generally (Douglas and Ney 1998). What matters to Jamaicans using a phone is not limited to the specific innovations associated with the individuality and mobility of the cell phone. We first have to understand the ways in which people see themselves as frustrated and diminished by deficiencies in their ability to communicate, but also whether they feel enriched or quite possibly betrayed and threatened by new forms of communication. Furthermore, we need to understand these things initially, not in terms of an imposed language of poverty and communication, but through the idioms and language by which a population comes to experience and express their relationship to the phone. The contribution of anthropology lies in the ability to acknowledge and then convey this specificity of experience. We have therefore chosen to focus upon one example of such a local idiom, the concept of 'pressure', because the term is well known from Jamaican dialect and music and effectively conveys the importance of trying to understand both poverty and communications in specifically Jamaican terms.

'Pressure': a Brief Introduction

The experience of modernity in the Caribbean has created particular attitudes towards an individual's relationship to work and leisure.[1] As Roland Littlewood (1998) explains for Trinidad:

> The term *pressure* refers simultaneously to the subjective pressures of paid employment, poverty, worries and the pace of town life but also to *high blood* or *high pressure*, understood variously as over-rich blood, the recording on the doctor's plethysmograph or blood moving up to one's head ... Low pressure is experienced as weakness and thus stout beer, used as a build up, may cause pressure. (83, author's emphasis)

Like Trinidadians, Jamaicans believe that 'pressure' is the result of too much blood and creates symptoms such as severe headaches (Sobo 1993: 37–38). According to Elisa Sobo, women are particularly prone to 'pressure' because 'male bodies do not tend to accumulate blood, which leads to "pressure", like women's do' (59). This propensity to accumulate blood and thus 'pressure' is associated with the female reproductive system, menstruation and the concern with cleansing the body. From the perspective of many Jamaicans, 'pressure' is the result of an imbalance. This unsteadiness can be physiological, such as the accumulation of blood, but is also related to social, sexual and spiritual imbalances, which in turn have an impact on the internal physiological state. Anyone familiar with the lyrics of Jamaican music, from Bob Marley to contemporary dancehall, will appreciate that from this basis 'pressure' has become central to the way Jamaicans express their relationship to the wider world and modernity's own propensity to create new factors that build up 'pressure' in the individual.

Just as men's and women's bodies may be differentially affected by the experience of 'pressure', there are also gendered distinctions associated with the release of 'pressure'. For men 'pressure', stems from the obligations to the household as well as from the outside world (often described by men in Portmore as 'the system'), and their escape from the system occurs in the practice of 'cooling out' or 'liming' either during the day or after work. 'Cooling out' effectively means 'to relax', or to relieve 'pressure' and often occurs in marginal spaces, such as in rum bars, on fences, under trees or in other undefined public spaces. Chevannes (2001) notes that even young boys are socialized to escape from the female influenced household by going out on the street (see Wilson 1966; Barrow 1996; Branche 1998). Among Trinidadians, Littlewood argues that 'cooling out' often involves the drinking of alcohol, such as rum, which, he explains:

> is praised for its effect in lightening mood, in enhancing relaxation after work, for improving sociability, for lowering inhibitions, for helping to ease pressure and in a controlled way easing social tensions. Drinking is a measure of reciprocity, of obligations remembered and discharged a measure of trust. (Littlewood 1998: 94)

In addition to alcohol, ganja and cigarettes may also be used during periods of 'cooling out', although Littlewood notes that Trinidadians do not believe that ganja is an appropriate medium for relaxation because it does not release any substance or 'pressure'. However, in Marshfield, where we found ganja use to be almost ubiquitous among men, these connotations do not appear to be prevalent. Instead, the sense of inappropriateness is applied to the discussion of 'harder' drugs such as crack, cocaine or heroin.

In contrast to men, where relieving 'pressure' is often a social act shared among other men, women are often left to relieve 'pressure' through sex or menstruation, each of which 'releases excess blood that would otherwise accumulate and bring on "pressure", thereby cleansing the body' (Sobo 1993: 59; see also Chevannes 1993b). In addition to sex and menstruation, 'pressure' may also be relieved through worshipping. Like menstruation, which expunges toxins from the body, Pentecostal services, such as those described by Diane Austin-Broos (1997), release the impurities from the believer's body with the process of filling in the body with the breath of the Holy Spirit, an act that becomes evident through dancing, involuntary physical movement and speaking in tongues. The complementary process of infilling transforms the soul and the body and creates a healthy spiritual and bodily state. Moreover, 'women have a strong sense that in-filling involves entry of the Spirit through the vagina', which counteracts the unhealthiness of lack of regular sexual activity with a male partner (Austin-Broos 1997: 146). Not insignificantly, these Pentecostal services are led by key male figures, who guide their church sisters through the process of release through the Holy Ghost (see Toulis 1997). As with women who receive the spirit in the Pentecostal church, women cleanse their spiritual, emotional and social selves through forms of expression such as singing, dancing and talk, and their renewal therefore comes through the process of infilling with 'the spirit', be it the Holy Ghost or the spirit of friendship and community.

The cell phone, much in the same fashion as alcohol, ganja, sex and more religious forms of purification, may allow release of the 'negative vibes' and the pressures of everyday life, such as worry, insecurity, struggling to get by, loneliness, lack of friendship and guidance. In common with other substances, it also contains the ability to be abused and misused, therefore exacerbating rather than relieving the problems that cause 'pressure'. The remainder of this chapter outlines how men and women respectively utilize the cell phone, as an object of communication, for the release of 'pressure'.

'Nuttin na Gwaan fi Wi': Men's Experience of 'Pressure'

As so often occurs in Jamaica, each gender has a particular regime of expression for what otherwise might be analogous conditions. The very term loneliness tends to evoke the relationships between women since the quantity as well as quality of relationships is seen as basic to their lives. Men do not often talk about loneliness, but they are constantly aware of the pressures that boredom can bring, a condition expressed by the comment 'nutting na gwaan fi wi' (nothing is happening for us). A critical difference is that boredom for men is not a condition of isolation but a condition of their sociality. Woman feel lonely within the isolated private domain of the house, while men appear as bored hanging around with groups of other men in the public domain, which is where most of their time is spent.

Traditionally, the rum bar or, in rural areas, the makeshift shop that also sells rum and other spirits, has been the space where male 'crews' collectively gather to pass the time drinking and playing dominoes:

> We talk about work, or I ask if he wanna do something, or he likes to play dominoes, or he might ask for a link with one of my cousins or those things, with is girlfriends or those things, he likes to, you know, we have a lot of different talks, you know. All depends on what it's all about.

In other words, crews are effectively male support systems, which can bear the same emotional, but also social and economic, connections that women's networks possess. Chevannes (1999) notes that, for many young men, crews and other peer groups 'virtually replaces mother and father as the controlling agents' (30).

In these friendships, equality remains absolutely central to the development and maintenance of a crew, even when the situations of individual members may vary dramatically. An employed member of a crew in Marshfield illustrates this:

> And yuh have a little bar deh roun the road weh we go more time a night time and cool out and tek as little one roun cause the people them round deh see say we regular and them like we vibes. Them will just say 'alright', cause the last time me go round deh me neva have nuh money, and the girl seh 'so wha oonu a drink tonight?' Me seh me bruk. She seh 'yuh can tek something man.' Me say 'eeh-ehh [shakes head no]. Give me a half pint a Appleton and a pepsi, how much that come to?' She say '$120.' Me seh '$120 and a six a we drink out a that.' We just take we time and sip, sip. Everybody drink and everybody nice, yuh see me? So a really a unification thing.

> [And you have a little bar over there around the road where we go a lot at night and relax and drink one little round of drinks because the people around there [who own the place] say we are 'regulars' and they like our vibes [attitudes, outlooks, friendliness]. They will just say 'alright' because the last time I went around I didn't have any money and the girl [at the bar] said 'so what are you drinking tonight?' I said I was broke. She said, 'you can take something man.' I said 'no, give me a half of a pint of Appleton (brand of rum) and a Pepsi. How much does that come to?' She said '$JA120.' I said, '$JA120 and six of us will drink out of it.' We just take our time and sip, sip. Everybody drinks and everybody feels good, you understand? So it's really a unification thing.]

A crew is a mode of communication, about money, work and information. As Wilson (1966) observed in Providencia, 'crews and their network linkups may indeed be considered as the foundation of a noninstitutionalized grass-roots structure of information dissemination and, possibly, mobilization' (181). Often this mobilization comes in the form of work, whereby one member of the crew might be commissioned to paint a house or build a tomb through one of his connections. He in turn calls his working partners to join in the activity and either shares out the pay for the work or helps in some other form (see Wilson 1966; Olwig 1985).[2] In Orange Valley crews were involved in house construction projects or with helping to pick fruit or working in the 'bush', but in Marshfield crews often came together for work on the 'ends' (see Chapter 3). For example, Tyrone occasionally received a call from the local councillor about money to organize a group of men for a day's work cleaning the 'ends'. He in turn calls members of his crew to volunteer to do this, negotiating with the councillor for a price. To keep himself on equal grounds with the other members of the crew, Tyrone directly informs them about these monetary arrangements. He thereby communicates that he has a 'link' with a local councillor, but that he is not complicit with the big men and remains one of the crew.

'Pressure' and Respect

The cell phone plays a central role in maintaining such connections around work and sharing, but cell phones also share a more fundamental relationship to the situation felt by most crew members: boredom. Men are socialized to separate themselves from women and escape to the corners or the ends (Branche 1998; Chevannes 1999, 2001). Because of its visibility, the cell phone's place in relation to boredom is much more evident than it appears for loneliness experienced by women within the confines of the home. Whenever men are hanging around, what they seek is an answer to the ubiquitous question 'Wa gwaan?' They crave simply for something to be going on, for there to be an event, an opportunity, a 'something' that constitutes a happening – whether to watch some quarrel unfold, to get involved in some kind of hustling, some sport, some relationship, just something to pursue. But, if there isn't anything and one is fed up playing dominoes or kicking a ball around, then at least one or two individuals can be on the cell phone, playing games, sending text messages or just scrolling through names, looking for someone who might have enough credit on their phone for a chat. But that which relieves 'pressure' through 'cooling out' can also become the impetus for further 'pressure'. This was discussed by a group of men in Marshfield:

> Man 1: Some man put a $100 card pon dem phone everyday. Some man spend all $3,000 fi the week, some man spend all $3,000 per day for the card. Them a look it hustle it fi buy it.

> [Some men put $JA100 card on their phone everyday. Some men spend all of $JA3,000 for the week, some men spend all of $JA3,000 per day for the phonecard. They look for ways to hustle to buy it/afford it.]

> Man 2: If him did employ and have a job it wouldn't have time fi deh pon the phone, cause him would a work, but because him deh yah so and idle and nuh have nutten fi do then, yuh understa' me, him stay so bap and spend cause him waan fi talk to somebody who maybe gi him a hope.

[If he was working and had a job, he wouldn't have the time to be on the phone because he would be working, but because he is sitting there so idle and doesn't have anything to do then, you understand me, he stays so bored/down and spends because he wants to talk to someone who might give him hope.]

Man 3: Or a go send a thing come gi him, do a little thing fi him now and then.

[Or someone who would send something to give him or do a little thing for him now and then]

Man 1: Yeah, or talk to him little girlfren who a go get pregnant two months down the sideline, and she get pregnant hardship come on more cause him have more responsibility, yuh understan, but if him did a go work now him wouldn't spend the money fi talk pon the cell phone.

[Yeah, or talk to his girlfriend who is going to get pregnant two months down the line and when she gets pregnant it is going to get harder because he'll have more responsibility, you understand, but if he was working now he wouldn't spend the money to talk on the cell phone.]

Man 2: Alright listen to me, say yuh want to take a bus transportation, is so expensive, so yuh girlfren live a town, right, it a go cost yuh $200 fi go town, seen? So instead yuh card and just put pon it and say 'wha gwaan baby, wha'ppen, ray ray, me miss you ray ray' and it done, instead a yuh go out go tek a bus go town fi that. That's the only benefit, yuh understand, when we yuh want to link up.

[Alright, listen to me, say you want to take a bus (or some transportation) and it's so expensive because your girlfriend lives in Kingston, right, it is going to cost you $JA200 to go to Kingston, you see? So instead you just buy a card and just put it on your phone and say 'wha gwaan baby, what's happening, etc. etc. I miss you, etc. etc.' and it's done instead of going to take a bus to go to Kingston to do that. That's the only benefit, you understand, when we want to connect.]

In other words, boredom and the physical manifestation of space in Marshfield may highlight a much deeper issue in the poverty of relationships than merely what is suggested by having not much to do. However visible the men 'pon di corna' may be, as each month and each year pass they become increasingly invisible. On the road to success, their friends eventually learn to see the youths sitting on the wall; the 'yout dem', who make their presence known vocally by making rude and humorous comments (Abrahams 1983), become part of the wall that one must learn to ignore as one seeks one's own futures beyond the confines of the walls and boundaries of Marshfield. The youth on the ends feel betrayed by the people who have started to become 'big' and entered the 'system' of churches, businesses and universities.[3] These so-called big people were once 'likl yout dem' just like them who ran around in the street making trouble. The big difference is between those who remember their communities and those who appear to have 'forgotten' their roots on the ends. Even family members may have 'forgotten' them or tried to ignore their presence, which stands as a reminder of what could have been. It is a paradox of the pursuit of freedom that one cannot escape from the burdensome presence and oppressive sense of constant relationships without to some degree losing the emotional support of those same relationships.

This also makes the cell phone central to a trajectory that is commonly held to link boredom and crime (Moser and Holland 1997; Bailey et al. 1998; Branche 1998;). Citing Herbert Gayle's study of coping strategies, Chevannes (1999) notes that 'men are expected to "make life" by fair means, juggling, or by foul means, hustling. Juggle, if you can, but hustle if you must. But you must do something. To do nothing is to be judged and branded "worthless"' (28). Many bored young men seek a form of success that means finally everyone in the area must now pay respect to an individual who now has a presence that cannot be ignored (see Levy 1996). Even the family, which denigrates a man who has no income to contribute, now becomes dependent upon the ability of the criminal or ultimately the don to provide for and protect them. As one young man attending tertiary school in Marshfield put it:

> ... The older guys are still on the corner. The younger guys that I use to see in khaki [boys' school uniforms] and whatever, now they graduated from school and has graduated to the corner ... No school nothing ... Where the outside interference is coming in, in the form of a gun where in which person are going outside and getting gun and carrying them in ... Because on the corner now yuh guarantee to find at least one gun. Equal to a gang or 2 or 3 so them rule this end and a next gang rule that ends so you go have that plus that equal to turf war. Therefore you have more than now a lot of gun relate[d] activities and it reach a stage where persons are just walking fearlessly.

One of the common responses to our general fieldwork question, 'What do people use cell phones for?' was a variant upon 'Men use them to target the people they are going to shoot.' Cell phones are associated with this sense of the modern criminal world and with the privacy and autonomy when someone standing around is talking on their cellular. The conversation might be innocent, but one would never know if otherwise. It is also something that feeds into low-level crime as an obvious target of theft and the sale of 'second-hand' phones.

This trajectory towards crime is commonly remarked upon both in the social science literature and by young men, but it is in fact only one of many trajectories. An alternative is a 36-year-old man in our urban site who has become very successful at developing the role known as 'an elder', mainly through low-level patronage of events such as community football or other activities that can alleviate the 'pressure' associated with boredom. In possession of one of the more desirable phones and unusual in his use of predictive text, his phone becomes instantly associated with his skills as an organizer. Similarly, Damian, a young man struggling with a background of poverty and abuse in Orange Valley, develops himself through an incredibly active participation in a local church. Although this extensive use of his phone placed a real burden on his very limited resources, Damian recognized that the cell phone was a worthwhile investment because he could accumulate contacts and then mobilize them to form church gatherings, outings and prayer meetings, which constituted the other major route out of boredom and 'pressure'. In other words, just as much as criminality, a series of respected routes out of hanging around and boredom have become associated with the potential of the cell phone in the hands of the right man to activate others and therefore make things happen.

'Pressure pon mi 'ead': Women's Experience of 'Pressure'

Trekking up the hills of central Jamaica to settlements strung along distant roadways that seem to speak to the heart of traditional community, it is hard to imagine that loneliness could be a real issue, especially when one is aware of the degree of intermarriage and the dense network of relationships. Even in urban Jamaica there are strong connections and associations between neighbours and friends, family, workmates, church sisters and brother's mutual friends and acquaintances, work and voluntary associations. Not surprisingly, Jamaica is a place where it is considered unnatural to be and to live alone. Being alone runs contrary to the ethos of pooling and social networking that are viewed as central to the workings of life. A single person living alone is subject to constant gossip from neighbours and friends as to how lonely they must be. Over and over Jamaicans contrast their experience with that of 'foreign', where it seemed common and unproblematic for individuals to be allowed to live alone. Indeed, one of the most disturbing stories that circulated between Jamaicans living in places like Brooklyn and their friends and relatives at home was the quintessential story of some elderly man or women who died alone in a large apartment complex, their decaying bodies found days or even weeks later, when someone detected the smell of the rotting corpse drifting from the locked apartment. Most Jamaicans we met were quite certain that this sort of event could never happen in Jamaica – if your neighbour did not see you come out or open up your windows, they would come around and look for you just to see 'if you're alright'. To a foreigner, this level of intervention can sometimes be perceived as 'nosy' and, indeed, it is accepted that the communal resistance to being alone is also one way of getting inside people's business. It is not that people are unconscious of a 'downside' to this intense sociality, but rather that they accept the assumed distinction between metropolitan countries, where this kind of sociality is viewed as something lost, and their own retention of communal interest in the individual and its attendant lack of privacy.

The phone seems an obvious medium with which to uphold these principles. Mrs Wright, an agile seventy-year-old widow, started living on her own after her daughter Kimberley received a job offer in Kingston. Fearful of being completely alone, she decided to transform part of the house into a rental unit. Unlike many metropolitan countries, renters in Jamaica are expected to become part of the extended household in some fashion, even when they have their own cooking and bathroom facilities. Their children are often allowed to wander into the landlord's house, where they may be offered food or snacks, and the women of each household will often sit together talking while cooking, washing clothes or relaxing during the afternoon heat. Having someone at your house, even a renter, is viewed as 'a company'.

In Mrs Wright's case, the two women turned out not to be much company at all, spending most of their time with their boyfriends and relatives, who came through the gate late into the night. On her regular visits back home, Kimberley began to notice the tension in the yard and she started calling her mother weekly. Not accustomed to having emotional conversations over the phone, Mrs Wright talked quietly and tried to be brief in her answers. Her daughter could tell she felt down. Later she began to complain of headaches and not feeling well, which (not unintentially) lured Kimberley back to Orange Valley for a visit. On her visit home, Kimberley helped her mother give the women notice and spread the word among her friends that she was seeking more suitable company for her mother. After returning to town, she also started calling her mother at least three or four times a week, even though It was quite expensive to call from her Digicel cell phone to her mother's Cable and Wireless house phone; it resulted in the purchase of two extra ($JA100) phonecards each week. Yet the added expense seemed well worth her while as now her mother sounded happy and at ease. Mrs Wright, like many elderly women, still views the phone as a pragmatic object and has never adjusted to talking in great detail about her worries and concerns over the phone. In her eyes, the phone can never replace her daughter's visits, but it has clearly made a considerable difference to her mental well-being and in alleviating Kimberley's worries.

As in many other countries, the phone, then, plays a significant role in the management of loneliness, but it can also extend the more specific issues of 'pressure', such as the sense of feeling overburdened. Over and over again, we found unemployed women sitting in their homes in the day worrying over how they were going to meet their expenses and the demands of their children. Sonia is a classic example of this. Since Sonia fell pregnant fifteen years ago, she has been determined to be a 'real' mother to her son. Sonia was a 'barrel child', the term Jamaicans use for the many children who are left in Jamaica with relatives while their parents seek better fortunes and futures abroad. Sonia's mother left when she was eight years old and, given the sparse telecommunications situation at that time, most of her contact was by a few calls or letters a year and the arrival of an annual barrel shipment filled with clothing, shoes, soap, rice and other food (see Soto 1987; Olwig 1999b). As a child Sonia recalled being excited about the arrival of the barrel and remembers how she would find ways to make it known to her friends that a shirt or a pair of shoes came from her mother in 'foreign'. But even then Sonia realized that, for her, the objects could not compensate for her mother's hug or advice about how to be a young woman. Although other friends and family live abroad and have offered 'to send' for her, she turned down opportunities 'to travel' in order to care for her son. Now she seemed to be moving backwards. Although she recently had an offer to work in home care, she calculated that this paid her little more than transport costs and would not be any better than her income from the house shop and as a part-time helper. More importantly, this job could in no way meet her son's school fees.

Over the course of the summer, she began to fret, constantly repeating 'pressure gone to me head'. At the beginning of August, she finally broke down and asked her boyfriend for $JA200 to purchase a phonecard, which she used to call her mother to 'beg' money for her son's secondary school fees. While she was relieved to have the money, the phone call only intensified the 'pressure' she felt. While it is very common in Jamaica for parents and grandparents overseas to be responsible for large annual expenses, for Sonia it meant a loss of pride and the acknowledgement that she was not making it. More significantly, it forced her to re-engage with her estranged mother, with whom she spoke only briefly three or four times per year.

'"Pressure" pon di Inside'

'Pressure' also lies behind a common genre of contemporary phone use in Jamaica, which is known as 'counselling'. A professional psychiatrist costing upwards of $JA3,000 for an hour's session is well beyond low-income budgets and the more accessible doctors and nurses in Jamaica are not viewed as people with whom one discusses problems extensively. In fact, many Jamaican women pride themselves on the idea and stereotype that they are 'strong' compared with women in 'foreign' and do not need to seek help from professionals. Not surprisingly, there is a stigma associated with mental illness (Wilson 1972; Hickling and Gibson 2004). In contrast, 'counselling' is readily acceptable because the genre derives not from medicine, but from religion. Unlike Euro-American models of quiet affirmation, Jamaican counsellors are expected to evaluate the situation and to provide judgements, which are often linked to the person's spiritual state and the need to reconnect with God. Most, if not all, of these informal counselling sessions end with prayer. In the public domain, the 'Ask the Pastor' column of the *Jamaica Gleaner* and equivalent call-in radio programmes provide models of how to advise people, especially about relationships. Because counselling is ultimately about the spiritual path and most Jamaicans feel they are qualified to talk about God and spirituality, they are often on the lookout for a counselling opportunity. In one case, a woman even reported receiving a call from someone with the wrong telephone number and described how in the course of determining it was a wrong number she began a conversation that eventually led to a counselling situation. Since then she admits she secretly hopes for more wrong numbers. Others use their phone to call to 'check people', which sometimes results in extensive discussions of a person's situation, counselling and even collaborative prayers held over the phone. In fact, because of this potential for spiritual counselling, many view missing a telephone call as a disservice. There may be an opportunity to do God's calling at any time and you have to be ready. While the cell phone is vastly more expensive than a landline for such sessions, for some it may seem worth it.

But there is an even more basic relationship between the cell phone and 'pressure', which stems from the belief that 'pressure' is created from the lack of communication itself. It is significant that Abrahams's (1983) seminal book on communication in the Caribbean is called the *The Man-O-Words in the West Indies*, because in many ways women were simply unable to find equivalent outlets for communication. Sobo (1993) observes that women can only exchange news and advice when a 'mission' takes them out of the yard, but that these conversations must take place quietly and subtly. Indeed, other female kin are often asked to accompany women when they go 'on the road' to avoid the suspicion of gossip and indecency. Men, on the other hand have sanctioned public spaces, such as rum bars, where they can converse, but women who sit and tuck their skirts between their legs and chat all day by the roadside are often disparaged. As Sobo recognizes, 'Although men "labrish" too, women are more often called out for it. Perhaps because men generally talk little about their personal feelings they do not realize that women, for a variety of cultural and psychosocial reasons, do. Women talking are not necessarily "chatting" others: often, they talk about themselves' (Sobo 1993: 106–107). This lack of opportunity to communicate therefore frustrates what many women understand to be a basic need.

From the perspective of many women, one of the critical advantages of the cell phone in terms of its ability to alleviate pressure comes from its potential for private communication. Monique, for example, views her missions 'on the road' as a performance. Sporting her blue-tinted trendy glasses and slinky, strappy dresses, which hug her ample breasts, stomach and hips, she lures people in with her wit and infectious laughter. Less evident is the fact that she had a four-week-old son and was struggling with her relationship with her husband and that, as she soon admitted, 'It's all smiles on the outside and shit on the inside.' The reasons became clear over the subsequent weeks. Although in public she laughed and even seemed to embrace comments about her 'curves', which were often more brazenly exclaimed as 'Whoa, Monique, yu put on weight,' she was concerned that she had reached over 300 lbs during her pregnancy. Although she loved her new baby, the timing was her husband's rather than her own, and he now was rarely at home, spending his days working or with one of his other women. Only a week before she gave birth, a 'friend' called Monique on the cell phone just to tell her that her husband was 'hitting on' her; Monique suspected that this friend had actually slept with her husband and was using the phone call to Monique to get something out of him. This tension was evident in her calls to her husband. No matter how animated or excitable her conversation, when the phone rang and his name appeared on the screen of the cell phone, we instantly stopped talking and Monique's voice became quiet and stern, muttering only brief words and responses to his queries. Their face-to-face interactions are considerably more animated – they quarrel, she threatens to leave and he threatens to take the baby. Monique feels trapped, so trapped that she contemplated taking her own life.

The distinction between Monique and Sonia is largely that Monique remains committed to a public performance as the life and soul of her social network. For Monique, the key to holding at bay this negative spiral into individual depression had to be the maintenance of her social connections, which placed a premium on her phone use. Monique spent over one-sixth of her weekly expenditures on cell phones, buying at least one card daily to keep in touch. Critical to her adjustment from being a working woman to a stay-at-home mother, the phone had now become her only real connection to the world. But there was an edge to this dependence that gave her relationship to the phone a quality of addiction. In contrast, Sonia seems relatively prudent with its use (often timing her calls) and keenly distinguishes between calls to landlines and to cell phones.

Like Monique, Natalie became something of a 'phone addict' in response to a cycle of failure and depression. Natalie returned home to live with her mother after going through a separation from her husband of three years. Suddenly without income, Natalie became increasingly depressed. As someone everybody predicted would 'go far', she was woefully embarrassed about what had happened to her and the way that her life had shifted, virtually overnight, after she learned about her husband's transgressions with other women. Before, she had felt that this was something that would not, even could not, happen to someone like her; everyone always commented on how 'close' they were. Humiliated and then depressed, she began hiding in her room, avoiding the people she could no longer care about, for days, then months, then a year. As her relatives grew increasingly concerned, her family commissioned their local pastor to come and bless the house, summoning the evil spirits to leave. But none of this seemed to help Natalie. However, she did have one outlet: two sisters, whom she was close to and felt she could confide in. But they lived in the States. Over the course of a month, Natalie called one of her sisters almost every day, often talking late into the night, when she could not sleep. Her sisters were concerned about the phone bill, but Natalie lied and told them that their mother knew she was making the calls. Inevitably a bill of $JA12,000 ($US200) arrived, which left her family in a state of absolute shock, torn between anger and sympathy for Natalie. They could not pay this bill and had to negotiate with C&W for a payment plan. They then cancelled the ICAS service and started to force Natalie to come out of her bedroom and start contributing to the family and the running of the household. Natalie was granted a $JA200 phonecard each week to call her sisters abroad, an act that brought her in line with what had become a national institution – 'when the card finish', she 'finish'.

For many women, the phone has provided an additional outlet for the release of stress, tension and 'pressure', particularly where traditional social networks have failed or let individuals down. For Natalie and Monique, whose stress and depression have reached a more serious level, the phone allows them to cleanse themselves of the stresses and troubles in their lives. Much like the testimonials of Pentecostal services, women become 'filled' or fulfilled by the fact that they have friends, family and other support that, while not necessarily physically present, sustain them through the difficult times. In turn, the ability to be connected and a source of comfort to others provides friends and family with a sense of fulfilment. Grace gives an example:

> It's so funny that my mind would be on somebody so much that sometimes I am just prompted to give them a call and it's either for a good reason, take for example, my friends sister Kamesha, who just had the baby. My mind was just on her. I have never ever called her apart from the fact when Paul was here ... But for that day I just knew something was wrong and when I called her she wasn't due to have the baby until 2 weeks before I called and she actually had the baby same day I called. And it was ... a terrible birth. I don't know how she survived it and she spent hours in labour and it just happened that my mind was just on her and I was like I have to call her and I did. I followed my instincts and called and I was relieved that she was okay.

The phone has become readily accepted as a means to relieve 'pressure' simply by feeling connected to others and to feel part of that natural (i.e. social) state of being that defines Jamaicanness. But while this use of the phone alleviates and prevents further 'pressure', as with other substances that relieve 'pressure' it can also become subject to abuse, addiction and overuse, which in turn can create and compound 'pressure'.

Conclusion

The intention of this chapter was to convey something of the potential of ethnography in order to establish what we meant by an anthropology of communication. Although the cell phone figures centrally within this account, its mobility and individuality are inseparable from the properties it shares with a landline as creating the very possibility of mediated communication. As such, it goes to the heart of the role of communication itself in creating and maintaining relationships that seem vital to an individual's sense of him/herself as a social being. As we have demonstrated, the phone is central to the way women in Jamaica cope with 'pressure' associated with the loneliness that may arise both from having children, and from children leaving home. It is equally central to the way men deal with the 'pressure' they associate with boredom, often experienced within the more communal setting of hanging around at street corners. In both cases, it may become the means for alleviating 'pressure', but when overused can also become an instrument that exacerbates 'pressure'. It also supports Douglas and Ney's (1998) contention that when speaking of poverty we need also to consider the poverty that can be experienced as a lack of access to communication itself, rather than merely the contribution of communication to the ability to cope. Simply to receive a call, hear someone's voice or realize that someone is thinking about you makes people 'feel good', that 'someone cares'. 'Pressure', and its attendant expressions of stress and depression, has always been associated with this absence of connection and communication.

–8–

Welfare

The final chapter of this volume will be concerned with an overall assessment of the impact of the cell phone on low-income households, but much of the evidence behind that evaluation will be presented here. In both cases, it is the processes of evaluation as well as the cell phone as the object of evaluation that are of concern. In the previous chapter, the concept of 'pressure' was utilized to understand how Jamaicans express and understand that which acts against people's welfare. In contrast, this chapter begins with fields delineated by the conventions of international development and other governing bodies, such as health, in which this assessment appears to be relatively unproblematic. We then proceed to more difficult sectors, such as schooling and crime, where the assessments of the cell phone's uses are rather more difficult, since there is strong evidence for a deleterious as well as a beneficial impact. Finally, we turn to a consideration of the church and of luck or fate, in order to comprehend the key idioms through which the benefits and costs of the phone are evaluated locally and the forces that people see as critical to the determination of their welfare.

Health

A simple and direct questionnaire that, for example, concentrated on the use of the phone for the dissemination of medical information or access to medical services would probably have suggested that the cell phone has had only a very modest impact, since these were rarely mentioned in our studies. Rather, it is the larger ethnographic embrace of context that helps draw out the critical relationship between the cell phone and health. A concept that has been essential is that of 'communicative ecology'. As noted in the introduction, the term ecology implies that each 'species' of technology becomes part of a larger communicative environment that gives it its specific place within communication as a whole (Slater and Tacchi 2004). The phone links downwards to word-of-mouth reportage, sideways to the dissemination of information through the media and, when it reaches its limits as a technology, upwards to another form of communication, transport, which then extends its ability to bring people and information together. All of these may be considered as part of the phone's integration into the larger social ecology of health. For example, rather than conveying health information, the critical role of the phone in a medical emergency may be the way it facilitates communicating the crisis to those best able to help fund the cost of the treatment or its use in linking up with the taxi service or with flights that can bring help from abroad.

Acknowledging this wider communication ecology is significant because assessments based on development agendas tend to focus on more immediate medical communication. Whether it is United Nations-funded programmes or academic reviews, such as the online *Journal of Medical Internet Research* (http://www.jmir.org/2003/1/e5/), the emphasis tends to be on communication technology as a means of disseminating medical information of benefit to populations. Our evidence suggested that, if the cell phone were judged on such criteria, it does not yet represent a significant development. Indeed, it is surprisingly absent even in arenas where one would anticipate an immediate appropriation, such as scheduling appointments or establishing reminders about routine medical examinations. Despite near-universal phone access, it is still rare to make appointments or seek out medical advice from professional doctors or nurses via the phone. It has become more acceptable, however, to use the phone to contact a nurse especially when they are a neighbour or family friend. Although outreach workers in Marshfield reported using their personal phones to arrange meetings with their clients who had young babies, in general such preventive care was rare. With respect to the dissemination of more general medical information, it is the media that have now garnered a central role in this task and there are now a number of high-profile HIV/AIDS campaigns utilising television, pamphlets and newspaper articles. Popular phone-in radio programmes also provide critical information for a wide audience and in a number of cases carefully clarify misconceptions about the spread and treatment of HIV/AIDS. In contrast, there was little evidence that the phone has become particularly important in spreading formal medical information by word of mouth or text messaging.

From the perspective of many members of the medical community, it is difficult to see how disseminating information through the cell phone would be productive, given the ways in which many Jamaicans spurn medical advice. For example, it is common for a doctor to prescribe a course of medicine, such as penicillin, and to instruct the patient to continue to the end of the course irrespective of when the symptoms have gone. This advice is usually ignored. Patients take the medicine for the first few days until the symptoms appear to have abated and then store the rest of the medicines until the next time they feel they have a similar illness. From a medical point of view, this is about the worst thing they can do. Not only is this detrimental to forming resistance to the illness but the medicines may be in a very poor condition when they finally take them. Yet we found that even families with children attending university routinely treat medication in this way, justifying it as economic prudence both in saving them from future doctor's visits and from wasting coveted and costly medication. In addition, parents and caregivers often have to make the difficult choice between which medications to purchase if they can only afford one of the three prescribed. Rather than trying to promote new practices, the various government ministries have tried to embrace new medications that might reduce reliance upon the conscientiousness of individuals to take their medicines properly, such as adopting the use of contraception through quarterly injections rather than relying on the more expensive and less manageable forms of 'the pill'. Still, there were many pregnancies attributed to forgetting to return to the clinic for these injections every three months. So, although the Ministry of Health used the media extensively to disseminate and make accessible useful advice and information about medication, their audience remains selective in their acceptance of this information.

As yet, the medical community has not explored the potential of the cell phone for administering or monitoring treatment or disseminating medical knowledge. Many work under considerable economic constraints. For example, alongside carrying out routine checks and treating ordinary illnesses, the free clinic in Marshfield also has to cope with problems such as gunshot wounds arising from violence. The clinic is not equipped for their immediate treatment, which takes place at Spanish Town Hospital or Kingston Public Hospital.[1] Because these public hospitals are understaffed and poorly equipped, patients are then shuttled off to their local clinics for their long-term and follow-up treatments. This means that the Marshfield clinic is expected to dress quite severe knife and gunshot wounds, which rapidly deplete their monthly allotment of dressings. The government states that a free clinic should not ask patients to pay towards treatment or supplies, but, finding themselves regularly short of materials to re-dress wounds, the nurses are often forced to require patients to purchase their own bandages before they return to the clinic for treatment. Most low-income households depend on these free clinics, which were held twice a week in Orange Valley and daily in Marshfield (except Sundays). The alternative, a visit to the doctor, will set patients back at least $JA1,000, or around half a week's income.

Given the limited free facilities and expense of doctors, the phone is much more likely to be used to find alternatives to formal medical treatments or at least to minimize the cost of treatments. Women, in particular, chat extensively about ailments, comparing experiences to determine whether a current illness is actually the same as something seen before and therefore can be treated without reference to a doctor. Similarly, some Jamaicans use the cell phone to compare the cost of medicines. Many of the elderly returned residents in Mandeville afflicted with diabetes, arthritis, high cholesterol and heart conditions, also found it much easier to comparison-shop for medication through the phone and to share information such as if a pharmacy was overcharging for a medication (see Horst 2004b). The phone was also used to spread the reputation of a particular doctor with a good bedside manner or a home-remedy treatment that was highly effective.

In emergencies, it is the link between the phone and the transport system that has become critical (see Jain 2002; Ito et al. 2005). The vast majority of people in Orange Valley live along various hillsides. Before the cell phone, it was possible to ask a taxi to continue from the main road to drop a person home, but it was not possible to summon a taxi to one's home; the only way to find a taxi was to walk down to the main road. The basic relationship between the population and their transport system has changed entirely as a result of the cell phone. Time is of the essence in most emergency situations and for residents of Orange Valley the nearest hospital is approximately forty minutes away. Nadine, a mother of two children, believes that the cell phone saved her son's life. Jared, Nadine's three-year-old son, is asthmatic. One winter evening Jared's coughs and wheezing took a turn for the worse and Nadine began to fear that he might stop breathing. However, because he has fallen ill so regularly, Nadine has been unable to hold down a job and cannot afford the $JA6,000 needed to purchase a nebulizer for his recurrent asthma attacks. The only way Jared could receive treatment was at the hospital, so Nadine tried to contact a neighbour who owned a car, but he was not home. Two phone calls later, her mother found a taxi driver to drive them to the hospital. While Nadine's rush to the hospital remains the norm, there are instances when the cell phone can be used to summon emergency services, such as when a twelve-year-old child called the paramedics because his mother was ill and unable to talk. He was counselled over the phone as to the appropriate action to take and to help determine the kind of assistance required.

Often with illness the problem is the timing, as when Heather's (co-author) son fell ill with bronchitis one Saturday night in Orange Valley. The only way that her son received treatment was thanks to her Jamaican 'sister', who remembered that one of her friends lived next door to a local doctor. She called the friend, who knocked on the doctor's door and spoke to him about the child. The doctor agreed to see him, but, again, transport and social connections proved to be crucial. Since all the taxis had returned home for the night, they ended up getting a ride from the same friend's husband's brother and temporarily borrowing some extra money in the event that the visit was more expensive than anticipated or an emergency-room visit was needed (the doctor's visit, penicillin and cough syrups came to $JA2,400 cash). With a 24–hour private taxi service, transport in Portmore is generally more reliable and the link between health and transport made much more explicit, with the list of taxi numbers and cars taped to the wall of the various clinics. In more extreme cases, it is air transport that is brought into the communicative ecology. For example, a woman from Orange Valley who kept having severe pain and other symptoms found that none of the local doctors could come up with a diagnosis for her condition. Her doctor asked if she had any relatives abroad, since he thought she might require medical treatment abroad. The woman phoned her family in New York and they pooled together to successfully apply for a visa and purchase a plane ticket, which enabled her to travel abroad. Once she was examined there, they determined that she should have her gallstones removed. Six months later, she returned to Jamaica.

Transnational connections may also become involved in simply meeting local costs. For example, Frances lived with her son and husband, as well as her ailing mother. After her mother had a small stroke, Frances took her to the doctor, who prescribed medication. With no one in the house working, Frances simply could not afford the medication, so she called her other sisters and brothers living in Orange Valley. However, they too were in a similar predicament and could not raise more than a few extra hundred dollars, so Frances decided to ask her relatives living abroad to send the equivalent of JA$2,000, which by remittance standards is a fairly small sum, but sufficient for her to be able to obtain the medicine. At one point, the process reached a bottleneck since she didn't even have the money for the phonecards to make the call and it was only when Frances 'begged' two cards from a local shop that she was able to proceed and thereby finally obtain the medicines.

A more complex case involved a seventeen-year-old girl named Veronica, whose new baby started to suffer from a skin condition. Unfortunately, the medicine prescribed by the local rural doctor ended up making this worse, causing severe burning. Clearly she needed to get to Kingston to see a qualified dermatologist, but this required various forms of coordination, garnering money from relatives as well as sorting out the logistics of where Veronica could stay while the baby was undergoing treatment. Veronica was known to be generally lackadaisical about finances and her forthright personality had alienated many members of her extended family, who might otherwise have been expected to come to her aid; indeed, there were some suggestions that she had disregarded the advice of her relatives and continued to slather lotions and baby oils on her baby which also exacerbated the condition (see Sobo 1993, 1997). For this reason she had to enlist the aid of her mother, who was working in Canada, to persuade these local relations to take pity upon Veronica's baby. Her mother made the detailed arrangements, including the coordination of the money, over the family's many cell phones and the baby was finally able to reach Kingston for the requisite treatment. Often the literature on the cell phone stresses its role in micro-coordination (e.g. Ling and Yuri 2002), but, in the case of Jamaican families, where this level of complexity is not rare, it is often more a kind of macro-coordination that comes to the fore.

The final two stories illustrate the way the phone doesn't just connect Jamaica with 'foreign' but thereby juxtaposes two kinds of sensibility with respect to illness and treatment. In one of his conversations with his wife, who lived in Brooklyn, Julian detected that her voice did not sound right. Julian's wife admitted that she had been working hard in a call centre and this seemed to be contributing to a problem with her throat. Noting that she had just been in Jamaica the week before, Julian (who believes in 'natural' medicine) told her that her return to the cold, damp weather of New York had been a shock to her system and was stressing her body (see Chevannes 1993b, 1994). When his wife responded by saying she was going to go to the grocery store to purchase some cold medication, Julian told her not to waste her money but to go home and make some chamomile or other natural tea with honey, which was better than taking some 'foreign' substance into her body (Sobo 1993). This should be followed by a special 'bush' tea he had given her, which would cleanse her system. Julian's wife protested and said she thought it would just be easier to buy a pill and sleep it off, but Julian kept insisting that she take the natural route to better health. Frustrated that, being in Jamaica, he could not oversee this process, he bought another phonecard and called again three hours later to reiterate his advice. She had to promise him that she had boiled the tea.

Working in the opposite direction, Sharon had been having trouble sleeping until she called an old friend, now a nurse in the USA, who reminded her that soursop tea was a traditional remedy for nervousness, which many Jamaicans believe is the cause of insomnia (Sobo 1993). Sharon remembered one big house on the hill in Jerusalem where the family had a soursop tree and she sent a message begging a bunch. Once the leaves dried, Sharon boiled the leaves in water and proceeded to drink the tea. That night, and several nights following, Sharon slept like a baby and subsequently started calling her friends all across the island to see if they had soursop leaves and, if so, whether they realized what a treasure they possessed. Both these stories reinforce the general sense that the phone is most often used to find alternatives to formal consultation with doctors, rather than either to arrange such a consultation or to disseminate official medical knowledge.

In conclusion, we found little evidence that the cell phone achieved a direct medical impact, but, when understood within the wider communicative ecology, it plays an important indirect role in managing health and welfare. The more one includes factors such as transport, paying for bills, international links and the broader concepts of medicine, such as folk remedies, the more the phone seems to be an integral part of health care. This is not to dismiss the potential of more direct uses. There are specialist campaigns that use or plan to use particular properties of the phone. For example, an AIDS worker used the phone to establish a more effective relationship to those with the illness, since a mobile phone makes it easier to keep in touch with individuals and inform them that a clinic is cancelled or the venue has been changed. Potentially it could be used to remind people to take medicines at particular times. The privacy associated with the cell phone can help individuals with HIV consult anonymously until such a time that they are ready to present themselves in person at a clinic. In other countries the potential for texting, thereby giving 'voice' and 'ears' to the deaf, is being exploited with highly positive results. These are the sort of specialist services one can expect to see developing in Jamaica. But, as yet, these official medical uses have impinged upon Jamaican society much less than the broader effects described above.

Crime and Security

In general, there was a widespread belief that the phone had been instrumental in reducing crime, dealing with the consequences of crime and increasing the sense of personal security. For example, a woman told of using her phone when the father of her half-sister was shot by gunmen in Portmore Mall and another woman called the police when her nephew was shot. Older Jamaicans also noted that they felt less isolated and vulnerable and parents found it comforting to know they could keep in contact with their children or phone in an emergency. Indeed, children were quite aware of the pull of safety and security in their attempts to persuade their parents to purchase a phone for their own use. In practice, the cell phone functioned as part of the everyday sense of security, of knowing where a child was at a given moment of time, and also the logistical security of being able to get on with one's own life and not waiting or being dependent upon the vagaries of children's use of their own time (see Kasesniemi and Rautianinen 2002). This, and the general expectation that, if a child receives a phone, then, in return, they should inform their parent or guardian where they are, seemed to fully justify the investment.

The cell phone was also seen as helping people feel secure within their home, and people noted that the cell phone was safer than a landline because with a landline the outside wires could be damaged or cut by criminals intent on breaking into the house. For those living in isolated houses or hamlets around Orange Valley, this sense of security hinged upon the ability to phone the police. One woman told us how suspicious people in the area felt since a neighbour three houses away had been shot three months before in a botched robbery attempt. Since then, she had felt fearful and admitted that she recently used the cell phone to phone her neighbour and the police when she heard some unusual noises and strange voices. For her, the primary advantage of the phone was that she did not need to turn on the light in order to make these calls, thus mitigating the possibility of being revealed as an informer and potentially the subject of retribution, a common motivation for violent crime in Jamaica.

Particularly in areas without landlines, there was a sense that criminals could have attacked in the past with impunity, given the impossibility of summoning help. The mere ability to call the police was also viewed as significant in preventing minor altercations from turning into major violent incidents. The police stressed this tendency for murder and violent crime to sometimes build up slowly from a more minor altercation; these were the murders that a phone was most likely to prevent. Even the knowledge that people were likely to have phones in the vicinity of an incident was seen as a major deterrent. As part of a general discussion, a police sergeant stationed in Orange Valley surmised that cell phones decreased crime in the area by 18 per cent. Such a figure seems artificial and arbitrary, but, if one wanted to summarize many different conversations, it also seemed about right.

The police station itself used only a rather antiquated radio system, and they were aware that having a phone made a big difference to their ability to respond to calls, typically reducing response times in Orange Valley from sixty minutes to twenty minutes. None of the police in Orange Valley or Marshfield received financial assistance for their use of the phone on the job, which meant that they were effectively subsidizing the cost of their work by using their private cell phones. But this seemed an accepted practice and they readily gave out their private phone numbers as part of their work. Everyone had stories about the cell phone as instrumental in combating or preventing crime, from schoolchildren phoning their parents when gunshots were heard in the vicinity of the school or a taxi driver alerting police when someone fitting the profile of a known criminal was seen. The police also saw this increased and often clandestine ability to communicate with informants as an important facility. Sadly the phone was also important when crime was not prevented. A woman in Orange Valley explained in detail how, after her 22-year-old nephew was shot by gunmen, the phone was used not just to tell the police, but also to rapidly inform family and friends both in Jamaica and abroad of his murder, including the victim's mother, who was living in England.

The phone could be also used to commit crimes. The Orange Valley police rarely bothered to send patrol cars along the road since the kinds of people they were hoping to catch, such as illegal street vendors, would always be rung ahead by others who had spotted the police driving down the road. This formed part of a general attitude that the phone could and should be used to help the police deal with serious crime but could also be used to thwart the police in trying to deal with activities most people supported, such as small-scale vending. The phone had an obvious function in the coordination of crimes by groups, who could, for example, post lookouts much more easily. Another tactic the police noted consisted of criminals phoning in a fake crime in some other place to keep the police occupied and unable to attend the real crime at hand. Generally, the sentiment was that the 'good' outweighed the 'bad' and even the most law-abiding citizens acknowledged that some of this subversion of police was merely preventing what they saw as unwarranted 'oppression'. In Marshfield, the latter would include any interference with the extensive marijuana trade and also attempts by police to close down noisy but popular dancehall parties.

The cell phone also stimulated crime inasmuch as stealing phones was a very common cause of break-ins to the home and petty crime on the street. In

Marshfield, it was assumed that, if one was prepared to pay enough for a particular handset, then someone was prepared to steal it to order. The other side to this, breaking codes and changing SIM cards to enable phone use beyond the control of the phone companies, was viewed as a mundane part of life. A man from Marshfield described the situation:

> Them thief phone regular, and because people now aware of that, him put phone locks on him phone. Although … no matter how much code yuh want have pon it, yuh have man out deh weh will pull it same way.

> [They steal phones regularly and because people are aware of this they put a lock on their phone [password protected]. Although no matter how many passcodes you put on it, you have men out there who know how to decode/break the code just the same.]

While accusations of phone theft could become more serious, such as a murder that arose in a neighbouring rural town out of such an accusation, in general the phone was seen as a symptom rather than a cause of such violence. To summarize, while the murder rate in 2004 was as high as it had ever been in the ghetto areas of Kingston and Spanish Town, for lesser crime, especially in rural areas, there was a sense that individuals were more cautious in committing crimes because there was so much more chance of victims summoning help or a crime being reported to the police.

Schooling

The significance of the cell phone for schools was most evident from a discussion with the headmistress of a primary school near Orange Valley. Until obtaining her cell phone two years ago, the school had never had any kind of phone. In fact, a few years ago the school received a grant to gain Internet access but without a landline the principal had to return the money, an act that drove her to tears. Even the public call box located near the school was out of order for long periods of time, leaving the school effectively cut off from hospitals and the police, as well as parents and government ministries. Despite a promise to connect all schools, C&W had never responded to her endless requests for a landline.

Before the arrival of the cell phone in the hinterlands of Orange Valley, contacting parents was a hit-and-miss affair, with children being notoriously unreliable in giving their parents written or verbal messages. In its place, the church became the nearest thing to a local public address facility, and information concerning schooling, fees, meetings with teachers and other events was most successfully passed on at the local Baptist church. But, now that she is equipped with her own cell phone, the principal feels she finally has some means for contacting a reasonable proportion of parents who have supplied her with their phone numbers and can check on long-term absence. Short-term absence was simply too common to be followed up, given that around a quarter of pupils did not attend the primary school on a given day, claiming lack of money to pay for lunch or transport. As with the police, the cost of all such phone use comes out of the principal's personal salary.

At Orange Valley Comprehensive High School (OVCHS), approximately 60 per cent of students carried a cell phone to school, which most students claimed would be more but for the school policy, which restricts cell phones on campus. The punishment involves a fine of $JA500 and the school retains the cell phone until the end of the school year. At Marshfield High School the figure is closer to 30 per cent. Most phones are set to 'vibrate', turned off or kept in bags during class time. This policy was not necessarily enforced uniformly and teachers were not seen as overly strict as long as an effort was made to conceal phones. Without this effort, teachers generally viewed use of the phones as disrespectful and tried to make an example of the students they perceived as not taking their authority seriously.

Teachers themselves were allowed to bring phones and use them openly, carrying them on their belts or around their necks, in handbags or simply in their hands. Stealing phones from teachers was not unknown. On one occasion, even the school vice principal had his phone stolen while his back was turned by a student who had been called in over an issue of discipline. When confronted, the student denied the offence and claimed his parents had given him money for a new cell phone. The school decided to call the student's parents, who reported that his statement was untrue. Wary of history repeating itself, one teacher opted to tuck her cell phone into the gap between her skirt and waist, or even her underwear. She admitted this sometimes ended up with her doing an odd little dance, in the middle of standing in front of her class when teaching in order to keep the phone in place, but she simply couldn't imagine not keeping the phone on her body. She also admitted to times when she had stopped teaching to respond to the vibrating phone – not every time, just when she was expecting an important call.

Another teacher, who sold phone cards on the side, tried to bring about five cards to school per day to sell. If she ran out during the course of the school day (and she often did), she simply called her daughter at home to scratch off a card to reveal the number, which was read on the phone or sent by text. Often these transactions took place through a favourite or reliable student, who would be given the money during class time to walk over to the teacher/phonecard vendor and return with the card. Recognizing the double standard posed by this flaunting of phone use, most teachers were relatively lax on the students' personal use of phones. Only one of the twenty students asked at Orange Valley High School had had a phone confiscated, although three others had been given stern warnings after being caught using them.

Many schoolchildren happily confirmed a widespread conviction that Jamaicans of their age had become almost obsessive about the cell phone. For example in Portmore one schoolboy asserted, 'Without my cell phone I would die. I am a very determined little fella, and you see once I want it I going to get it. It nuh matter how big or small it might be. It nuh matter how expensive. I going to want it. So phone is a thing weh me love and I can't live without my phone.' A girl from the same school put it more in terms that reflect the passions of first love. When asked how often she called her boyfriend she replied, 'Every second I get I call and talk to him 'cause I don't know how long he has to live you understand. Anything can happen, so I call every second, to find out if anything happen to him. So I call every second to find out if everything is ok and he calls me every second as well.' For teenagers in particular, the phone had quickly become as essential and as inseparable as clothing.

Students were therefore prepared to make a number of sacrifices to acquire credit in order to use phones at school. For girls who could not gain credit from parents or a boyfriend, the most common method was by scrimping and saving from their lunch money (see Henry-Lee et al. 2001). Those who received $JA150 daily could make do with lunch under $JA100 and within a couple of days they could buy a phonecard. Those with less sometimes shared lunch with a friend, buying on alternate days. Some girls, such as Chantal, only received a minimal $JA50 a day. Chantal skipped lunch at least two times per week, saving $JA100 for her phonecard; on the third day she skipped a patty, saving enough to make $JA120, the cost of a card. The girl she relied on for doing this, Tracey-Ann, often let her down because, being attractive and flirtatious, she often managed to get not only a free lunch but often also free rides home from taxi drivers or a boyfriend. On those days Chantal would either skip another lunch or spent the weekend without credit. Another girl, Amina, relied on her father. On one morning he had less money than expected so he made an arrangement to leave the money with the security guard at the school entrance. Amina kept her phone on silent during class and, just before twelve, felt it vibrate, asked to go to the bathroom and saw the text 'dolla 2 sk' meaning that he had left the money with the security guard. Particular students had identified 'spots' on the campus where they could sneak a phone call to a boyfriend or girlfriend. In all instances students said they used the phone in the classroom itself 'only for emergencies'. A typical example of such an 'emergency' was when Lee Ann was running late one day and left the house without her nutrition book, within which she had left the class assignment. It would have taken her three hours to return for it, so she excused herself to use the bathroom and dialled her mother, who then retrieved the assignment and brought it in by taxi. What such stories indicate is that, for many school pupils, the ability to make calls had become the absolute priority of day-to-day life.

While students avoided flaunting their phones in the classroom, at other times it was an entirely different matter. During lunch students openly huddled in groups with their phones, playing games, sending text messages and making phone calls; in effect, a focal point for students has come to be sitting collectively and experimenting with their phones. Students with Internet phones (most often boys) made themselves well known among the student body and used this time as an opportunity to go online and check the results of a football match or look at porn sites. Some allowed their friends to use the phone to go online, but this was when Digicel offered the Internet service without a fee. Schoolgirls also used lunchtimes, breaks and after school to make the phone a focal point of leisure time, for example, to help their girlfriends make a decision about what to say to a boyfriend, or in one case to help compose a friend's text message after a major fight had broken out between this friend and the friend's boyfriend. A schoolgirl described such concerns: '[We] talk about life. It is stressing for us young people as well – life – we will sit and, no nuh really sit cause a don't what the other person is doing at their house, but we like talk about our past relationships, boyfriend, now, how is life, schoolwork, what you doing right now, sometimes we would a call and ask if them can braid we hair tomorrow.' Occasionally the phone performed a useful function in organizing pupils' academic lives. For example, Janoy's school drama teacher assigned a new play, but, given the school's limited budget, she could only obtain three copies. Most of the pupils were keen to have star roles, but only had one week to read and practise the play. All fifteen students agreed to exchange cell phone numbers (the one without, gave her mother's number) in order to circulate the few precious copies amongst them.

The manner in which the phone might change the relationship between teachers, pupils and parents also proved critical. During her fifteen years of teaching, Diane had become quite skilled at developing her relationship with particular students and their parents. Unlike most teachers, Diane had extended this into obtaining gifts, ranging from snacks to a sweater. Although she always claimed these were unsolicited and only revealed the extent to which her students loved her or thought she was performing well as their teacher, other teachers were often jealous. This, combined with a notoriously bad attendance rate, meant that schools had often refused to renew her contract and she moved from school to school. It seemed that the schools found her 'too beggy beggy'. With the cell phone, all of this changed. Diane was now able to give out her number to her students and their parents, who could call and ask for clarification of class assignments. Soon she found parents ringing her up to eleven at night asking for help in explaining some aspect of homework. Parents also phoned when their child was sick to determine what they had missed, or to confirm their child's claim that they did not have homework or a test the next day. They phoned for details about school trips, such as how much money was required. Although rare, a few parents have asked Diane to help their daughters or sons find lunch money. In exchange for this accessibility, Diane received phonecards from these parents, sometimes amounting to several cards per week around exam time. Because it could be argued that this was improving her teaching and the phonecards seem justified, the cell phone helped her retain a job for two years straight. With respect to her other problem of timekeeping, the cell phone allowed Diane to phone either the principal or other colleagues to inform them that she would be late, which was common, given that she had to change multiple buses en route. In essence, Diane was not unusual, in that teachers along with police officers, firefighters and other civil servants increasingly give out their private phone numbers and regard this as a routine aspect of their job. Teachers who actually receive phonecards are rare, but it could be seen as reasonable given that their salary was only $JA20,000 to $JA30,000 a month and, as with other civil servants, they were never given phonecards or phone allowances from the Jamaica Teacher's Association (JTA) or the Ministry of Education.

These relationships could, however, go still further. Teachers of older students often gave out phone numbers to students they liked or felt some sort of mentorship with and these student–teacher relationships continued after the student completed school. Teachers often gave advice and encouragement concerning what to do with a student's education and religious guidance as well as relationship advice concerning parents and others. This was seen as a natural extension of the kind of counselling vocation that was a common genre of Jamaican phone usage (see Chapter 7). In addition, some teachers extend their commitment by becoming a kind of community servant, giving students lunch money or even helping with their continued education if the relationship became particularly close. This, as well as counselling, may be seen as closely related to their deep religious commitments but can also revolve around other, ulterior, motives.

Cell phones could also mediate as part of the more official relations between school and home. Like the primary school principal, the school guidance counsellor at OVCHS now routinely obtains parents' numbers to contact them if the student becomes a 'problem'. He was also trying to develop weekly meetings with these parents, which were organized through the phone. At first only a few of these parents attended these sessions, which included lectures and training on moral guidance and proper learning environments, but attendance began to increase over time. As such, the phone was playing its role with respect to what is probably still the dominant concept within the Jamaican school system – that of 'discipline'.

There were various claims made about the larger benefits of the phone for education. Even though Internet access through the phone was clunky and slow, it was being used for schoolwork, as by a Marshfield pupil, who reported:

> For instance you get a project right, you know you have to do a whole lot of research. When you have Internet access to your phone you know it's very easier. There's only

one fault with it. It's very hard to get Internet access to come, it takes a good while for it to come, so I wouldn't tell you to depend on the phone, if you can get it elsewhere you could try and get it. If you doing history or if you doing research, if you get a project to do research on say the heroes them and stuff like that you can go and search.

More generally, pupils used the phone to catch up on information about assignments they had missed while absent or to find out what was happening to students who hadn't turned up for school.

But, apart from this secondary effect of ameliorating the consequences of absenteeism, there was little evidence that the phone is used in any direct or positive way to enhance the educational experience or to gain knowledge (although see Ito 2002, 2004). In general, there is much more evidence that social relationships, such as boyfriend/girlfriend relationships, and general playing around with the phone have a major distracting impact, with negative consequences for concentration and school performance. They might be doing research on the Internet through the phone, but much more common than homework projects were other sorts of 'research', as one student in Marshfield admitted: 'Well you have some techniques in sex, OK, that people say a guy should know, and several of these techniques are on this site, so when a guy waan know something them just go to the site and download the pictures.' Even the homework research can be pretty inefficient, as one mother commented:

> Because sometimes some people now because they have the cell phone it gets to them, they are always on the phone. If them a do them homework them, deh pon the phone same way, and it nuh really relevant, so them a waste. The time when dem a waste pon the cell phone them should a in a them book.

Notwithstanding the fact that students acknowledged that they use the cell phone less during exam time, it is entirely possible that the cell phone has contributed to the decline in performance over the last few years. As a schoolgirl admitted, 'If you should go by the school and ask, when since the education in the school has been going down, and they will tell you from x time and you realize say is from the same x time that the cell phone come in.' This is not just apocryphal. There were several reports published during 2004 that suggested the overall performance of schools in Jamaica is currently in decline (e.g. Figueroa 1998; Bailey 2000; Anderson 2004; Jamaica Gleaner 2004; Miller and Horst 2005).

In conclusion, the key to understanding the cell phone's presence at school is its ambiguity, which allows a set of legitimations and justifications to make acceptable what otherwise would be a largely illegitimate practice. The dominant use of the phone by students and in the context of school suggests that it is best described as a kind of glorified toy that children can play with. Rather than enhancing the traditional possibilities of education and learning, it primarily distracts pupils from their educational work and experience. As such, it is likely that the draconian regime of fines and confiscation would have been rigorously applied until the phones disappeared. But the phone does not look like a toy. It masquerades as a functional instrument, which, in the hands of many parents and teachers, is precisely what it is used for – something that enhances communication and helps people to efficiently keep in touch and may, in some instances, become more important to paving the way for other opportunities. It is thus hard for adults to dismiss it as superfluous. Most importantly, there is the claim that the phone is essential for emergencies and therefore must be there to accompany the child. In practice, these 'emergencies', such as forgetting one's homework, rarely live up to their billing and in a genuine emergency the parents have always contacted the school. About the only usage that probably justified parental concern is the way the phone is used to keep in touch with pupils after the end of the school day when they are travelling on the road, and where the potential for contact enhanced the parents' feeling of security. But this instance does demonstrate something profound about the quality of the cell phone, which is that, in some instances, the attribute that really matters is the discrepancy between actual usage and claimed need. The result is that it is very hard to maintain any kind of clear or legitimate policy for possession and use of the cell phone.

The Church, Fate and Blessing

There are many other genres and areas of use that could be discussed here, but the central theme of this chapter is a desire to move from assessment based on the categories of welfare that derive from external agencies to something closer to Jamaican's own evaluations of the cell phone's impact on Jamaican life and welfare. With schooling one can start to see the tensions between observations of usage and the various legitimations given for usage. In this final section we have deliberately juxtaposed what might otherwise be seen as two highly disparate areas of use, religion and gambling, because of the way they reflect upon these same tensions. In practice, the church is not an isolated part of life concerned only with spirituality but often the key link between various profane worlds enmeshed in poverty and communication. This is especially true of Pentecostalism (Austin-Broos 1997), the dominant form of Jamaican Christianity today. Even those who do not belong to formal Pentecostal churches such as the Church of God have found that their Seventh Day Adventist or Baptist churches have taken on many characteristic attitudes of the Pentecostal church.

One effect of this dominance is found in the prevailing attitude to money and economic well-being. In some of the older churches influenced by Baptist and Anglican rites (Besson 2002), the use of scriptural material was more a form of reassurance with regard to poverty, that lack of money did not signify lack of moral values. Indeed, there are many scriptural references, such as the Sermon on the Mount, that appear to endow poverty with moral superiority. Much of the teaching is directed towards compassion and concern for the state of poverty. It is relatively rare in such churches to be confronted with preaching in which the prevalent message is that Christian activity is in and of itself a way to gain wealth.

In contrast, in the many evangelical messages that permeate contemporary Jamaican life through television, radio and billboards, the constant message is that devotion to the church and giving directly to the church has the potential to pay 'interest' inasmuch as, amongst the various blessings that may accrue to those who seek them, there is certainly the possibility of wealth. There are countless stories not just of people finding Jesus but also finding good fortune. Where once the quintessential example of good fortune might have been the blind who are now able to see, today it seems to be the poor suddenly finding they have means. The image of gaining interest is quite an explicit one, since so much of the service is punctuated by direct appeals for money to be given to the church followed by promises that such devotion will not go 'unrewarded' by God, as witnessed by many examples of people in poverty who didn't know how they were going to cope suddenly obtaining some miraculous good fortune. This is not an occasional aspect of devotional practice; it is fundamental.

Consequently, many religious Pentecostals believe in these benefits with fervency. Winsome is completely certain that her money is coming; she doesn't know when and in what form, but there are no doubts entertained at all. Indeed, in her case, this led to a complex quandary over whether she is allowed to accept money directly from the church. Winsome possesses few resources and has a desperate struggle to make ends meet. She should be one of those who could go directly to institutions such as the church for poverty relief, but she is not sure. She really does not want to go to ask money from the church, because that does not fit her sense of the miraculous and unexpected fortune that is her due. She resolves her dilemma through her belief that surely her pastor will know directly from God who should or who should not be helped by the church. She believes that, if he turns her down, that is simply an expression of God's plan that she should wait a little longer. Recently, she was desperate because she could not find money to pay her daughter's school fees. Without a certificate showing the fees have been paid, her daughter would not receive a book voucher for her coursework. But one day a letter came from the bank with a voucher. Since this was clearly a mistake, Winsome's daughter wondered whether she should return it. Her mother replied instantly, 'Shut your mouth, collect your books and give thanks to God!'

The issue for Jamaicans living in poverty is that money is not generally something that derives from consistent work, since this is very hard to find in itself. Money and good fortune are much more likely to be a result of a windfall or the munificence of others, either relatives living abroad or some local patron. As a result it is easy to see the receipt of money as the primary evidence of blessing. In theological terms this is in many ways a 'vulgar', in the sense of more immediate and calculated, example of the wider Protestant tradition of wealth as the evidence that one is indeed saved, famously analysed by Max Weber (1992). Stories circulate about how individuals who are down to their last $JA100 and worrying about how they were going to eat have received calls from their family abroad out of the blue, which involved money from Western Union. One woman described how one day her nephew called on his cell phone from New York and said, 'Write down this number.' As she noted upon later reflection, 'God must have been with me that day since I remembered I had my documents with me and I was able to walk straight into Western Union and there it was, my money.' Such events reinforce the strong belief that service to the church and devotion to prayer are the best source for ensuring that money will somehow come your way, probably through an unexpected source. One of the main ways in which people demonstrate their devotion is through regular donations, which may be equivalent to the biblical tithes but most often are simply a weekly donation as befits the means of the person, small amounts such as $JA20, $JA30 or $JA50 for regular attendees. If one then examines the subsequent financial relationship between individual and church, we find a system by which a small but regular amount is spent on the church by the individual, but that individual believes that occasional windfalls of large sums are coming to them as a direct result of that commitment of income to the church.

The obvious analogy when living in Orange Valley is the fervency of attachment to another source of potential windfall money: Lotto or Cashpot. For people living in the settlements around the hills, the phone has become instrumental to their regular participation. As one middle-aged woman put it:

> This is the backdoor deal man yuh understand, so is like me have him number when me ready – cause yuh know. Say we not going to Orange Valley as regular and Cashpot play three time a day now. So like we ready now, we just call him and give him our number. Beg somebody send down the money fi we. So sometime we just gather up all who want number and give him a one call.

Here the structure of financial relationships is very similar to that of the church. The individual commits a small but regular income to gambling of this kind. In return they expect an occasional but large windfall sum to come their way, which would not be possible without this regular commitment of money. In both the lottery and the church, the belief is that the money that comes to the individual is much greater than the money that is spent. A sceptical outsider might suggest that the truth is exactly the opposite.

The connection is furthered since in a place such as Orange Valley almost all expenditures on Lotto and Cashpot are based on the interpretation of dreams. These forms of gambling derive from the original Chinese numbers game, in which different symbols represent particular numbers and the best indication of whether these symbols will come up on a particular day is dreams (Chevannes 1993a, Wardle 1999, 2000). As a result, when one looked closely at budgets and expenditure, it was found that the lottery was a significant expenditure. But then so were phone calls. On enquiring further into the main content of the conversations that accounted for these high phone charges, one of the main topics of conversation was people's dreams and the discussion as to what numbers to bet on in the Lottery. The local lottery shop saw the cell phone as having a direct impact in that as individuals can more easily spread the word about a significant dream so the proportion of people betting on the same number on a particular day increases. As in the case of the church, there is seen to be a kind of spiritual or transcendent dimension to luck, which in turn is closely connected with the idea of blessing.

Organizing church functions and betting on the lottery are probably the two major genres of cell phone use by adults after basic social intercourse and gossip. Both are also in part explained by the sense of respectability that pertains in these Pentecostal areas (Austin-Broos 1997; Toulis 1997). Many of those talking on the phone are neighbours or near neighbours, but they talk by phone rather than going around to each other's houses because of the particular expressions of respectability associated with going 'on the road'. Within the house women can walk around happily in nightwear or even undergarments, but if they leave the house they are expected to be carefully dressed in a manner that represents a considerable amount of time and effort (see also Chapter 7). As a result the phone, where people can afford this, is much preferred as a means of communication even amongst those who live close by each other.

Given the increasingly strong connection between the cell phone, the church and the lottery, particularly in Orange Valley, it is not surprising that the cell phone itself is commonly looked upon as a form of blessing. For people so far removed from the levers of power, whether of government or companies, there is no obvious way to explain why things do or do not come their way. It would have seemed rational to them that, since C&W make money from phone calls in the past, they would have supplied landlines to those that needed them. But on the whole this did not happen or took extraordinary efforts to secure. In contrast, the sudden arrival of Digicel and the apparent ease with which everyone could now be supplied with a cell phone that could have a clear reception, even in such a remote area, were themselves seen as a blessing, in which the company was the intermediary to a higher source.

This explains some of the remarks that were reported in Chapter 2. The eschatology of the Pentecostal church lends itself to a theology that sees events in terms of the work of Jesus or the work of Satan and, to a degree, it seems the rival companies have been located within this structure of belief. Many people in both field-sites talked about Digicel in remarkably benign terms, as the source of blessings.

It was not just the advent of the phone itself, but the various high-profile gestures of support that Digicel made through some brilliant marketing that suggested that almost every good thing or interesting sporting or cultural event originated with this completely benign company. In contrast, C&W was not just a company people disliked, but something that could cause visceral disgust that suggested almost satanic tendencies. It was common to place C&W within a general set of satanic and oppressive forces, which could include colonialism, slavery, Babylon and ultimately the Devil's purposes. We are not suggesting that there was any actual sense of temporal power ascribed to the company, nor did such sentiments necessarily impinge upon the evaluation of economic issues. For example, C&W's system proved more robust than Digicel after Hurricane Ivan and, combined with a two-for-one promotion at the end of 2004, it experienced something of a revival of fortune, although this may also be because it now seemed that fate was not always on the side of Digicel. It is not that religion is the only idiom through which people judge telephone companies, but rather there is certainly a tendency to appropriate familiar structures and discourses of good and evil when judging both the phone and the phone company.

For those who were deeply involved in the church, there could arise a much more detailed and careful argument about the theological pros and cons of the phone. For example, Damian, a young Pentecostal who hoped later to find a career in the church, went through several changes during the course of the year as to how he should assess the overall cost and benefit of the cell phone in spiritual terms. At first he expounded on the basic idea of a blessing:

> The word of God says 'be not confounded to this world, but be transformed by the renewing of your mind'. I think personally that many souls are going to be saved, and the phone is a medium in which we can help persons who don't know Jesus Christ, to help them find Jesus Christ by this partnership of prayer and encouragement and counselling. I think the phone is a blessing from God since this is the medium through which I can help many persons.

Damian recounted many stories within which the phone took on an active role in the overall trajectory that led to an individual becoming saved.

On the other hand, Damian sees a darker side to this technology, which included the way it could disturb a church service and the conflicts that arose through gossip and temptations that came to one through the phone. He also sees a more sinister implication in the spread of communication, which leads to the conveying of information about an individual. This could form part of the 'Prophecy of the Mark of the Beast', where Satan uses his knowledge of individuals to prevent them from being saved. As he commented, 'I heard there is a chip called a Digi-angel that can pick up 2,000 informations on one person in about one second.' As the year progressed, Damian became clear that the phone is not in itself either simply an instrument of good or evil; it depends entirely upon the state and motivation of the user. The phone even starts to come into his preaching. He now preaches to his increasing flock:

> Before you run to the phone, run to the throne. When something happens to some people they will call their friends and say some bad thing happened at church. They call and create mischief. But they should first run to God and talk to him first before they talk to anyone else.

Damian does not worry that his phone will be stolen since he has 'covered it under the blood', that is, he has prayed to God to protect his phone under the blood of Jesus against the deeds of Satan, which is also why he does not feel the need to back up the numbers in the phone. In any case, he notes he could easily get back most of these numbers because he is involved with most of these people directly, not just by phone. Covering the phone under the blood is not the only way a phone can be Christianized. Phones can be secured on a string that says 'I ♥ Jesus' or marked by a Christian screen saver such as a cross or a Bible verse. They can also be Christianized through ringtones. At first, Damian was tolerant of secular ringtones, but as time went on he increasingly saw these as an abomination, not surprisingly, given the racy titles and lyrics of popular Jamaican dancehall tunes that are commonly used for local ringtones. Fortunately there are Christian alternatives. He has several on his phone, which also has the facility to record music directly and turn this into a ringtone. These include 'No matter what they say, I made up my mind I am a fool for Christ', 'My God is an awesome God, he reigns for evermore' and (without irony) 'Oh God you are the only one, that's why I am holding on so long'.

The phone also has a more mundane relationship to church business. Members of the church choir used the cell phone to coordinate rides to and from church and called each other to make sure that they knew what to bring for special events. A number of the women from whom we collected phone address books had contact numbers for friends and church sisters they talked to when they were worried. Charmaine, for example, had four numbers in her short phone list that consisted of persons she called and who 'encouraged her' to pray about her situation and get involved in the church. Grace had over twenty numbers in her phone book from people she talked to about her struggles; she also reciprocated occasionally by sending out 'positivity text messages', including scriptures. Michelle used her phone during a spiritual crisis, calling everyone she knew of varying religious beliefs to solicit advice about whether she should take the leap and become a member of the Church of God, which she had been attending regularly for the past few years. Born and raised a Methodist, Michelle felt this was a very large commitment and one which her family, who were also Methodists, might have approved or disapproved. She herself had some reservations about the dangers of speaking in tongues and receiving the spirit, but she enjoyed the support from the church and felt that the services really ministered to her. Yet she did not feel right about letting herself go, after spending her life in the relatively conservative Methodist environment. In the end, she did not convert, but still felt more comfortable with her decision after all the counselling she had received by telephone.

Conclusion

In the three main case studies discussed in this chapter, schooling, health and the church, what emerges conforms to a common observation about the beliefs that are most consistent with the experience of poverty. For those in the middle class, there tends to be a strong idea and ideal that people make their own destiny by hard work and entrepreneurship, even when in practice they obtain fortune largely through inheritance and patronage. For those living in poverty, where a commitment to hard work has often been of little help, given either the impossibility of finding work or the sparse remuneration that comes either from labour or from extensive studying at school and obtaining further qualifications, this relationship looks rather unconvincing. Instead there is much more evidence that wealth is largely a matter of luck, windfall or blessing. It is more likely that a family member was fortunate enough to obtain a visa to go abroad that accounted for their success. Someone has won the Lotto or one developed a relationship with a wealthy individual. These are what seem to make the difference between poverty and sufficiency, if not wealth, in the same way that misfortune, such as illness, comes not from bad behaviour but emerges from a twisted warp of fate.

In these circumstances the phone itself is seen as an unexpected but welcome piece of good fortune, there being no obvious reason why at one stage one couldn't obtain one for love or money and now companies seem to virtually give them away. When it comes to the dominant genres of phone use, the evidence here is consistent with our discussion of link-up, where we argue that the idea is to continue to create possibilities through personal networking. The phone is not used to gain employment or carry out entrepreneurial work so much as it is used to spread the social network or to consult about how to engage with the church or the lottery to obtain the benefits of prayer and gambling. In the model of link-up, a large number of small conversations cast out the net of social communication widely enough for one to hope finally to catch a big fish. This is similar to the expectations of a windfall economy, where consistent investment in fate, whether through Cashpot or the church, will finally bring big dividends, or at least create social networks and communication for their own sake.

At this point we can return to the concept of communicative ecology with which the chapter began. The initial point made with regard to the medical benefits of the phone was that, if we focused our attention too narrowly on the kinds of benefit that most development agencies were looking for, such as the spread of medical information, the effects were, as yet, very limited. But, if we change the lens to a wide angle and consider the background landscape, then there are many ways in which the phone has become integral to the way people deal with medical emergencies. The relationship between different forms of communication, whether this be the dovetailing of the phone to the local taxi system, which can take a sick child to hospital in an emergency, or as a communicative link to the transnational family as the source of remittances that can pay for that child to go to hospital, suddenly becomes enormously significant. What might have been regarded as externalities, to use the economist's language, now seem to radically transform our assessment of the benefits of the phone.

This was also true of schooling, but it worked in a different fashion. If we focused narrowly on the phone as an instrument of learning, it added little but probably doesn't do much harm either. But, if we focus on the overall impact of the phone on the wider environment of learning, including the way school operates on a day-to-day basis and the various relationships between pupils and teachers, then we start to see a different possible assessment, in which the phone could be said to have a significant negative effect on education as a whole.

When using the term communicative ecology, it is other forms of communication such as the taxi service or media generally that come to mind. But, if we think of this from the perspective of many Jamaicans rather than from the viewpoint of the programmes of aid agencies, then actually the most important communication of all is often held to be that which takes place between the individual and God. Indeed, in many Pentecostal churches this is a very immediate and intense relationship so, in an important respect, what we achieve by opening up the idea of the phone as communication in the last part of the chapter is directly analogous with the way we have opened it up in the consideration of health and medicine in the first part of the chapter. In both cases we are trying to apprehend the wider sphere that would need to be considered if we want to make a proper evaluation of the cell phone. Welfare, as it emerges from ethnography, tends to require an evaluation that goes well beyond the more immediate narrow criteria that are often applied. While in these last two chapters we have tried to expand from a given concept of welfare to see the implications of examining local terms and the wider context of welfare, in the final chapter we need to return this material back to a more conventional use of this term because we now need to transcend the particular case of Jamaica and allow the case study to become a resource that is used by bodies concerned with comparative, if not global, impacts of the cell phone.

–9–

Evaluation

If yuh nuh have cell phone now him a nuh part a Jamaica. If a man lose him phone now is a headache, 'Lawd, lawd me phone.' No man, the people hold them phone like how them value them house key. If you lose that phone it come in like you lose a vital part of you. Cause the phone is essential, it come in like people heartbeat right now. If yuh nuh have a cellular, yuh nah move.

36-year-old man in Marshfield

On the front cover of a recent edition of the journal *The Economist* stands a young African boy holding to his ear a fake cell phone made of mud under the title of 'The real digital divide'. The accompanying article, one of several in that issue examining the role of technology in mitigating the 'digital divide', concludes that 'Rather than trying to close the digital divide through top-down IT infrastructure projects, governments in the developing world should open their telecoms markets. Then firms and customers, on their own and even in the poorest countries, will close the divide themselves' (*The Economist* 12–18 March 2005, p. 9). In effect, *The Economist* is making two main points. The first favours the cell phone over the Internet as a vehicle for the elimination of poverty. The argument, repeated over several articles, is that the Internet requires too many skills and too much knowledge to be the force that can actually bring people out of poverty in the first place. Based on inspection of development-based facilities provided in South India, the publication claims that 'rural ICTs appear particularly useful to the literate, to the wealthier and to the younger – those, in other words, who are at the top of the socio-economic hierarchy. In the 12 villages surrounding Pondicherry, students are amongst the most frequent users of the Knowledge Centres' (*The Economist* 12 March 2005, Technology Quarterly, p. 22). The second claim is that the cell phone, supplied through the market, is what actually provides people with greater income and that plenty of evidence suggests that the mobile phone is the technology with the greatest impact on development (*The Economist* 12 March 2005: p. 9). The topic is also discussed in its weekly page, called 'Economics Focus', where economists assert that 'in a typical developing country, an increase of ten mobile phones per 100 people boosts GDP growth by 0.6 percentage points' (p. 94).

The Economist is about the closest thing social scientists are likely to read these days that stands as some kind of 'spokes-vehicle' for the market, the general stance being that the market is generally a more effective means for the alleviation of poverty and the improvement of welfare than is government, while not denying that government has its place. *The Economist* justifies its stance on the basis of the freedom of choice it provides for people, who are the best arbiters of their own fate, and the journal is as consistent in its advocacy of a certain liberal politics as it is in its faith in the power of markets. But *The Economist* is also renowned for its intelligence and discrimination and not just for its ideological position. It is entirely capable of castigating any form of capitalist enterprise or theory it takes issue with and it also has a strong sense of what might be called 'bottom line' priorities. Indeed, the emphasis on the digital divide illustrates its argument that the furtherance of capitalism can be based on a concern for the welfare of the poorest populations and is not just an ideological preference for the market as an end in itself.

There is one more significant factor at play here: *The Economist* is also a reflection of the power and influence of economists, the discipline of economics and its practitioners and the way they tend to view the world. Indeed, and as argued elsewhere (Miller 2003), the sheer power of contemporary economics is such that often the discipline is best described as performative (Miller 1998; MacKenzie and Millo 2003) or even virtualist, that is, having the capacity to remould the world in its image. At the level of global institutions, such as the World Bank, and through the global system of credit and debt, economics can punish institutions and countries for the degree to which they fail to conform to the model of behaviour that is required for economic modelling to become more relevant to the world. For this reason, *The Economist* is not just discussing the impact of ICTs on poverty; it also reflects the power of professional economists to define poverty, most commonly in terms of a bottom line, such as insufficient GDP.

This is obviously of central importance to a project such as ours, which was funded by the British Department for International Development. DFID views its role largely in terms of the responsibility of wealthier countries to help reduce poverty, which, at least in semantic terms, coincides with another movement that was prominent over the last year, the movement to 'Make Poverty History', which has often been in the news fronted by figures such as Nelson Mandela and Bob Geldorf. The specific task of our project was to help assess the degree to which ICTs should be a priority in funding by organizations like DFID. In short, the question posed was the relative effectiveness of ICTs in this task. A larger (and later) assessment of our project is intended to compare the four countries in which ethnographies were conducted, that is, India, Ghana and South Africa as well as Jamaica, and will be based not only on the cell phone but also the Internet and wider communicative ecologies.

In this volume, we have the thankfully narrower task of trying to evaluate only the cell phone in Jamaica, but this still pitches our task as outside that of purely academic anthropology since the very term evaluation is something that implies and acknowledges the power relationship that exists between bodies such as economists or government departments, on the one hand, and anthropologists and other social scientists, on the other. The purpose of this chapter is to try and build some kind of bridge or translation that will enable the material presented in the previous eight chapters to have a presence within the discussions of organizations such as DFID, which in turn must examine and relate to the overarching power of economics, its language and its practitioners. We shall attempt this in stages, the first of which involves an evaluation in terms of the more traditional concerns of economists with the market and with income. Then we turn to a more familiar anthropological viewpoint, which briefly summarizes and emphasizes the evaluation of the cell phone by the people we worked with. The third task concerns possible ways to create a bridge between these two, starting with a consideration of the writings of Amartya Sen. We conclude with a second and final evaluation of our material in the light of Sen's contribution and its limitations.

Bottom-line Economic Evaluation

We are not so foolish as to try and characterize all the many branches and stands of a discipline as vast as economics. Rather, we shall start with what we would argue is at least colloquially seen as its primary concerns, those reflected in the issue of *The Economist* with which we began. These perspectives involve the role of the market and the capacity of the cell phone to alleviate poverty through its contribution to GDP and income generation. We take these to be the 'bottom line' of economic evaluation. Starting with the issue of the market, at first glance the material in this book might be thought to back up the stance taken by *The Economist* admirably. It could appear as the overwhelming conclusion of the book as a whole. If the Jamaican population could give credit for the blessing that is represented by the rapid spread of the cell phone, then their praise would first go to God since Jamaica is a highly religious country. But, as one participant phrased it, 'after God then Digicel'. Furthermore, the degree of affinity between capitalism, as a general concept, and Digicel, as a particular company, is probably only apparent if one is actually spending an extended period in Jamaica. Once there, it is clear that the two telecommunication companies dominate the Jamaican landscape like no other force. It is as though almost every billboard and available advertising space are given over to their rivalry. Such is the level of sponsorship that it sometimes seems as though every dancehall party, every sporting event, every philanthropic announcement or television quiz is somehow beholden to these two giants of the capitalist world and the largesse that results from the market-centred competition between them for the hearts, minds and, above all, the wallets of the Jamaican population.

Digicel is certainly emblematic of modern capitalism and Digicel deserves much of the credit for the proliferation of the cell phone in Jamaica since 2000. It achieved 1 million subscribers within five years on the basis of highly competitive pricing and highly aggressive marketing. But, as noted in Chapter 2, C&W is just as much a candidate for a characterization of 'capitalism' as is Digicel. Both are simply commercial firms trying to make a profit, but the two firms differ in almost every respect. C&W represented a completely different style of capitalism, one now seen as conservative and old-fashioned compared with the flat, more egalitarian structure of Digicel (although by 2004 C&W was also trying to update itself). Clearly, though, if most Jamaicans were to use C&W as it used to be, they would regard capitalism as a highly exploitative force that in many respects was the bottleneck that prevented the permeation of new technology into lower income levels and was much more concerned to secure its profit margins at the expense of the population it served. Whether true or not, the popular voice saw C&W as a form of capitalism that was about as beneficial to the population as the colonialism it had grown up with. So, taking a longer-term view, capitalism has often looked as close to the demonic view taken by its critics, an instrument that fosters inequality and poverty, as it has to the benign view taken by its adherents and represented by Digicel for the period of 2001 to 2004.

'But', one might imagine a journalist from *The Economist* replying, 'that is the point.' It is the market that is favoured by the journal not simply the existence of firms, and it was the WTO policy of liberalization and competition that allowed for the advent of Digicel and also led to the internal transformation of C&W in response to that competition. The evidence in Chapter 2 largely supports this argument, but it also draws attention to its limitations. There is, after all, a third company on the horizon, MiPhone, and their perspective is, not surprisingly, rather different. They acknowledge the extraordinary achievement of Digicel, but in part this success can be attributed to the intense dislike of C&W as the incumbent. They also claim, that once Digicel achieved its position of dominance, it started to change its policy. Instead of constantly looking for ways to cut prices, it established a cosy duopoly with C&W so that prices for most services became effectively stable and identical. In short, MiPhone is suggesting that a duopoly is likely to form and remain, because the structure has shifted so that profitability is going to be secured in the future by a duopoly, which may turn out to be as problematic as the earlier monopoly because at least a monopoly looks like something that government should attempt to overthrow while a duopoly looks more like a 'market'. MiPhone also suggests that, even if the market is completely open, a third force (such as itself) may not be able to overturn the duopoly because there are so many difficulties in establishing sufficient presence as to become attractive to consumers and, unlike Digicel, it does not have the advantage of a disliked incumbent. As things stand, MiPhone can cut prices all it likes (and at just over $JA14 per minute for an international call they are the cheapest). Yet few people have MiPhone and the prices for inter-network calls are so much higher than intra-network calls that it doesn't make much sense to use MiPhone, even if the calls within their network were completely free. Again, this reflects the perspective of MiPhone's current position and probably not what one would hear from the other newcomer, Cingular.

It is clear that we face a plethora of perspectives on both capitalism and the market. First, we are faced with capitalisms, not capitalism (Miller 1997). There are many different styles and forms of the way companies operate and the fight between Digicel and C&W became, in some measure, a fight between opposing models of capitalist organization. Secondly, the market simply left to itself would have little reason to do other than revert to a pattern of exploitation whenever and wherever that boosted profitability. The factor that must always be taken into account and not relegated to some kind of externality is that of regulation. The other key player in Chapter 2 was the Office of Utilities Regulation (OUR). It was the OUR which issued the licences that broke up the initial monopoly and it is the OUR that is currently trying to push forward a new cable, which will liberate Jamaican Internet access from the stranglehold of C&W. But their success depends on a careful balance of liberalism and protectionism. For example, C&W have bitterly complained that the one place where the OUR provided a perfectly free market was in the payment for termination of calls, which has resulted in the loss of what C&W regard as a proper reward for investment and for Jamaica as a whole, a huge stream of income. To simply support an ideal of the free market makes it impossible for a company to commit to long-term expensive investments that are essential to the welfare of both the firms and the consumers.

Miller's (1997) study of Trinidad suggested that a purely free market is decidedly detrimental to the forces of local capitalism. In the context of Trinidad, Miller argued that a pure capitalism based on economists' notions of the free market was as likely to be in opposition to as on the side of what he called 'organic', that is, home-grown, local capitalism, which took the form of highly successful local enterprises. In Jamaica, a pure market may not prevent a duopoly of companies entrenching their positions through structural imbalances that make the cost of entry of new competition simply prohibitive. Capitalism is just too complex. Simply providing for an unregulated market does not in and of itself ensure competition; this is more commonly the product of state regulation, rather than deregulation. Similarly, a more open market may prove beneficial to the population only to the degree that regulation prevents its reduction to an instrument for short-term profit-taking. At the end of this chapter, we shall make a similar critical appraisal of other candidates that have been offered as the 'solution' for Jamaica, which includes an equally critical examination of the state as the source of regulation, the people, as the source of choice, and technology itself. In the meantime, it should be clear that left to itself the market would not solve the digital divide but would probably exacerbate it. Nonetheless, a sufficiently regulated market seems to be an essential part of any solution.

There is, however, a second aspect to this bottom-line assessment, represented here by *The Economist,* which is the contention that, to best understand the potential of the cell phone as a contribution to the elimination of poverty, we need to consider first its contribution to increasing GDP, in particular, and income generation, more generally. When we started our project, we felt committed to looking for evidence that new communication technologies were becoming a source of income generation. That this is possible is clear from the results of the other three studies, in South Africa, Ghana and India, (Skuse and Cousins, personal communication; Slater and Kwami, personal communication; Tacchi and Chandola, personal communication). But, as discussed at length in Chapter 6, within our own study, the results could only be seen as severely disappointing.

Certainly we could find examples of the phone being used to help facilitate entrepreneurship. People are able to find out about prices, supplies and competition in far more efficient ways. Work that requires mobility is no longer tied to an office in order to remain in touch. But, considering these possibilities, few low-income Jamaicans had made the significant switch into seeing their phones as effective mobile offices that allowed them to suddenly turn themselves into fully fledged entrepreneurs. In this respect, Jamaica is significantly different from Ghana, South Africa or even Trinidad (www.isrg.info; Miller and Slater 2000). There is no major new spirit of enterprise based on either the cell phone or the Internet. Indeed, this lack is made more evident by the exceptions to this generalization. One was the music business. Almost half the men we knew under the age of forty did see some new potential in playing music, hiring bands, making CDs and somehow making it 'big' in secular or religious music. There is no sign that this is actually happening, but it demonstrates that, where there is an imagination of a certain kind of commercial future, then phones are understood immediately to be a means to transform these into possibilities. Another exception would be the taxi driving business, which is so integrally linked to the phone as to form a vital part of this communicative ecology. In this case, the difference made by the phone is substantial. But these are exceptional cases.

We should also note that it is entirely possible, indeed, we suspect probable, that the situation was very different for middle-class Jamaicans. We came across several hints that such Jamaicans saw the cell phone's potential to generate new forms of entrepreneurship. However, this was not part of our remit and we have no clear evidence to support this statement. The other main sector in which we sought evidence for ICTs being used to assist income generation was the search for employment. Although there were cases of people being told about job adverts by phone, the general consensus was that this was a very minor use of the phone, simply because it was felt that the vast majority of jobs were accessed through social connections and patronage and not through simply matching opportunity to qualifications. We therefore concluded that the expected opportunities for income generation through the phone have largely failed to materialize.

What Chapter 6 did reveal was the significant impact of the cell phone in enabling people living in conditions of poverty, or indeed destitution, to get by. In terms of DFID's priority of poverty alleviation, the cell phone could be said to have proved a highly effective mechanism. In Jamaica the cell phone has penetrated the most impoverished sections of the population, who, as we have demonstrated, make considerable use of it. As many studies of poverty have shown, the problem is that people in such conditions are in an almost constant state of crisis posed by every new demand for funds, whether this is a school uniform for a child or filling a prescription given by a doctor. There is simply no surplus of funds available for additional or unanticipated expenditures. A great many of the short stories that punctuate this volume have demonstrated the effectiveness of the phone in resolving these crises. Individuals and households in crisis constantly use their cell phone to deal with immediate needs, often scrolling down their phone lists, not just to see who might 'have it' but who might 'have it' at that particular point of time. So the primary impact of the cell phone on poverty is through the changing temporality of low-level redistribution, which can now be achieved quickly and effectively, whether through a remittance via Western Union, a taxi driver, or the redistribution of microcredit through texting phonecard numbers and the use of 'call-me' texts. Our conclusion at this level is that the cell phone is highly effective for ameliorating the worst forms of suffering associated with poverty. It has become integral to a system where our careful analysis of micro-budgets shows that more than half of household income is accounted for by who you know and not what you do.

We have, then, two important conclusions of relevance to bottom-line economics. On the one hand, the cell phone is not central to making money, but it is vital to getting money. Although it is hard to provide firm evidence, there is at least a clear logic that can connect these two. In many respects the relative lack of entrepreneurship amongst low-income people throughout the Caribbean has been associated with what might be called economic individualism (Safa 1986; Robertson 2002; Wilk 2003). The degree to which money remains associated with the individual and not with the household means that even the small amount of capital represented by the household as aggregate is not available for investment. This lack of capital is a major factor in the lack of entrepreneurship and the cell phone appears to exacerbate this trend. The evidence from Chapter 6 and the repudiation of the landline as a collective household form of consumption, discussed in Chapter 4, clearly feed into this underlying economic individualism. The cell phone, then, seems to reinforce the tendency to distribute income within low-income areas from those who at any given time 'have it' to those who 'have not', often through the intervening mechanism of gender relations. This plays into a system we have also discussed, the widespread tendency to give money and assistance even where there is no kinship or other formal obligation to give. So it seems reasonable to conclude that this more effective redistribution downwards in the resolution of small-scale crises of poverty reduces still further the pool of capital available for any kind of investment that might be employed in actually making money.

With respect to the traditional expectations of welfare and development economics, as reflected by the agenda of DFID or the journalism of *The Economist*, we have an important conclusion. There is a general expectation that technology will assist in the alleviation of poverty by becoming a foundation for new forms of entrepreneurialism and income generation, which ultimately will be reflected in aggregate figures such as GDP. However, our evidence suggests that this conflates what can become radically opposed trends. The very fact that the cell phone is used for the immediate amelioration of suffering is closely linked to the degree to which it is not part of any such development of entrepreneurialism. The money that might have been used for capital accumulation is instead filtered downwards to help alleviate regular crises of poverty. If the phone does help with income generation, and thus GDP, it is likely that it does so for those who already have the capital and education to work from a much higher baseline. Our conclusion for the cell phone in Jamaica would follow *The Economist*'s argument for the Internet: that it probably requires too high a level of prior capital of various kinds to make this kind of impact. Contrary to the assumption implicit in the argument made by *The Economist*, this turns out to be precisely because it is effective in poverty alleviation.

Anthropology and Jamaican Evaluations of the Cell Phone

Economists are by no means the only group concerned with evaluating the impact of the cell phone. There is also the emergent social science literature, especially in the last two years, which considers the wider impact of the cell phone on society. The debate introduced at the beginning of Chapter 5 is concerned with arguments by Manuel Castells, Barry Wellman and other sociologists about the rise of individually focused networking and the way this related to another general debate about the decline of 'social capital'. As noted, researchers who actually study the impact of the cell phone in detail have suggested that the evidence to date does not support these general arguments (Harper 2003, see also Ling 2004: 169–195). The importance of our anthropological contribution is not simply to weigh in on one or other side of such debates but rather to demonstrate how the basic terms and assumptions may make little sense when dealing with regions outside traditional sociological domains.

This is one of several ways in which it is hoped that a volume such as this one might radically expand upon an emergent literature, which could become much too parochial if, for example, it became over-dominated by concerns with the appropriation of the phone by teenagers in Scandinavia or Japan, important though that might be to commercial interests. For example, in the prevailing literature, the question of micro-budgeting and the integration of the cost of phone calls with other costs generally focuses upon this youth market because of their relatively limited disposable income. This turns out to be highly relevant to the Jamaican situation, not because of the high usage by young children, but because so many low-income adults are in an analogous situation of having very limited resources but an equally powerful dependence upon the phone. In this volume we have also documented the many and creative ways in which Jamaicans fund their phone use, which would seem to us just as creative as those of metropolitan youths. Similarly, compared with the main literature (Ling 2004), we have paid less attention to favoured topics such as micro-coordination or the phone as intrusive noise in public space, but perhaps more attention to other topics such as the importance of the phone in terms of feelings of personal security or the use of religious idioms in its assessment. Also, and in contrast to much of the commercially driven literature, we are also not primarily concerned with predicting future trends – although we shall venture a speculation that there will be an interesting match between the wealthiest and the poorest countries in terms of being in the vanguard of Internet access through the cell phone. Because low-income Jamaicans cannot afford computers, there is an enthusiasm for using cell phones in this way that is probably rather more immediate than that found in higher-income regions.

Most anthropologists would be entirely happy to see their work as a contribution to these various external evaluations, whether coming from economics or social science. Almost inevitably, however, anthropologists want also to at least start their own analysis from a quite different point of departure. To conduct 'an ethnography' implicates the researchers in a radical movement away from such external evaluations as found in economics, sociology or media studies, and towards a general participation in the lives of the people of a region and an attempt to empathize with those lives. This is based on a commitment to try and view the object of enquiry through attempting some kind of alignment with the perspective of those who participate in the research. In turn, the people one is living amongst are not simply the users of a technology; they are inevitably and vigorously involved in their own evaluation of that technology and that involvement tends to become the starting point of anthropological evaluation.

With regard to Jamaican evaluation, it is clear that the vast majority of Jamaicans regard the cell phone as of considerable benefit, a benefit not isolated to one or two aspects of their lives but of importance to Jamaicans across the board. Indeed, there were several writings about the notorious areas of downtown

Kingston which made clear that, even before the rise of the cell phone, people in these areas already saw the telephone as one of their priorities for the future (Levy 1996; Moser and Holland 1997). These overarching evaluations varied from the most local frustration with the previous technology to the most general statements of the phone as a symbol of modernization. An example of this sense of immediacy comes from the following statements:

> It very good and helpful, you see when mi never have a phone mi had to tek bus and go a call box. And sometimes you go di call box, sometime di call boxes full a people and you can't talk any thing private. Every body crook dem ear fi listen to what you saying.

> I had to leave house at whichever hour I wanted to, walk whatever distance to a pay phone. Wait in line and when you actually get on the phone you have people in yu ears, telling yu 'hurry up an' get off the phone mi waan use it'. Yu have people passing you and noise whatever so it was very uncomfortable for me. Having a cell phone now it was much better because I could be in my own private place whenever, wherever, however and be on the phone, on my cell phone … it's more private, it's more convenient.

Examples of these more general positive appraisals are reflected in the quotation with which this chapter began and the comment made by an elderly farmer living in the hinterlands of Orange Valley when we asked him if he thought the cell phone made a difference to life in Jamaica: 'It uplift de country. It uplift de country. It develop it … Develop mean uplift de country. In Jamaica when you have a cellular company come in dat mean de country not so poor. It build de country.'

Clearly, it is not difficult to find this kind of 'aggregate' appraisal, but ethnography also reveals a vast number of much more specific attributions, both positive and negative. Some of these appraisals link quite easily with the concerns of economists and development workers while others reflect quite parochial concerns. Furthermore, many of these, as it were, home-grown evaluations are ambiguous or contradictory. To start with the more straightforward evaluations, the recent World Bank assessment of the economic situation in Jamaica highlighted crime as one of the key bottlenecks in economic development and tried quite hard to give a quantitative assessment as to the level of negative impact that this had had on the Jamaican economy as a whole (World Bank 2004). In the previous chapter, we documented an overall feeling that the cell phone improves the personal sense of security and has been instrumental in a substantial reduction of crime in isolated rural areas, which previously had no means of even calling for help when attacked by criminals. Yet there was another side to this. When we asked general questions about 'the influence of the cell phone on Jamaican life', or more colloquially if they thought the cell phone was a 'good or a bad thing', a surprisingly common response was some version of 'Men use the cell phone to target the people they want to kill' (see Chapter 7). In a location such as Marshfield this cannot be dismissed as some kind of paranoia. Too many of the people we met either had at some time been shot, had had a close relative or neighbour who was shot or had recently witnessed the result of some shooting. We only met one individual who (plausibly) claimed that he himself was a professional assassin and did indeed use the phone in this way, but then there are limits to participant observation.

The point is that, with respect to almost every genre of discussion, one could devise a scale of consequences from positive to negative and there were usually some dramatic examples that helped fix each end of that scale. A further example from the last chapter was the case of usage in schools. On the positive side there was the need to keep contact between children and parents and positive usages such as finding out about homework that had been missed. Fixing this positive end of the scale could be achieved by the considerable impact the phone made on an isolated rural primary school keeping in touch with a population where most children couldn't afford to come to school on a regular basis. In contrast, there was considerable evidence from children, parents and teachers for the detrimental impact of the cell phone on education at the other end of the scale. There is no way we can quantify the impact of the cell phone on education, but our guess would be that it is conceivably a contributory factor to a decline in standards within the Jamaican educational system and that the potential to connect Jamaican schoolchildren with the same resources as schoolchildren in other countries has not yet been fully realized.

With areas such as crime, health and education, we remain in terrain happily occupied by external evaluators trying to gauge the costs and benefits of a new technology. But, if we remain true to the ethnography, then we find other genres of use that are much harder to assess in those terms. For example, probably the single most common negative assessment made of the cell phone by men comes from what we could term their 'euphemistic discourse' about plural sexual relationships, euphemistic in that men did not usually say the problem was that women were able to overhear their conversations, interrogate their address book and therefore find out about such relationships. Rather what they gave us, again and again, were more or less plausible examples of how women could make mistakes in thinking that they had just overheard an illegitimate conversation or discovered an illicit number on the phone.

Certainly this was a matter of evaluation. It was often highlighted as the principal reason why men (and sometimes women) would claim they wanted to give up their phone or suggest that their lives had been blighted by this single problematic consequence. Implicit in this discussion was an acknowledgement that the cell phone had proved largely beneficial in actually organizing multiple and simultaneous relationships. As evident in Chapter 5 and the details of individual names saved on the cell phone, this really is both a major usage and a consequence of the phone. Although there was a gender bias, this aspect of phone use proved to be important for a great number of women seeking such relationships, as well as for men. We do not claim any direct evidence of negative consequences that might be of interest to development agencies such as the impact on HIV/AIDS (Fox 2001). Rather, the point is that this is part of what is experienced as simply a given of Jamaican life, as much as schooling or crime. The emphasis was on whether the phone made these relationships easier to organize but also more open to revelation. What is rather more difficult is to see quite how we would link this evaluation to bottom-line economics or sociologists discussing social capital. It is not just that there is no particularly obvious link to economic development, but that it is pretty hard to see this as even part of an external appraisal of welfare within development. In short, what may seem most important to Jamaicans themselves may be dismissed as outside the frame of reference by external evaluation. This same point followed from the analysis of the Jamaican concept of 'pressure' in Chapter 7. It is hard to imagine an appropriate definition of well-being in Jamaica that did not give considerable attention to this experience of 'pressure', or to the term 'respect', but it is equally hard to see quite how to fix this within an external discourse about welfare or development.

A final example of this problem, and the most fundamental for this volume, regards the underlying importance of an anthropology of communication and our suggestion that link-up represents a Jamaican imperative in its own right. While we can consider how communication becomes an important resource within what we have termed coping strategies, we cannot ignore a symmetrical dimension within which people also exploit their own difficulties and make them grounds for expanding their communication networks. What is clear and unsurprising is that everyone regards the cell phone as facilitating extensive social networks. With the exception of ambivalence over these increased sexual liaisons, such social networking is itself regarded as positive. As such, the term link-up could refer not only to the way people create social networks but the way our analysis has to recognize the connectedness between the different genres we tend to reduce our observations to, that is to say, economic, social, communicative and others (see also Horst and Miller 2005). Link-up represents the anthropological sense of holism as the ordinary experience of individuals who have no reason to compartmentalize their own desires and interests into conventional academic categories.

All of this suggests that the ideal of evaluation and ethnography are not easily reconciled. On the one hand, we want to bring together the criteria of evaluation that would be used by the participants of this study with those used by external bodies such as development authorities. The task, given the wider aims of this chapter, seems to be to acknowledge and translate concepts such as 'pressure' and 'respect' into something more generalizable, such as welfare. The concept of communicative ecology provided one route to a solution, in that it showed how much depends upon what is included within the frame of evaluation (see Callon 1998). This point became clear in Chapter 6, where economic improvement emerged more from social networking than from directly using the phone to obtain jobs. If the focus was narrow, such as on the dissemination of medical information, then the impact was minimal, but, if it included paying for medicines and international communication, then the impact was substantial. This suggests that somehow evaluation has to be both more focused on local experiences and more inclusive of the wider contexts of those experiences than might otherwise have been considered in an evaluation exercise.

Amartya Sen

In the previous sections we have suggested that bottom-line economics does not offer much assistance in determining the parameters of welfare, such as how to deal with plural relationships or concepts such as 'pressure', which need translation into more conventional languages of welfare – that is, unless one wants to follow Becker (1996) and reduce all human activity to some kind of simplistic furtherance of individual interest (see Fine 1998). Fortunately, academics involved in development over many years have been concerned to bridge this gulf between economistic discussion and practical, applied and development work. Different proposed solutions have come and gone over the years. For example, the term 'social capital' seemed to forge links between social and economic perspectives, but has been roundly criticized (e.g. Baron et al. 2000; Fine and Green 2000). We could also have engaged in an extended discussion about issues of 'livelihoods' or 'welfare economics' and various forms of 'applied anthropology'. Out of this range of models, we find the work of Amartya Sen most intriguing, largely because this represents a body of ideas that have already been taken up by Caribbean social scientists concerned with issues of poverty and development, such as Aldrie Henry-Lee (2002).

Sen also seems particularly appropriate since he clearly rejects bottom-line economics (see, for example, Sen 1987, 1992, 1999a, b; also Ackerman et al. 1997). His work on poverty and famine examines much wider forces than simply the market, and he also rejects any definition of poverty that is reduced either to GDP or income generation alone. Furthermore, his primary concern has been to offer alternative ways of considering what we mean by the welfare of populations. As Robeyns (2003: 62) explains:

> This line of Sen's work, known as the capability approach, postulates that when making normative evaluations, the focus should be on what people are able to be and to do, and

not on what they can consume, or on their incomes. The latter are only the means of well-being, whereas evaluations and judgments should focus on those things that matter intrinsically, that is, on a person's capabilities.

Sen himself summarizes his approach as follows: 'Our chosen approach concentrates on our capability to achieve valuable functionings that make up our lives, and more generally, our freedom to promote objectives we have reason to value' (1992: xi).

For Sen and those who follow his approach, well-being consists of identifying these basic functionings and then examining what contributes to or inhibits those capabilities that are required to realize these functionings. But integral to both is an element of choice that gives people a say in prioritizing such capabilities. The literature that has subsequently emerged is vast, but primarily comprises a discussion of these terms. Indeed, in some respects, this constant return to semantics is precisely what is so depressing about it. One recent example of a concerted attempt to make something of Sen's approach is a double issue of *Feminist Economics* aimed at acknowledging and examining Sen's desire to open up issues of diversity, including gender. Sen is a contributor, as is one of his most important interlocutors, the philosopher Martha Nussbaum. It is noticeable that, although Sen seems to imply an engagement with development that reaches down from the heights of highly abstract economic modelling, most of the discussions move horizontally to the equally abstract discipline of philosophy and their common concern with semantics. There are astonishingly few direct references to or debates with social science. In *Feminist Economics*, Nussbaum (2003) observes that it is hard to operationalize Sen's model without specifying some basic capabilities. Robeyns (2003) observes that capabilities have to be relative to particular times and populations. But both contributions are largely attempts to build consensus around the terms. As a result, the main practical outcome to date has been at the level of highly aggregate statistical characterizations of populations, most noticeably the United Nations' welding of Sen's concept of capability with his notion of positive freedom in order to create new indices of development that include factors such as education and human rights (Wengland 1997).

Within the *Feminist Economics* volume there is one honourable exception to the general discussion of concepts, a paper on women's choices of contraception in Mexico which strives to ground the ideal of choice, not in some abstract argument with the philosopher Rawls, but as something that is only with great difficulty accredited to Mexican women (Beutelspacher et al. 2003). The authors argue that this is because apparent choices cannot be separated from pressures, for example, from husbands and relatives and, more subtly, from the normativity we gloss as culture. Contraception fostered by the state is shown by them to have been accepted by those who want it, but equally accepted by those who do not.

Certainly Sen's ideal of individual choice is difficult to reconcile with most contemporary social analysis. One does not need the legacy of Marx and Foucault (although both are of considerable help) to appreciate that choice itself is often an aspect of, rather than external to, ideology and power. Should Jamaicans be said to choose to become Pentecostal, when faced with constant insistence that failure to be saved will lead to eternal damnation? Nevertheless many do not. More problematically, should Jamaican children be said to choose to be educated when educationalists would be just as firm in claiming the necessity of education to the salvation of a population? Again, it seems that unfortunately many do not. Yet the term 'choice' is not terribly helpful in either case, so anthropologists prefer to situate 'choice' within the historical conditions of normativity, or to recognize what Bourdieu (1977) called *doxa* as well as habitus.

Rather than starting from the issue of choice, there is another attempt to critically appraise Sen that is more directly related to our contribution. As part of a larger assessment of Sen, Douglas and Ney (1998: 46–73) argue that one of the major gaps in work like Sen's is that the issue of communication itself has been largely ignored. In contrast, they assert that 'a social being has one prime need – to communicate' (46). What is implied in their critique is that the kind of individualist stance often associated with concepts such as choice is ill-fitting for an anthropological engagement, while communication reroutes the encounter through a more social trajectory. Communication, which for them includes not just language but the whole world of goods and symbols, is intrinsically a social activity and the foundation for larger social norms and expectations. Communication must therefore be understood as ends and not just means.

This certainly brings us closer to the heart of our own analysis. In our chapter on link-up, we contend that many of the apparently economic actions of Jamaicans, such as the constant and complex giving of money and help to others, is best understood not as reciprocity, or indeed as altruism, but as motivated in some measure by a drive for the expansion of social networking in itself (see also Horst and Miller 2005). This is why different social scientists have ended up with a focus upon extensive networking even when, as far as they were concerned, the topic of investigation was essentially kinship, as with R.T. Smith (1988), or coping strategies (Henry-Lee et al. 2001). In Jamaica the potential of the cell phone that is most fully realized lies in its ability to facilitate this social networking. This is not something best understood as individualistic choice, but rather a realization of social normativity that comes from a long gestation in Jamaican history and experience (Smith 1988).

But even if in general terms we can envisage how an anthropology of communication could contribute to Sen's project, to actually build this bridge requires much more specificity. We can start by considering how Sen moves downwards and anthropology moves upwards. Sen, for his part, starts with his critique of the economists' model of 'revealed preferences'. In short, a pure market logic is based on the idea that we have no way of really knowing much about demand except through the evidence of its expression in the consumer choices of the population. The preferences of an individual are deemed to be revealed by what they choose to buy, and there is no reason to investigate demand any further. Sen dismisses this simplistic equation of purchase with demand and insists that we directly investigate the complex world of demand with all its contradictions, pressures and choices. We can embrace this critique as the first step downwards by economists trying to reach towards the kinds of materials encountered in anthropology.

In response, an anthropology that seeks to engage with policy has to repudiate its own version of revealed preferences. One could imagine a simplistic version of populist and relativist anthropology that sees itself as there largely to give 'voice' to a population. To work for the welfare of a population, all we need is to go out there and listen to this authentic voice of the people and record what they declare to be their preferences. In this case, 'revealed preference' is not what they buy, but what they say. Olivier de Sardan (2005) provides a well-argued critique of this tradition of anthropological populism. Few anthropologists would be this simplistic, but within the discipline there are many discussions that hinge on the value of information garnered. For example, in opposition to the top-down tendency of development work, anthropologists fought hard for the recognition of indigenous knowledges. As long as policy is dominated by top-down expertise, there is a clear call to anthropology to force the agenda to turn its attention towards and listen to the very population it claims to want to help (see Gardner and Lewis 1996, Sillitoe and Bi 2002).

Remaining a discipline founded in listening and observing, reaching upwards towards policy requires anthropology to transcend its own version of revealed preferences. The strongest alternative, and one that helps transform ethnography into anthropology, has been the emphasis upon larger continuities that are regarded as locally grounding some general phenomenon. These may be constructed quite formally, as when Sahlins (1987) examined structural continuities in historical transformations in the Pacific, or more loosely, for Jamaica when Smith (1988) tries to account for contemporary forms of kinship through the history of slavery and colonialism. This latter account can be rendered still more specific, as in Besson's (2002) analysis examining history from both sides, that is, more formal archival history and history as the memory and traditions of villagers, in order again to account for the relationship between kinship and land.

One version of this stress on historical continuity that may be applied to the propensity to engage with a new technology is what Miller and Slater called expansive realization (2000: 174–178), a social value or normative aspiration that previously existed but is now realized to some greater extent, thanks to the technological capacity of the cell phone. This recognises that things change as a result of a new technology, but, instead of some technological determinism, one is starting from the viewpoint of the frustrations any given population already possessed as a result of aspirations that were previously unfulfilled. It seemed reasonable to suggest that this is the first usage that is likely to be exploited. For example, much of Horst's previous research in Jamaica has been an attempt to understand the trajectory of Jamaicans' lives from individual autonomy through to the establishment of the house and more communal and transcendent goals that lead finally to the enormous emphasis upon funerals in Jamaica (Horst 2004a). In her study of returned migrants, she has shown how the house itself is used as an attempt to reintegrate people with the land, but that this aspiration is only fully realized through the funeral itself (Horst 2004b). While much of this research occurred prior to the rapid spread of the cell phone, this perspective became extremely important in helping us to understand the different ways in which the cell phone has become integral to contemporary Jamaican life. As we have indicated, there are elements of cell phone use that are highly individualized and personalized and emphasize privacy as exemplified in the various discussions within Chapter 4 on possession. This affirms many of the general arguments about the way the cell phone differs from the landline in its potential for individual association (Ling 2004). But, before this descends into some version of technological determinism, we see that older, especially elderly, Jamaicans actually resist this kind of relationship. Their emphasis is often on the way the phone facilitates social mobilization around collective events, most especially the organization of funerals, and they insist that the phone should always be regarded as a functional instrument rather than as an expressive aspect of the individual person. So the term 'expansive realization' makes sense when we put together Horst's previous research with the evidence for how the phone is used both to expand and to realize projects that existed prior to people's knowledge and use of the cell phone. Although this may seem a long way from the language of Sen, we would argue that, where changes can be understood in terms of these trajectories of the normative, we may start to see an anthropological perspective that achieves Sen's aim of articulating a concept of welfare that meshes a population's specific ideals with those coming from unprecedented new developments. It is a version of Sen's ideal that seems to accord much more easily with the way that anthropologists understand social relations and could be applied to an anthropology of communication. However, this still begs certain questions.

Responsible Contradictions

Anthropology spans approaches that vary from trying to vicariously represent a popular voice to an analytical construction of historical trajectories. We have suggested that neither perspective alone seems sufficient to constitute the forms of evaluation that are more easily appropriated by those concerned with policy and development. Both approaches also tend to ignore the more nuanced and contradictory realities often faced in fieldwork. Populism tends to homogenize this voice of the people, while an emphasis upon historical continuities tends to a conservatism that regards successful appropriation as Jamaican only to the extent that it meshes with some prior practice. In contrast, if one is trying to engage with policy, then the major concern is often change, especially unprecedented developments. In health, education or entrepreneurship the main worry is often with what was not and is not present, so an anthropology focused only on historical continuity is not terribly helpful. Secondly, the main problems of policy arise from the lack of a homogeneous constituency, and for this reason policy cannot pretend it is responding to some simple and consensual popular voice. As a result, a populist anthropology of the people's 'voice' is not terribly helpful either. If that were the case, elections would look rather different from the way they usually do. The political struggle faced by people working in policy is usually to resolve contradictory demands either between different sections of the population or within a given population.

In our final section we want not just to acknowledge, but to foreground the ability of ethnography to contribute to an anthropology of communication by focusing upon these issues of change and conflict. Sen himself clearly recognizes that the desire to move forward on the ideal of choice can flounder on the jagged edges of contradiction. It is not only that a population's choices may themselves be contradictory, but observed usage may be considered detrimental to the welfare of users. Properly employed, the primary contribution of ethnography can be to turn the phrase 'it all depends' from a negative critique of policy into the positive foundation for policy. What seems appropriate at one point of time has to remain under scrutiny for its effects, which are often unintentional, fortuitous and best seen from the ethnography of consequences. We recognize that policymaking is almost inevitably an attempt to seek out a 'best fit' reconciliation that is concerned with ameliorating the negative consequences that are often intrinsically bound up with a well-intentioned proposal.

We can apply these principles, in turn, to each candidate that puts itself forward as the true instrument of welfare. For example, at the core of our argument is the evidence that Jamaicans make extensive use of the cell phone as part of what we called coping strategies, but as already noted this may be to the detriment of more collective forms of economic unit that could accumulate small amounts of capital and use this to establish micro-entrepreneurial endeavours (see Wilk 2003). From the point of view of the Jamaican government, it could be argued therefore that a policy that favours household instruments of communication, such as the landline or the computer, are in the long term of greater benefit to the population than the more individualistic cell phone. In discussions with officials at the Ministry of Commerce, one could sense this troubling contradiction because this would mean acting in opposition to an individualism that is often respected as an authentic Jamaican tradition. Given this trajectory, should government seek to respect an individualistic stance that was regarded as in some ways typically Jamaican? After all, this was the government of Jamaica representing the Jamaican people. Or, since its role was partly to help Jamaicans survive in a global market, should the government rather take a paternalistic stance with respect to their own population and favour what helped build collective interests?

This conflict came to the fore in government documents such as the proposal for a Universal Access Plan, which saw the market as best placed to deliver the cell phone and the government as best placed to promote the Internet as part of future strategy. The implication was that the market had catered to demands that were individualistic in origin and consequence, while the government had to take charge of the collectivist ambition that was essential if Jamaica was to compete within a global capitalist market. Contrary to many assumptions about economic progress, it had become evident that economic progress depended more on fostering collective action than on individual liberal entrepreneurship.

In our policy recommendations to the Jamaican government (Miller and Horst 2005), we take issue with the Universal Access Plan. On the one hand, we recognize that the market is the most effective means for reflecting micro-choice in the population and in making the technology cheaply available to that population. But that is only true when the market is subject to insistent and carefully updated regulation and monitoring that keeps open competition, favours long-term investment over short-term profit-taking, forces companies to enact policies driven by the welfare demands of populations and balances global markets with local interests. The market can only serve the welfare of the population if driven to do so by government, but the danger is that this makes the government seem like the alternative panacea that is the guarantor of people's welfare. This also ignores the fact that these benefits are often coming not through regulation, but through the regulated market. The state can benefit the population through a regulatory structure, through collaborative schemes with commerce, such as seen in the building of Portmore, and through all the arms of welfare, from education to policing, but it also needs to be carefully monitored and limited. After all, about half the social science literature on Jamaica is concerned with the catastrophic effects of state patronage on crime and violence (Stone 1980; Robotham 2001; Sives 2002). Jamaica is a country where any claim as to a destructive market can be matched by evidence for a destructive state. Both seem to be potentially positive when constrained and equally destructive when left to their own devices and interests.

The Universal Access Plan envisages channelling large sums of money into government-led initiatives, financed through a tax on the telecommunications companies. The plans range from establishing a large network of community computers to attempts to use virtual teaching to combat the depressing fall in educational standards. It is backed by a major loan from the Inter-American Development Bank, something not necessarily to be welcomed given the current state of Jamaica's debt. In our review of policy, we have suggested that much of this money might be wasted, being based on wishful thinking rather than research (Miller and Horst 2005). This happens because, just as capitalism left to its own devices is primarily concerned with profit, not welfare, so the state will also tend to develop its own interest-led agenda, based on top-down thinking, rather than becoming deeply involved in the intricacies of the welfare of low-income Jamaicans.

Policies based on community computers and communications were appropriate in South Africa, where the relationship between the state and the population was intensive, sustained and central to South African daily experience (see Skuse and Cousins 2005). But it made no sense at all in Jamaica. Such a policy tends to reflect the influence of NGOs, which take the successes of development from one part of the world and assume these can be reproduced in quite different arenas. These policies ignored the failed attempts to establish such community-based initiatives in the past and ignored what we found to be local-level scepticism (Miller and Horst 2005). Even in Orange Valley with its seemingly stable population, there was no evidence at all for anything approaching the 'community' assumed by such proposals, or indeed, any evidence that people desired such a thing, with the exception of the churches. Of course, the state may have a very positive potential role in developing widespread computer access, but this is unlikely to arise directly out of such top-down or important development agendas.

But just as the market and the state have to be seen as contradictory forces that, left to follow their own interests, can slide from being positive to negative in their impact, so too can an oft-proposed alternative, that of the 'voice' of the people. As it happens, the last time *The Economist* decided to dedicate an article to the situation in Jamaica, it was precisely to discuss the popular voice of the Jamaican people. Some of the best-loved and most authentic Jamaican troubadours, artists such as Beanie Man and Sizzler, were being refused access to play in the UK and elsewhere because their lyrics suggested that gays should be killed. This had come into international media prominence as it was realized that this popular voice was strongly and staunchly homophobic. Although there are many academic contributions that show this is far more complex and nuanced than the way it is portrayed in foreign media (e.g. Cooper 2004), nothing in our own research suggested that this was anything other than authentic. Indeed, it was one of the few issues that united the whole spectrum of popular opinion amongst low-income Jamaicans, from the stridently Pentecostal, for whom liberal attitudes to homosexuality were a complete anathema, to their internal enemies, the voices of dancehall. The problem with this romantic notion of the authentic popular voice is that it presupposes that the people with the least resources, least education and least access to the larger forces that bear on them are nevertheless, because they are the subject of academic study, best placed to be the determinant of their own and each other's interests. At one level, this is an honourable premise that is shared with the principles of democracy, but, at another level, it ignores what are bound to be clashes and contradictions between various forms of modernist, governmental, religious and diverse expressions of value.

There is a strong strand in Jamaican academic and other literature that valorizes this popular voice, in particular as it has been given expression by popular culture, not only the analysis of dancehall lyrics by Cooper (1996, 2004), but also the many books devoted to the study of political processes close to the experience of the urban ghettos (Stone 1980; Levy 1996,). Anthropology is often cast in this perhaps slightly strange role of the outsider that becomes the authentic voice of the insider. We started our study with the hope of retaining sensitivity to differentials in power and education, and committed to an ethnography steeped in the humility of learning from others. Although we were not Jamaicans, Jamaican officials had neither the time nor, in some cases, the desire to engage with low-income populations and we soon found ourselves in the uncomfortable position of being buttonholed by government officials as 'experts' on what most Jamaicans do, say and think. Certainly this book is largely a condensed description of what we observed people do with a new technology. But when ethnography is fetishized as a vicariously popular voice or revealed preference, it too becomes more hindrance than help to the population that participates in this research. We are quite clearly not the voice of the Jamaican people and, in claiming to represent some kind of popular voice, the potential for anthropological hypocrisy is endless.

This romantic ideal of a popular voice, either somehow located in the field or indeed in the ethnography, tends to ignore unwelcome elements, such as a homophobia, that do not suit our ideological stance in favour of the popular. It also tends towards an abnegation of professionalism, including the professionalism of anthropology. The effects on policy recommendation are often absurd, as can be seen when governments share the same stance. For example asking villagers about precisely how the OUR should deal with the issue of termination payments for international calls, because government and academics want to pretend that everything should be determined by 'the people' or by 'consumer choice', is obviously ridiculous. Yet this can happen, as Miller discovered in a study of local government in London (Miller 2003), where local councils were only allowed to express an opinion on some complex point in the Mayor's long-term urban strategy if they could get ordinary citizens to claim to have shown an interest in this issue through a highly contrived 'pinpoint' focus group. For entirely benign reasons, we had reached a point where no one was allowed to formulate policy unless it could be shown to represent the actual voice of 'consumers' as users of services. The results were farcical.

Finally, there are also the contradictions intrinsic to focusing upon an item of material culture, the cell phone. For decades modernism and science fetishized 'the new' as intrinsically liberating, creating a backlash green movement that came to see science as intrinsically destructive. One of the most revealing books about the spread of the cell phone has been Burgess's (2004) monograph which focuses not on the spread of the phone, but on the spread of the various scares, such as health scares, that accompanied the introduction of the cell phone. From our introduction, we have tried to distance ourselves from various versions of technological or social determinism. In contrast, our evaluation of the cell phone is almost always based on close observations of its contradictory effects. The cell phone can be used by criminals and to stop crime. It has a potential for education, but is currently detrimental to education. It can save money, but also becomes an unbearable cost. It can help short-term coping, but possibly at the expense of long-term wealth. And it can make sexual liaisons easier to arrange, but also harder to keep private. It is worth transcending these contradictions in order to confirm a larger evaluation that, overall, the cell phone's potential to become what Jamaicans call a blessing is much stronger than its negative effects. But this is also true of all the other institutions discussed here: the market, the state and the voice of the people.

In each case, we argue that there are negative effects when any one object or institution becomes fetishized as either a principle or a thing whose consequences are intrinsic and given and when it is allowed to follow the 'interests' that come with the ascription of agency. In other words, unconstrained and left to follow its own interests, almost everything turns into a disaster. Good policy is always based on a recognition of these contradictions. In turn, an ethnography is a snaphot of these contradictions that can help inform policy, but which needs to be continually updated and monitored since when turned into policy it too will lead to unforeseen consequences. As a result, our policy recommendations tend to represent a 'twist' in expected advice, but always accompanied with caveats. For example, we were sceptical about the impact upon childhood education, but see new technologies as of considerable benefit in adult education, which happens to be of particular importance in a country where many individuals seem to go through a sudden switch when young adults. Having paid little attention to education when schoolchildren, they then do develop a serious interest in a future career and taking responsibility for their children. This often includes a passionate commitment to their own education, but at a stage in their lives when free education is no longer available. So we would suggest the major potential of ICTs in Jamaica lies not in school education but in adult education. This may seem typical of anthropological devotion to localization by finding a solution that is quite specific because of quite specific aspects of Jamaican society. We follow this with a caveat, which suggests that localization is not always the best solution. For example, we would argue that the NGOs and development bodies want educational material to be increasingly localized to fit 'cultural' relevance. But we found that Jamaicans, with their cosmopolitan outlooks and transnational connections, tend to judge educational material by international standards. As a result, local materials produced with good intentions are viewed as patronizing and a lowering of standards. Far from showing respect for local traditions, as intended by their creators, they are likely to be viewed by many low-income Jamaicans as not taking Jamaicans seriously.

This is the way we feel ethnography should advise policy. We provide an example of localization in the sense of helping to tailor a policy to the specifics of the Jamaican situation, but we then recognize that, like everything else, localization itself can become seen as intrinsically good, so we follow with a caveat in the form of an example where localization is clearly inappropriate. It is hardly surprising if an ethnography ends with this contradiction of the local, because anthropology remains entranced by the specificity and diversity of the world and yet, in its commitment to comparison and here to policy, has also to connect with the generalized and the unprecedented.

Quite possibly, no other region has quite this form of coping strategy or communication networks quite like that of 'link-up' and there is no direct translation of the concept of 'pressure'. The particular impact of the phone on the Pentecostal church, the national lottery and crime will also be in some measure unique. Much of this volume is presented through small-scale stories because even the term 'Jamaican' often feels like an unwarranted generalization that needs to be broken up into the very particular experiences of individuals, who also need to be respected as individuals, rather that as tokens of 'Jamaica'. At the same time, we need to acknowledge generalizations that come across not just as new forms of normativity that can properly be termed Jamaican, but also the requirement of generalization given by policy, by academic theory and by other forces we regard as potentially benign in their impact. Finally, as we stated at the beginning of this volume, this is not a study of the appropriation of the cell phone by Jamaicans. It is a study of the changes that document and demonstrate what a cell phone can turn into in the hands of a Jamaican, and what a Jamaican can become when they have their hands on a cell phone. It is this dialectic that permeates the entire volume and became the only principle we could consistently adopt in a final chapter concerned with the process of evaluation.

Notes

Chapter 1 Introduction

1. Friday, 24 November 2004.

2. The use of the term 'youth' signals age but is also associated with unemployed men engaging in criminal activities. 'Scandal bags' are the ubiquitous black plastic bags used throughout Jamaica for shopping, garbage and food and are valued for their ability to conceal the objects contained inside.

3. The term cell phone will resonate with US readers rather than with much of the rest of the world, where the term mobile phone is more common. However, our choice of terms is intended to respect the conventions of Jamaica, where mobile phones are usually referred to as cell phones (and sometimes cellular).

4. Our comparative results will be published elsewhere, as will material on other technologies such as the Internet. For interim results see the publications of the *Information Society Research Group* at www.isrg.info.

5. Here we are speaking more directly about academic anthropology, rather than the sub-discipline of applied anthropology, which has developed complementary techniques for a variety of aims.

6. Our central premise of objectification remains closer to that of Miller (1987) than the manner of its employment by Silverstone.

7. According to Patterson (1967), due to fear of rebellions Jamaican slaves needed tickets to leave the plantations after 1696. Slaves called the tickets 'talkee-talkee' (84).

8. This occurred quite literally in our experience of living in rural and urban households. In our urban location, gospel radio and television played throughout many houses during the night and the radio was often left on throughout the day, even when members of the family left the house.

9. For a comparison of the significance of transport in Jamaica, see Douglass 1992 and Wardle 2000, who emphasize the importance of movement and mobility in understanding the social geography of Kingston.

10. This public verbal argument is called 'tracing' in Jamaica (see Sobo 1993: 104–105).

11. Cooper (1996) has called this practice (h)ideology.

12. In Besson's (2002) chapter on the Baptist church and revival practices,

Pastor Roberts notes that 'the drum can send message like a telegram. There are different ways of sounding the drum … they can sound the drum and the whole district understand that a bands is here. When is sound fe dem, deh know that it sound fe dem 'cause a de different sound dat it give. So de drum carry a message' (253).

13. While the traditional term 'informants' is used to refer to those individuals who work with and collaborate with anthropologists, we have specifically chosen not to use this term throughout this volume. Due to the negative connotations of informing in Jamaica (associated with 'snitches', 'traitors' and others who cooperate with the police and government agents), which could potentially harm those (anonymous individuals) who assisted us with this study, we prefer the term 'participants'.

Chapter 2 Infrastructure

1. Jamaica is party to the WTO General Agreement on Trade in Services (GATS) agreement of 1995, including the annex on the Agreement on Basic Telecommunication Services, and also subscribes to the Connectivity Agenda for the Latin American and Caribbean Region.

2. E.g. by DFID, the British development agency that funded our research.

3. The OUR website provides an often highly revealing picture of the sometime vitriolic debates within the industry

4. The rate of exchange was fluid during our fieldwork but a reasonable approximation was $JA100 to £1 and $JA60 to $US1.

5. Our analysis of the subsequent events draws heavily on the work of Inger Boyett, who carried out extensive interviews with all the major figures in Digicel.

Chapter 3 Locations

1. We are presenting here formal figures from various international sources. We feel these represent one perspective on the situation, but our ethnography suggests that many such figures are both simplistic and misleading. For example, the very notion of a clear division between employed and unemployed fails to correspond to our experience, where formal employment is quite limited. Indeed, our rural survey would suggest that the figure of 16 per cent is closer to the population that is formally employed, rather than as given in official statistics the figure for those formally unemployed. We feel it best to provide both perspectives.

2. Life expectancy is relatively high, at 74.8 (World Bank 2004: 8).

3. Mintz's often overlooked contribution to our understanding of gender and space still represents one of the most nuanced contributions to the discussion of reputation and respectability in Jamaica.

4. M.G. Smith viewed the white elite as the epitome of Western European values, functioning virtually outside Jamaican society. Douglass (1992) argues that the small number of privileged families known as white Jamaicans possess and operate with a Creole kinship structure rather than a separate European world view, but that this structure is experienced differently based on current economic status and gender (see Gordon 1987).

5. Some have viewed R.T. Smith's earlier exegesis of matrifocality as a process of survival.

6. While this is a study of low-income Jamaicans as they were apparent in our ethnography, we want to make clear that we have not explicitly confined ourselves to understanding a particular class of Jamaican society nor would we want to suggest that 'low-income Jamaicans' are any more authentic than other income strata. Due to our choice of fieldwork sites, as well as our very rough income guide used to characterize participating individuals or households (i.e. earning less than $JA5,000 weekly in our urban site and less than $JA3,000 weekly in our rural site), most of the people we interviewed defined themselves as 'poor' or 'not so poor but not rich'. Indeed, the nature of Jamaican society and particularly the transient nature of work and income (as well as occupational multiplicity) can in some ways negate the significance of class or even occupational status.

7. Generation was also an important feature of our study. For example, many of the elderly individuals we encountered still upheld the values of older class-based hierarchical societies from the period of British colonialism (Horst n.d.) and many Jamaican youth were influenced by global consumerism and American popular culture shown on cable television and heard through African-American music. Attitudes towards and uses of the cell phone reflected this distinction. In the past many of the older participants noted that in their youth they wanted to obtain a 'good job' in traditionally esteemed occupations such as teaching, nursing or other stable jobs and they perceived the cell phone as a potentially useful object for obtaining information about and access to such positions. Today, however, esteem is derived from access to money and, as we demonstrate in Chapter 6, the cell phone is a key resource for maintaining 'links' with those who have money. As Robertson (2002) observes, 'The amount of money people earned or received through networks was also a factor in judging who was rich, poor or worthless. Occupation itself was not an indicator of rank … Rank actually depended on how someone maintained control over their person in the pursuit of money and what they did with it' (130). The degree to which an individual was successful in extending these networks could, therefore, transform their economic status, income and esteem.

8. Government and local sources agreed that the official figure of 160,000 was outdated.

9. Marshfield and Orange Valley (and the names of the districts in the area) are

pseudonyms employed to protect the anonymity of the communities and individuals we worked with in Jamaica.

10. The police station is in a state of disrepair and a fire truck is a rare sight these days, the official truck either being repaired or relocated to the main fire station in May Pen.

11. Primary education through Grade 6 is free at public schools in Jamaica. While in Grade 6, students take the Caribbean Examination Council (CXE) examinations, the highest-scoring students are placed in 'colleges' and lower-scoring at 'high schools', such as OVCHS. Although students are allowed to mark their top three preferences for schools, students are often placed at schools involving a considerable distance from their homes and, in turn, expense, with little chance of appeal unless one has influence in the community.

12. We carried out a household survey of fifty homes in Orange Valley and fifty homes in Marshfield. Part of the survey focused on assessing the living conditions of households in each research site and included information about the size and constitution of the household, access to water and other sanitary resources, as well as basic household income and expenditure, which could be contextualized within the wider study of living conditions biannually conducted in the Jamaica Survey of Living Conditions. The second portion of the survey assessed the use of new communication technologies within the household, such as number of cell phones owned, access to and ownership of computers, as well as telephones, television and other media.

13. £UK45,000 (or approximately $JA4,725,000) passes daily through the offices in the two weeks leading up to Christmas (cambio owner, personal communication).

14. The reconstruction of the causeway as part of a major upgrading of the highway in St Catherine remained a constant source of controversy, beginning with the relocation of the illegal causeway fishing village along the main road. Upon termination of fieldwork, protests were being organized over the plan to make the causeway into a toll road, based upon the financial hardship it would bring to those Portmore residents travelling to and from Kingston daily for work and school.

15. We thank Deborah Duperly-Pinks for clarifying this distinction.

16. 2005 and 2006 continue to be plagued by high homicide rates.

Chapter 5 Link-up

1. The phone also reflects a rather obvious issue of the relationship between biological baby-mothers and fathers as against girlfriends and boyfriends, who may actually be rather closer but have not fathered or given birth to a child.

2. The volume forms a major bridge between the foundational work on Jamaican anthropology, best represented by Clarke (1966), and current work by

Besson (1995a, b, 2002), which focuses upon unrestricted cognatic descent and ego-centred bilateral kinship. Together with work of R.T. Smith, they demonstrate that kinship relations are extensive and multiple rather than tightly structured.

3. The studies were mainly carried out between 1967 and 1972.

4. Baby-father is a term used in Jamaica to describe the relationship between a woman and her biological child's father. The use of the term itself presumes neither the continuation nor the termination of the relationship between the couple.

5. This is something readily attested to even by quite young girls of fifteen or less who begin as schoolgirls. While schoolgirls may have relationships with schoolboys, they may prefer to associate with 'older men', whose 'pockets run deeper' than the schoolboys their own age, and the extent to which mothers and other family members look the other way (or even encourage their daughters to engage in such relationships) remains a constant source of concern to the wider Jamaican public.

Chapter 6 Coping

1. Our more policy-oriented conclusions will be published elsewhere (Miller and Horst 2005).

2. 'Partners' is the rotating microcredit scheme that many Jamaicans with regular income use for saving money (Kirton 1996; Besson 2002).

3. Our most extensive study concerned the taxi trade; this study we hope to publish in detail elsewhere since it is far too extensive to be included here. It is a prime example of the larger communicative ecology, as will become clear in the discussion of health in Chapter 8. From the point of view of the drivers, it provided vastly greater independence, because they were now able to use their personal cell phones rather than a business radio system in order to network and coordinate with customers.

4. There are certain areas where this sort of activity has taken on more significant meaning, such as in tourist areas. For example, in Negril an entrepreneurial fisherman was seen taking a cell phone with camera attachment on his boat and checking with the local hotels when he caught a large fish. He called to ask his 'link' in the hotel if the particular fish was what they wanted. If not, he would return the catch to the sea. He also summoned friends on discovering a large shoal of fish.

5. See Riak Akuei's (2005) article on the stress that Dinka refugees feel once they arrive in 'the West' and the burdens associated with economic support of their relatives in Sudan, Cairo and elsewhere.

6. In Horst's (2004b) study of returning residents in Mandeville, residents noted that they managed to send back small increments of money in letters during the 1950s.

7. There has been significant debate in Jamaica over the wider ramifications of remittances. Certainly, the Jamaican government has expressed a commitment to encouraging Jamaicans abroad to contribute and invest in the island. However, others have argued that this recreates dependency as well as placing an undue burden on relatives living abroad. During our research we asked if people felt they were receiving more remittances. In general, individuals felt that remittances had increased as a direct result of being able to contact relatives by cell phone. In many cases, they argued that the investment in the phone was itself effectively paid for by this increasing income.

8. Given the more dispersed nature of Portmore and the fact that Marshfield constitutes only one of the many communities there, figures from the Western Union and Money Gram office in that area could not be analysed in the manner we have employed for the relatively isolated Orange Valley.

Chapter 7 Pressure

1. In his analysis of more severe mental illnesses, Littlewood argues that Rastafarians in village Trinidad blame madness upon the social pressures of the modern world.

2. In nineteenth-century St John, Olwig (1985) characterizes three forms of exchange that occurred: partnership, clubs and 'lending a helping hand'. In a partnership, two or more men worked together or alternated working for each other and shared profits from their work. In clubs, friends or relations of particular households worked together to complete a task, such as tomb or house building, which culminated in shared meals and drinks. The third category, lending a helping hand, was more mundane and occurred at short notice when jobs needed completion, such as carrying something from the market or sewing a dress.

3. Men in Marshfield often used the language and idioms of Rastafarianism (such as 'the system') to describe the world and their role in it. However, very few men we encountered were practising Rastafarians and there was a general sense that this practice was on the decline (Chevannes 1994, 1995).

Chapter 8 Welfare

1. Indeed, one of the long-standing concerns of the Portmore community is that, despite its population growth to 200,000, the municipality does not have a hospital, and there have been movements over the past decade petitioning for the funds for such an establishment and/or the upgrading of many of the main clinics in the wider Portmore area.

Appendix

Technical Infrastructure

In order to fully understand the story of the companies introduced, a short excursion needs to be made to the more technological side of the cell phone. If there remains this general perception of C&W as the bottleneck that prevents further development, there is one place where this seems most literally to be the case: the ownership of the cables that provide most of the data access to and from Jamaica. These cables are literally submarine cables laid by special ships. The first leg of C&W's fibre ring, called TCS-1, was set up in 1992. A second major leg running into the Cayman Islands from Jamaica and then to the USA was constructed in 1994. The fibre-optic cables have two outlets, and C&W also operate a fibre ring around the island, which is enhanced by a digital microwave network. It recently invested further in its South Coast Fibre System, increasing capacity by 50 per cent to handle 33,000 voice calls simultaneously.

The OUR claimed that C&W was charging its competitors too much for rental of its fibre-optic gateway, thereby curtailing further development of the Internet by overcharging the ISPs. One source suggested that to gain network access was costing 'somewhere in the neighbourhood of $US8,500 and $US8,600 per month' and further added that 'you could buy the same facilities in North America from between $US450 and $US700 a month' (Phillip 2003). With regard to voice traffic, all calls originating in Europe, Africa and Asia are routed through Miami. Digicel uses a US third party for routeing to Jamaica but was planning its own hub in Miami. In 2004 the government negotiated for a massive new cable that would effectively end C&W control, though C&W claimed its cables were at full capacity by 2004. C&W consistently defends its record on the basis of the considerable past investment represent by the current 'backbone' to Jamaican communications (Whitehorne 2003), and the considerable taxation it has paid to the government over the years. Its competitors claim, however, that it has failed to unbundle and liberalize access thus hurting consumers and development. C&W is well aware that the USA spent $US1.3 trillion on telephony infrastructure and ended up with some of the largest bankruptcies in history.

The technical terms commonly used in relation to cell phones, such as GSM and GPRS, are explained in some detail on many sites available on the Internet. Briefly, the cell phone has experienced a number of transformations, which are typically discussed as 'generations', or G's. For most of its history, transmission was analogue, based on microphones and the conversion of voice into electrical signals. The development of digital communication has been incremental. In some cases, traditional voice communication was carried out alongside digitized data. Later, data or voice might be sorted into packages of information, the General Packet Radio Service (GPRS). GPRS split conversation into alternating segments that were experienced simultaneously, while advanced third-generational calls code each conversation separately. At this stage, the distinction between voice and data becomes redundant. Unfortunately, each stage has seen competitive and often incompatible systems evolve. The European route has been through what was termed GSM-based TDMA to GPRS, officially a 2.5 generation system, while the leader in the third generation is likely to emerge from another 2.5 generation system, called CDMA. Here again, Europeans have devised a w-CDMA, which is incompatible with the CDMA2000 favoured by the USA and East Asia. Indeed, an East Asian version called EV-DO has the fastest data capacity of all, and Korea and Japan have rapidly appropriated the new third-generation features (Ito et al. 2005). At the end of 2004, Japan had 20 million users of 3G, compared with fewer than 2 million in Europe (*The Economist* 16 November 2004). In Jamaica, Digicel was licensed for the European system of GSM, which is one of the reasons MiPhone are optimistic about their CDMA system for the future. Access to the Jamaican market is also through allocation of the SMA (Spectrum Management Authority). At present, Cable and Wireless operate at 800 megahertz and 1900 megahertz, Digicel operates at 900 megahertz and 1800 megahertz, MiPhone at 800 megahertz, and AT&T will share 1900 megahertz with C&W. One potential development may be at the 450 megahertz range, which only works for CDMA but because of its low frequency only requires a dozen or so towers to cover the whole island. These systems were under continual development. For example, in 2003 C&W rolled out ASDL and GSM services. In 2004 they overlaid their current GSM/GPRS 1900 megahertz with the lower frequency 850 megahertz and entered into an international roaming agreement with T-Mobile.

Bibliography

Abrahams, R.D. (1983). *The Man-O-Words in the West Indies: Performance and the Emergence of Creole Culture*. Baltimore and London, The Johns Hopkins University Press.

Ackerman, F., D. Kiron, N. Goodwin, H. Harris and H. Gallagher, eds (1997). *Human Well-being and Economic Goals*. Washington, Island Press.

Agar, J. (2003). *Constant Touch: A Global History of the Mobile Phone*. Cambridge, Icon Books.

Alcock, P. (1997). *Understanding Poverty*. London, Macmillan.

Alexander, J. (1977). 'The Culture of Race in Middle-class Kingston, Jamaica.' *American Ethnologist* **4**(1): 413–435.

Alexander, J. (1984). 'Love, Race, Slavery and Sexuality in Jamaican Images of the Family.' In *Kinship, Ideology and Practice in Latin America*, ed. R.T. Smith. Chapel Hill, University of North Carolina Press: 147–180.

Allen Consulting Group (2002). *A Jamaican E-commerce Blueprint Discussion Paper*. Sydney, prepared for the Commonwealth Secretariat and the Government of Jamaica.

Alleyne, M. (1988). *Roots of Jamaican Culture*. London, Pluto Press.

Anderson, G. (2004) Grades Plunge. Many Schools Performing Well Below Expectations. 16 May 2004. Jamaica Gleaner, http://www.jamaica-gleaner.com/gleaner/20040516/lead/lead1.html, accessed 16 March 2006.

Apter, A. (1991). 'Herskovits's Heritage: Rethinking Syncretism in the African Diaspora.' *Diaspora* **1**(3): 235–260.

Austin, D.J. (1983). 'Culture and Ideology in the English-speaking Caribbean: A View from Jamaica.' *American Ethnologist* **10**: 223–240.

Austin, D.J. (1984). *Urban Life in Kingston, Jamaica: The Culture and Class Ideology of Two Neighborhoods*. London, Gordon and Breach.

Austin-Broos, D.J. (1995). 'Gay Nights and Kingston Town: Representations of Kingston Jamaica.' In *Postmodern Cities and Spaces*, ed. S. Watson and K. Gibson. Oxford, Blackwell: 149–164.

Austin-Broos, D.J. (1997). *Jamaica Genesis: Religion and the Politics of Moral Orders*. Chicago, University of Chicago Press.

Bailey, B. (2000). *Issues of Gender and Education in Jamaica: What About the*

Boys? Kingston, Jamaica, UNESCO.

Bailey, W. (1998). 'Conflict and Accomodation: Female Gendered Existence in the Inner City of Kingston.' In *Gender and the Family in the Caribbean*, ed. W. Bailey. Mona, Jamaica, Institute for Social and Economic Research: 128–146.

Bailey, W., C. Branche, G. McGarrity and S. Stuart (1998). *Family and the Quality of Gender Relations in the Caribbean*. Mona, Jamaica, Institute of Social and Economic Research.

Baron, S., J. Field and T. Schuller eds (2000). *Social Capital*. Oxford, Oxford University Press.

Barrow, C. (1996). *Family in the Caribbean: Themes and Perspectives*. Kingston, Ian Randle Publishers.

Bartilow, H. (1997). *The Debt Dilemma: IMF Negotiations in Jamaica, Grenada and Guyana*. London, Macmillan.

Basch, L., N. Glick-Schiller and C. Szanton Blanc (1994). *Nations Unbound: Transnational Projects, Postcolonial Predicaments and Deterritorialized Nation-States*. Amsterdam, Overseas Publishers Association.

Beck, T. (1994). *The Experience of Poverty*. London, Intermediate Technology Publications.

Beck, U. and E. Beck-Gernsheim (2001). *Individualization*. London, Sage.

Becker, G. (1996). *Accounting for Tastes*. Cambridge, Massachusetts, Harvard University Press.

Beckwith, M.W. (1929). *Black Roadways: A Study of Jamaican Folk Life*. Chapel Hill, University of North Carolina Press.

Bernard, H.R. (1995). *Research Methods in Anthropology: Qualitative and Quantitative Methodology*. Boulder, Altamira Press.

Besson, J. (1984). 'Land Tenure in the Free Villages of Trelawney, Jamaica: A Case Study in the Caribbean Peasant Response to Emancipation.' *Slavery and Abolition* 5(1): 3–23.

Besson, J. (1992). 'Freedom and Community: The British West Indies.' In *The Meaning of Freedom: Economics, Politics and Culture after Slavery*, ed. F. McGlynn and S. Drescher. Pittsburgh and London, Pittsburgh University Press: 183–219.

Besson, J. (1993). 'Reputation and Respectability Reconsidered: A New Perspective on Afro-Caribbean Peasant Women.' In *Women and Change in the Caribbean*, ed. J. Momsen. Bloomington, Indiana, Indiana University Press: 15–37.

Besson, J. (1995a). 'The Creolization of African-American Slave Kinship in Jamaican Free Village and Maroon Communities.' In *Slave Cultures and the Cultures of Slavery*, ed. S. Palmié. Knoxville, University of Tennessee: 187–209.

Besson, J. (1995b). 'Land, Kinship and Community in the Post-emancipation Caribbean: A Regional Overview of the Leeward Islands.' In *Small Islands,*

Large Questions, ed. K.F. Olwig. London, Frank Cass: 73–99.

Besson, J. (1997). 'Caribbean Common Tenures and Capitalism: The Accompong Maroons of Jamaica.' *Plantation Society in the Americas* **IV**(2&3): 201–232.

Besson, J. (2000). 'The Appropriation of Lands of Law by Lands of Myth in the Caribbean Region.' In *Lands, Law and Environment: Mythical Land, Legal Boundaries*, ed. A. Abramson and D. Theodossopoulos. London and Sterling, Virginia, Pluto Press: 116–135.

Besson, J. (2002). *Martha Brae's Two Histories: European Expansion and Caribbean Culture-building in Jamaica*. Chapel Hill, University of North Carolina.

Besson, J. and B. Chevannes (1996). 'The Continuity–Creativity Debate: The Case of Revival.' *New West Indian Guide* **70**(3&4): 209–228.

Besson, J. and J. Momsen, eds (1987). *Land and Development in the Caribbean*. London, Macmillan Caribbean.

Beutelspacher, A.N., E.Z. Martelo and V. Garcia (2003). 'Does Contraception Benefit Women? Structure, Agency and Well-being in Rural Mexico.' *Feminist Economics* **9**(2 & 3): 213–238.

Black, M.L. (1995). 'My Mother Never Fathered Me: Rethinking Kinship and the Governing of Families.' *Social and Economic Studies* **44**(1): 49–71.

Bolles, A.L. (1981). '"Goin' Abroad": Working Class Jamaican Women and Migration.' In *Female Immigrants to the United States: Caribbean, Latin American and African Experiences*, ed. D. Mortimer and R. Bryce-Laporte. Washington, DC, Smithsonian Institution: 56–85.

Bourdieu, P. (1977). *Outline of a Theory of Practice*. Cambridge, Cambridge University Press.

Bourdieu, P. (1984). *Distinction: A Social Critique of the Judgement of Taste*. London, Routledge and Kegan Paul.

Boyett, I. and G. Currie (2004). 'Middle Managers Moulding International Strategy: An Irish Start-up in Jamaican Telecoms.' *Long Range Planning* **37**: 51–66.

Branche, C. (1998). 'Boys in Conflict: Community, Gender, Identity and Sex.' In *Gender and the Family in the Caribbean*, ed. W. Bailey. Mona, Jamaica, Institute for Social and Economic Research: 185–201.

Brodber, E. (1975). *A Study of Yards in the City of Kingston*. Mona, University of the West Indies.

Brown, B., N. Green and R. Harper, eds (2001). *Wireless World: Social and inter-actional aspects of the mobile age*. London, Springer.

Burgess, A. (2004). *Cellular Phones, Public Fears, and a Culture of Precaution*. Cambridge, Cambridge University Press.

Burton, R.D.E. (1997). *Afro-Creole: Power, Opposition and Play in the Caribbean*. Ithaca, Cornell University Press.

Callon, M., ed. (1998). *The Laws of the Markets*. Oxford, Blackwell.

Cassidy, F.G. and R.B. Le Page (2003). *A Dictionary of Jamaican English*. Kingston, Jamaica, University of the West Indies Press.

Castells, M. (1996). *The Rise of Network Society*. Oxford, Blackwell.

Castells, M. (1997). *The Power of Identity*. Oxford, Blackwell.

Castells, M. (1998). *The End of Millennium*. Oxford, Blackwell.

Castells, M., M. Fernandez-Ardevol, J. Linchuan Qui and A. Séy (2005). The Mobile Communication Society: A Cross-cultural Analysis of Available Evidence on the Social uses of Wireless Communication Technology. Los Angeles, California Annenberg School for Communication, University of Southern California.

Chevannes, B. (1993a). 'Drop Pan and Folk Consciousness.' *Jamaica Journal* **22**(2).

Chevannes, B. (1993b). 'Sexual Behaviour of Jamaicans: A Literature Review.' *Social and Economic Studies* **42**(1): 1–45.

Chevannes, B. (1994). *Rastafari: Roots and Ideology*. Syracuse, New York, Syracuse University Press.

Chevannes, B., ed. (1995). *Rastafari and Other African-Caribbean Worldviews*. London, Macmillan Press in association with the Institute of Social Studies, The Hague.

Chevannes, B. (1999). *What We Sow and What We Reap: Problems in the Cultivation of Male Identity in Jamaica*. Kingston, Grace Kennedy Foundation.

Chevannes, B. (2001). *Learning to Be a Man: Culture, Socialization and Gender Identity in Five Caribbean Communities*. Kingston, University of the West Indies Press.

Clarke, E. (1966). *My Mother Who Fathered Me*. London, George Allen and Unwin.

Clarke, M. (2002). 'Domestic Work, Joy or Pain? Problems and Solution of the Workers.' *Social and Economic Studies* **51**(4): 153–180.

Colen, S. (1990). '"Housekeeping" for the Green Card: West Indian Household Workers, the State and Stratified Reproduction in New York.' In *At Work in Homes*, ed. R. Sanjek and S. Colen. Washington, DC, American Anthropological Association.

Constable, N. (2003). *Romance on a Global Stage: Pen Pals, Virtual Ethnography, and 'Mail-order' Marriages*. Berkeley, University of California Press.

Constabulary Communications Network (2005). Constabulary Communications Network Release, J.C.F. http://www.jamaicapolice.org.jm/ccn_news_release.html, accessed 3 February 2005.

Cooper, C. (1996). *Noises in the Blood: Orality, Gender and the 'Vulgar' Body of Jamaican Popular Culture*. Durham, Duke University Press.

Cooper, C. (2004). *Sound Clash: Jamaican Dancehall Culture at Large*. Oxford, Palgrave Macmillan.

Day, S., E. Papataxiarches and M. Stewart, eds (1998). *Lilies of the Field: Marginal People Who Live for the Moment*. Boulder, Colorado, Westview Press.

Department for International Development (DFID) (2001). *Jamaica Country Strategy Paper*. Kingston, Jamaica, DFID Jamaica.

Dinham, P. (2005). Jamaica 2004: Year in Review. Jamaicans.com Website, http://www.jamaicans.com/articles/primearticles/yearreview2004.shtml, accessed 2 February 2005.

Douglas, M. and S. Ney (1998). 'Communication Needs of Social Beings.' In *Missing Persons: A Critique of Personhood in the Social Sciences*. Berkeley, University of California Press: 46–73.

Douglass, L. (1992). *The Power of Sentiment: Love, Hierarchy and the Jamaican Family Elite*. Boulder, Westview Press.

Economist, The (2004a). 'Debt in the Caribbean: Shadow on the Beach.' *The Economist*, 26 August, http://www.economist.com/displaystory.cfm?story_id=E1_PTNSJQV, accessed 3 September 2004.

Economist, The (2004b). 'Vision Meet Reality.' *The Economist*, 2 September, http://www.economist.com/displaystory.cfm?story_id=E1_PTVDSPT, accessed 15 September 2004.

Economist, The (2005a). 'A Spiritual Connection.' *The Economist*, 10 March, http://www.economist.com/research/articlesBySubject/displayStory.cfm?story_ID=3713955&subjected=894408, accessed 25 March 2005.

Economist, The (2005b). 'Mobile Phones and Development. Less is More.' *The Economist*, 7 July. http://www.economist.com/research/articlesBySubject/displayStory.cfm?story_ID=4151426&subjected=894408, accessed 8 August 2005.

Escobar, A. (1994a). 'Welcome to Cyberia: Notes on the Anthropology of Cyberculture.' *Current Anthropology* 35(3): 211–231.

Escobar, A. (1994b). *Encountering Development*. Princeton, Princeton University Press.

Eyre, L.A. (1986). 'The Effects of Political Terrorism on the Location of the Poor in Kingston.' *Urban Geography* 7: 227–242.

Figueroa, M. (1998). 'Gender Privileging and Socio-economic Outcomes: The Case of Health and Education in Jamaica.' In *Gender and Family in the Caribbean*, ed. W. Bailey. Mona, Jamaica, Institute for Social and Economic Research: 112–127.

Fine, B. (1998). 'The Triumph of Economics; or "Rationality" can be Dangerous to your Reasoning.' In *Virtualism: A New Political Economy*, ed. J. Carrier and D. Miller. Oxford, Berg: 49–73.

Fine, B. and F. Green (2000). 'Economics, Social Capital and the Colonization of the Social Sciences.' In *Social Capital*, ed. S. Baron, J. Field and T. Schuller. Oxford, Oxford University Press: 78–93.

Fischer, C. (1992). *America Calling: A Social History of the Telephone to 1940*. Berkeley, University of California Press.

Foner, N. (1971). *Social Change and Social Mobility in a Jamaican Rural Community*. Chicago, Department of Anthropology, University of Chicago.

Foner, N. (1978). *Jamaica Farewell: Jamaican Migrants in London*. Berkeley and Los Angeles, University of California Press.

Foner, N. (1983). *Jamaican Migrants: A Comparative Analysis of the New York and London Experience*. New York, New York University Center for Latin American and Caribbean Studies.

Foner, N., ed. (2001). Islands in the City: West Indian Migration to New York. Berkeley, University of California Press.

Fortunati, L., ed. (2002). *Italy, Stereotypes, True and False*. Cambridge, Cambridge University Press.

Fortunati, L., J. Katz and R. Ricini (2003). *Mediating the Human Body*. Erlbaum, New Jersey, Lawrence.

Fox, D.J. (2001). 'AIDS in Jamaica: The Grim Reality of HIV/AIDS in Rural Jamaica.' *Bridgewater Review*, http://www.bridgew.edu/NewsEvnt/BridRev/Archives/01Jun/jamaica.htm, accessed 23 February 2005.

Freeman, C. (1997). 'Reinventing Higglering Across Transnational Zones: Barbadian Women Juggle the Triple Shift.' In *Daughters of Caliban*, ed. C.L. Springfield. Indianapolis and Bloomington, Indiana University Press: 68–95.

Freeman, C. (2000). *High Tech and High Heels in the Global Economy: Women, Work and Pink-collar Identities in the Caribbean*. Durham and London, Duke University Press.

Galambos, L. and E. Abrahamson (2002). *Anytime, Anywhere: Entrepreneurship and the Creation of a Wireless World*. Cambridge, Cambridge University Press.

Gardner, K. and K. Lewis (1996). *Anthropology and Development*. London, Pluto Press.

Gleaner (1913). 'Mr Horn's Address.' *The Gleaner*. Kingston.

Godelier, M. (1999). *The Enigma of the Gift*. Cambridge, Polity.

Gordon, D. (1987). *Class, Status and Social Mobility in Jamaica*. Mona, Institute of Social and Economic Research.

Gordon, D., P. Anderson and D. Robotham (1997). 'Jamaica: Urbanization in the Years of the Crisis.' In *The Urban Caribbean: Transition to the New Global Economy*, ed. A. Portes, C. Dore-Cabral and P. Landolt. London and Baltimore, The Johns Hopkins University Press: 190–223.

Goulbourne, H. and M. Chamberlain, eds (2001). *Caribbean Families in Britain and the Transatlantic World*. London and Oxford, Macmillan.

Government of Jamaica (2002). *A Five-year Strategic Information Technology Plan for Jamaica*. Kingston, Ministry of Commerce, Industry and Technology.

Gray, O. (2004). *Demeaned but Empowered: The Social Power of the Urban Poor in Jamaica*. Mona, University of the West Indies Press.

Green, N. (2001). 'Who's Watching Whom? Monitoring and Accountability in Mobile Relations.' in *Wireless World: Social and Interactional Aspects of the Mobile Age*, ed. B. Brown, N. Green and R. Harper. London, Springer: 32–45.

Gunst, L. (1995). *Born fi dead: A Journey through the Jamaican Posse Underworld*. New York, Henry Holt.

Hakken, D. (1993). *Computing Myths, Class Realities: An Ethnography of Technology and Working People in Sheffield, England*. Boulder, Westview Press.

Halsey, A.H. (1972). *Education and Social Change*. Paris, UNESCO.

Handa, S. and D. King (2003). 'Adjustment with a Human Face? Evidence from Jamaica.' *World Development* **31**(7): 1125–1145.

Harper, R. (2001). 'The Mobile Interface: Old Technologies and New Arguments.' In *Wireless World*, ed. B. Brown, F. Green and R. Harper. London, Springer: 207–226.

Harper, R. (2003). 'Are Mobiles Good or Bad for Society?' In *Mobile Democracy: Essays on Society, Self and Politics*, ed. K. Nyiri. Vienna, Passagen Verlag: 185–214.

Harriot, A. (2001). 'The Jamaican Crime Problem: Some Policy Considerations.' *Wadabagei: A Journal of the Caribbean and its Diaspora* **4**(2): 123–152.

Harrison, F.V. (1988). 'Politics of Social Outlawry in Urban Jamaica.' *Urban Anthropology* **17**(2 & 3): 259–277.

Harrison, F.V. (1997). 'The Gendered Politics and Violence of Structural Adjustment: A View from Jamaica.' In *Situated Lives: Gender and Culture in Everyday Life*, ed. L. Lamphere, H. Ragone and P. Zavella. New York and London, Routledge: 451–468.

Harrison, M. (2001). *King Sugar: Jamaica, the Caribbean and the World Sugar Economy*. London, Latin American Bureau.

Henke, H. (1996). 'Mapping the "Inner Plantation": A Cultural Exploration of the Origins of Caribbean Local Discourse.' *Social and Economic Studies* **45**(4): 51–75.

Henriques, F. (1953). *Family and Colour in Jamaica*. London, Eyre and Spottiswoode.

Henry, F. (1994). *The Caribbean Diaspora in Toronto: Learning to Live with Racism*. Toronto, Buffalo and London, University of Toronto Press.

Henry, L. (2004). 'The Digital Divide, Economic Growth and Potential Poverty Reduction: The Case of the English Speaking Caribbean.' *Journal of Eastern Caribbean Studies* **29**(1): 1–22.

Henry-Lee, A. (2002). 'Economic Deprivation and Private Adjustments: The Case of Security Guards in Jamaica.' *Social and Economic Studies* **51**(4): 181–210.

Henry-Lee, A. and E. LeFranc (2002). 'Private Poverty and Gender in Guyana and Barbados.' *Social and Economic Studies* **51**(4): 1–30.

Henry-Lee, A., B. Chevannes, M. Clarke and S. Ricketts (2001). *An Assessment of the Standard of Living and Coping Strategies of Workers in Selected Occupations who Earn a Minimum Wage*. Kingston, Planning Insitute of Jamaica.

Hickling, F.W. and R.C. Gibson (2004). *Application of Research Findings in the Development of Community Mental Health Services in Jamaica*. Mexico City, Global Forum for Health Research.

Higman, B.W. (1988). *Jamaica Surveyed: Plantation Maps and Plans of the Eighteenth and Nineteenth Centuries*. Kingston, Institute of Jamaica Publications.

Higman, B.W. (1995). *Slave Population and Economy in Jamaica, 1807–1834*. Mona, Jamaica, University of the West Indies Press.

Hinrichs, L. (2004). "Emerging Orthographic Conventions in Written Creole: Computer-mediated Communication in Jamaica.' *Arbeiten aus Anglistik und Amerikanistik* **29**(1): 81–109.

Horst, H.A. (2004a). 'A Pilgrimage Home: Tombs, Burial and Belonging in Jamaica.' *Journal of Material Culture* **9**(1): 11–26.

Horst, H.A. (2004b*). 'Back a Yaad': Constructions of Home Among Jamaica's Returned Migrant Community*. London, Department of Anthropology, University of London.

Horst, H. A. (2006). 'The Blessings and Burdens of Communication: Cell Phones in Jamaican Transnational Social Fields.' *A Journal of Transnational Affairs Global Networks:* **6**(2): 142:160.

Horst, H.A. (n.d.). '"You can't be two places at once": Return Migration and the Problem of Transnationalism in Jamaica.'

Horst, H. and D. Miller (2005). 'From Kinship to Link-up: The Cell Phone and Social Networking in Jamaica.' *Current Anthropology* **46**(5): 755–778.

Hurston, Z.N. (1990 [1938]). *Tell my Horse Voodoo and Life in Haiti and Jamaica*. New York, Harper and Row.

Inter-American Development Bank (IADB) (2004). 'Project Abstract Oceanic Digital Jamaica (JA-0128)': http://enet.iadb.org/idbdoscwebservices/idbdocsInternet/IADBPublicDoc.aspx?docnum=416680.

Ito, M. (2002). 'Engineering Play: Children's Software and the Production of Everyday Life.' Ph.D. dissertation, Department of Anthropology, Stanford University.

Ito, M. (2004). *Technologies of the Childhood Imagination: Yugioh, Media Mixes, and Otaku*. London, Keynote Address at 'Digital Generations: Children, Young People and New Media', Centre for the Study of Children, Youth and Media, University of London.

Ito, M. (2005). 'Mobile Phones, Japanese Youth, and the Re-placement of Social Contact.' In *Mobile Communications: Re-negotiation of the Social Sphere*, ed.

R. Ling and P. Pedersen. New York, Springer-Verlag: 131–148.

Ito, M., D. Okabe and M. Matsuda, eds (2005). *Personal, Portable, Pedestrian: Mobile Phones in Japanese Life*. Cambridge, Massachusetts, MIT Press.

Jacobs, H.P. (1923). 'The Parishes in Jamaica.' *The West Indian Review*. Kingston: 14–17.

Jain, S.S.L. (2002). 'Urban Errands: The Means of Mobility.' *Journal of Consumer Culture* **2**(3): 419–438.

Jamaica Gleaner (2004). 'Ghastly Grades – CXC Exam Results Worse than Reported.' *Jamaica Gleaner*, 14 November, http://www.jamaica-gleaner.com/gleaner/20041114/lead/lead1.html, accessed 16 March 2004.

James, J. (2003). *Bridging the Global Digital Divide*. Cheltenham, Glos, Edward Elgar Publishing Ltd.

Kasesniemi, E.-L. and P. Rautiainen (2002). 'Mobile Culture of Children and Teenagers in Finland.' In *Perpetual Contact: Mobile Communication, Private Talk, Public Performance*, ed. J. Katz and M. Aakhus. Cambridge, Cambridge University Press: 170–192.

Katz, J. and M. Aakhus, eds (2002). *Perpetual Contact: Mobile Communication, Private Talk, Public Performance*. Cambridge, Cambridge University Press.

Kim, S.D. (2002). 'Korea: Personal Meanings.' In *Perpetual Contact*, ed. J. Katz and M. Aakhus. Cambridge, Cambridge University Press: 63–79.

Kirkpatrick, C. and D. Tennant (2002). 'Responding to Financial Crisis: The Case of Jamaica.' *World Development* **30**(11): 1933–1950.

Kirton, A. (2003). 'Major Internet Potential in Jamaica – JAMPRO'. *Jamaica Gleaner*: http://www.jamaica-gleaner.com/gleaner/20030702/business/business2.html.

Kirton, C. (1996). 'Rotating Savings and Credit Associations in Jamaica: Some Empirical Findings on Partner.' *Social and Economic Studies* **45**(2&3): 195–224.

Klak, T. (1992). 'Excluding the Poor from Low Income Housing Programs: The Roles of State Agencies and USAID in Jamaica.' *Antipode* **24**(2): 87–112.

Levy, H. (1996). *They Cry Respect: Urban Violence and Poverty in Jamaica*. Kingston, University of West Indies Press.

Licoppe, C. and J.-P. Heurtin (2002). 'France: Preserving the Image.' In *Perpetual Contact*, ed. J. Katz and M. Aakhus. Cambridge, Cambridge University Press: 94–109.

Ling, R. (1998). 'She Calls, (but) it's for Both of Us you Know: The Use of Traditional Fixed and Mobile Telephony for Social Networking among Norweigan Parents.' *R&D Report* **33**(98): http://www.telenor.no/fou/program/nomadiske/articles/10.pdf.

Ling, R. (2004). *The Mobile Connection: The Cell Phone's Impact on Society*. San Francisco, Morgan Kaufmann.

Ling, R. and B. Yuri (2002). Hyper-coordination via Mobile Phones in Norway. *Perpetual Contact*, ed. J. Katz and M. Aakhus. Cambridge, Cambridge University Press: 170–192.

Littlewood, R. (1998). 'From Vice to Madness.' In *The Butterfly and the Serpent: Essays in Psychiatry, Race and Religion*. London and New York, Free Association Books: 68–113.

Lundy, P. (1999). *Debt and Adjustment: Social and Environmental Consequences in Jamaica*. Aldershot, Ashgate.

McAfee, K. (1991). *Storm Signals: Structural Adjustment and Development Alternatives in the Caribbean*. Boston, South End Press.

McDonald, S.A.M. (2002). 'The Jamaica Food Stamp Programme: The Beneficiaries' Viewpoint.' *Social and Economic Studies* **51**(4): 211–242.

MacKenzie, D. and Y. Millo (2003). 'Constructing a Market, Performing Theory: the Historical Sociology of a Financial Derivatives Exchange.' *American Journal of Sociology* **109**: 107–145.

Manley, M. (1987). *Up the Down Escalator: Development and the International Economy, a Jamaican Case Study*. London, Andre Deutsch.

Market Research Services (2002) *All Media Executive Research Summary*. Kingston, Jamaica, Market Research Services.

Marvin, C. (1988). *When Old Technologies were New*. Oxford, Oxford University Press.

Massiah, J. (1983). *Women as Heads of Households in the Caribbean: Family Structure and Feminine Status*. Colchester and Paris, UNESCO.

Maurer, B. (2001). 'Islands in the Net: Rewiring Technological and Financial Circuits in the "offshore" Caribbean.' *Comparative Studies in Society and History* **43**(3): 467–501.

Mauss, M. (1954). *The Gift*. London, Kegan Paul.

Miller, D. (1987). *Material Culture and Mass Consumption*. London, Blackwell.

Miller, D., ed. (1988). *Material Cultures: Why Some Things Matter*. Chicago, University of Chicago Press.

Miller, D. (1994). *Modernity: An Ethnographic Approach*. Oxford and New York, Berg.

Miller, D. (1997). *Capitalism: An Ethnographic Approach*. Oxford and New York, Berg Press.

Miller, D. (1998). 'A Theory of Virtualism.' In *Virtualism: A New Political Economy*, ed. J. Carrier and D. Miller. Oxford and New York, Berg: 187–215.

Miller, D. (2003). 'The Virtual Moment.' *Journal of the Royal Anthropological Institute* **9**: 57–75.

Miller, D. (2005). 'Materiality: An Introduction.' In *Materiality*, ed. D. Miller. Durham, Duke University Press: 1–50.

Miller, D. and H. Horst (2005). *Understanding Demand: A Proposal for the*

Development of ICTs in Jamaica. Information Society Research Group Working Papers, http://www.isrg.info/ISRGWorkingPaper2, accessed 20 June 2005.

Miller, D. and D. Slater (2000). *The Internet: An Ethnographic Approach*. Oxford and New York, Berg.

Miller, D. and D. Slater (2005). 'Comparative Ethnography of New Media.' In *Mass Media and Society*, ed. J. Curran and M. Gurevitch. London, Hodder Arnold: 303–319.

Mintz, S.W. (1974). *Caribbean Transformations*. Chicago, Aldine Publishing Company.

Mintz, S.W. (1985a). *Sweetness and Power: The Place of Sugar in Modern History*. New York, Viking.

Mintz, S.W. (1985b). 'From Plantations to Peasantries in the Caribbean.' In *Caribbean Contours*, ed. S.W. Mintz and S. Price. Baltimore and London, Johns Hopkins University Press: 127–154.

Mintz, S.W. and D. Hall (1970). 'The Origins of the Jamaican Internal Marketing System.' *Yale University Publications in Anthropology* **57**: 3–25.

Mintz, S.W. and R. Price (1992). *The Birth of African-American Culture: An Anthropological Perspective*. Boston, Beacon Press.

Mintz, S.W. and S. Price, eds. (1985). *Caribbean Contours*. Baltimore and London, Johns Hopkins University Press.

Moser, C. (1998). 'The Asset Vulnerability Framework: Reassessing Urban Poverty Reduction Strategies.' *World Development* **26**(1): 1–19.

Moser, C. and J. Holland (1997). *Urban Poverty and Violence in Jamaica*. Geneva, World Bank.

Mossberger, K., C. Tolbert and M. Stansbury (2003). *Virtual Inequality: Beyond the Digital Divide*. Washington, DC, Georgetown University Press.

Munn, N. (1986). *The Fame of Gawa*. Cambridge, Cambridge University Press.

Murphy, L.D. (1994). 'Jesus Now More Than Ever'. University of Calgary, unpublished MA thesis.

Navas-Sabater, J., A. Dymond and N. Juntunen (2002). *Telecommunications and Information Services for the Poor*. Washington, DC, Discussion Paper 432, World Bank.

Nussbaum, M. (2003). 'Capabilities as Fundamental Entitlements: Sen and Social Justice.' *Feminist Economics* **9**: 33–59.

Office of Utilities Regulation (OUR) (2004). *Towards a Universal Access Obligation for Telecommunications Services in Jamaica*. Kingston, Jamaica.

Okabe, D. and M. Ito (2005). 'Keitai and the Intimate Stranger.' In *Personal, Portable, Pedestrian*, ed. M. Ito, D. Okabe and M. Matsuda. Cambridge, MIT Press: 205–218.

Olivier de Sardan, J.-P. (2005). *Anthropology and Development: Understanding Contemporary Social Change*. London, Zed.

Olwig, K.F. (1985). *Cultural Adaptation and Resistance: Three Centuries of Afro-Caribbean Life on St. John*. Gainesville, University of Florida Press.

Olwig, K.F. (1993). *Global Culture, Island Identity: Community and Change in the Afro-Caribbean Community of Nevis*. Reading, Harwood Academic Publishers.

Olwig, K.F. (1999a). 'Caribbean Place Identity: From Family Land to Region and Beyond.' *Identities* **5**: 435–467.

Olwig, K.F. (1999b). 'Narratives of the Children Left Behind: Home and Identity in Globalised Caribbean Families.' *Journal of Ethnic and Migration Studies* **25**(2): 267–287.

Olwig, K.F. (1999c). 'Travelling Makes a Home: Mobility and Identity among West Indians.' In *Ideal Homes? Social Change and Domestic Life*, ed. T. Chapman and J. Hockey. London, Routledge: 73–83.

Olwig, K.F. (2001). *Researching Global Socio-Cultural Fields: Views from an Extended Field Site*. Princeton, Transnational Migration: Comparative Perspectives, Transnational Communities Working Papers Series WPTC-01–12, Princeton University.

Patterson, O. (1967). *The Sociology of Slavery*. London, McGibbon and Key.

Pertierra, R., U. Eduardo, A. Pingoi, J. Hernandez and N. Dacaney (2002). *TXT-ING Selves: Cellphones and Philippine Modernity*. Manilla, De La Salle University Press.

Phillip, D. (2003). 'Unbundling Network Elements for Competition in Broadband Access.' In *The Jamaica Internet Forum*, ed. E. Wallace. Kingston, OUR (private circulation).

Planning Institute of Jamaica (PIOJ) (2003). *Jamaica Survey of Living Conditions 2002*. Kingston, The Planning Institute of Jamaica.

Planning Institute of Jamaica (PIOJ) (2004). *Economic and Social Survey Jamaica 2003*. Kingston, The Planning Institute of Jamaica.

Putnam, R.D., ed. (2002). *Democracies in Flux: The Evolution of Social Capital in Contemporary Society*. Oxford, Oxford University Press.

Rakodi, C. (2004). *The Livelihood Strategies of Poor Households in Downtown Kingston, Jamaica*, International Development Department, University of Birmingham.

Riak-Akuei, S. (2005). 'Remittances as Unforeseen Burdens: the Livelihoods and Social Obligations of Sudanese Refugees.' *Global Migration Perspectives* **18**(January), http://www.unhcr.ch/cgi-bin/texis/vtx/home/opendoc.pdf?tbl=RSDLEGAL&id=42ce49684, accessed 22 January 2005.

Robertson, L. (2002). *Dealing in Self-ownership: the Pursuit of Money and Personal Autonomy in Urban Jamaica*. Edinburgh, University of Edinburgh.

Robeyns, I. (2003). 'Sen's Capability Approach and Gender Inequality: Selecting Relevant Capabilities.' *Feminist Economics* **9**(2 & 3): 61–92.

Robotham, D. (1980). 'Pluralism as an Ideology.' *Social and Economic Studies*

29(1): 69–89.

Robotham, D. (1985). 'The Why of the Cockatoo.' *Social and Economic Studies* **32**(2): 111–151.

Robotham, D. (2001). 'Crime and Public Policy in Jamaica.' *Wadabagei: A Journal of the Caribbean and its Diaspora* **4**(2): 69–122.

Safa, H.I. (1986). 'Economic Autonomy and Sexual Equality in Caribbean Society.' *Social and Economic Studies* **35**(3): 1–21.

Safa, H.I. (1995). *The Myth of the Male Breadwinner: Women and Industrialization in the Caribbean*. Gainsville, University of Florida Press.

Sahlins, M. (1987). *Islands of History*. Chicago, University of Chicago Press.

Schejter, A. and A. Cohen (2002). 'Israel: Chutzpah and Chatter in the Holy Land.' In *Perpetual Contact: Mobile Communication, Private Talk, Public Performance*, ed. J. Katz and M. Aakhus. Cambridge, Cambridge University Press: 30–41.

Schneider, D. (1968). *American Kinship: A Cultural Account*. Chicago, University of Chicago Press.

Sen, A. (1987). *The Standard of Living*. Cambridge, Cambridge University Press.

Sen, A. (1992). *Inequality Reexamined*. Oxford, Oxford University Press.

Sen, A. (1999a). *Development as Freedom*. Oxford, Oxford University Press.

Sen, A. (1999b). *Commodities and Capabilities*. Oxford, Oxford University Press.

Senior, O. (1991). *Working Miracles: Women's Lives in the English-speaking Caribbean*. London, James Currey.

Sillitoe, P. and A. Bi, eds (2002). *Participating in Development: Approaches to Indigenous Knowledge*. London, Taylor and Francis.

Silverstone, R. and L. Haddon (1992). *Information and Communication Technologies in the Home: The Case of Teleworking*. Working Paper 17. Falmer, University of Sussex.

Silverstone, R. and E. Hirsch, eds. (1992). *Consuming Technologies: Media and Information in Domestic Spaces*. London, Routledge.

Sives, A. (2002). 'Changing Patrons from Politician to Drug Don: Clientelism in Kingston, Jamaica.' *Latin American Perspectives* **29**(5): 66–89.

Skuse, A. and T. Cousins (2005). 'Managing Distance: The Social Dynamics of Rural Telecommunications Access and Use in the Eastern Cape, South Africa.' Information Society Research Group Working Papers **1**: www.isrg.info.

Slater, D. (2005). 'Ethnography and "Communicative Ecology": Local Networks and the Assembling of Media Technologies,' paper delivered at Information Systems Department, London School of Economics, 17 November.

Slater, D. and J. Kwami (2005). Embeddedness and Escape: Internet and Mobile Use as Poverty Reduction Strategies in Ghana. ISRG Working Paper Series **4**. http://isrg.info/ISRGWorkingPaper4.pdf, accessed 30 June 2005.

Slater, D. and J. Tacchi (2004). *Research: ICT Innovations for Poverty Reduction*. New Delhi, UNESCO.

Smith, M.G. (1983). 'Robotham's Ideology and Pluralism: A Reply.' *Social and Economic Studies* **32**(2): 103–139.

Smith, M.G. (1984). *Culture, Race and Class in the Commonwealth Caribbean*. Mona, Jamaica, Department of Extra-mural Studies, University of the West Indies.

Smith, M.P. and L.E. Guarnizo, eds (1998). *Transnationalism from Below*. New Brunswick, New Jersey, Transaction Publishers.

Smith, R.T. (1988). *Kinship and Class in the West Indies: A Genealogical Study of Jamaica and Guyana*. Cambridge, Cambridge University Press.

Smith, R.T. (1996). *The Matrifocal Family: Power, Pluralism and Politics*. New York and London, Routledge.

Sobo, E.J. (1993). *One Blood: The Jamaican Body*. Albany, State University of New York.

Sobo, E. (1997). 'Menstrual Taboos, Witchcraft Babies and Social Relations: Women's Health Traditions in Jamaica.' In *Daughters of Caliban*, ed. C.L. Springfield. Bloomington and Indianapolis, Indiana University Press: 143–170.

Soto, I.M. (1987). 'West Indian Child Fostering: Its Role in Migrant Exchanges.' In *Caribbean Life in New York*, ed. C. Sutton and E. Chaney. New York, Center for Migration Studies: 121–137.

Stack, C. (1974). 'Sex Roles and Survival Strategies in an Urban Black Community. In *Women, Culture and Society*, ed. M. Rosaldo and L. Lamphere. Stanford, Stanford University Press: 113–128.

Stanley-Niaah, S. (2004). 'Kingston's Dancehall: A Story of Space and Celebration.' *Space and Culture* **7**(1): 102–118.

Stewart, M. (1997). *The Time of the Gypsies*. Boulder, Westview.

Stirton, L. and M. Lodge (2002). 'Regulatory Reform in Small Developing States: Globalisation, Regulatory Autonomy and Jamaican Telecommunications.' *New Political Economy* **7**: 437–455.

Stolzhoff, N.C. (2001). *Wake the Town and Tell the People: Dancehall Culture in Jamaica*. Chapel Hill, Duke University Press.

Stone, C. (1980). *Democracy and Clientelism in Jamaica*. New Brunswick and London, Transaction Books.

Stone, C. (1986). *Class, State and Democracy in Jamaica*. New York, Praeger.

Strathern, M. (1988). *The Gender of the Gift*. Berkeley, University of California Press.

Strathern, M. (1992). *After Nature*. Cambridge, Cambridge University Press.

Sullivan, D. (2003). 'Access in Schools, Libraries, Community Centres, Health Facilities.' In *The Jamaica Internet Forum*, ed. E. Wallace. Kingston, OUR (private circulation).

Tacchi, J. (2005). 'Finding a Voice: The Potential of Creative ICT Literacy and Voice in Community Multimedia Centres in South Asia.' ISRG Working Paper

Series **3**: www.isrg.info/ISRGWorkingPaper3.pdf.

Tacchi, J., D. Miller, D. Slater, A. Skuse, T. Cousins, T. Chandola, H. Horst and J. Kwami (2005). *Information Society: Emergent Technologies and Development Communities in the New South*. Final report prepared for the Department for International Development (UK), June 2005, http://www.isrg.info/ InformationSocietyFinalreport.doc.

Taylor, A. and R. Harper (2003). 'The Gift of the Gab? A Design Oriented Sociology of Young People's Use of Mobiles.' *Computer Supported Cooperative Work* **12**: 267–296.

Taylor, S.A.G. (1976). *A Short History of Clarendon*. Kingston, Ministry of Education Publications Branch.

Thomas, D. (2004). *Modern Blackness: Nationalism, Globalization and the Politics of*

Thomas-Hope, E. (1988). 'Caribbean Skilled International Migration and the Transnational Household.' *Geoforum* **19**(4): 423–432.

Thomas-Hope, E. (1992). *Explanation in Caribbean Migration*. London, Macmillan.

Thomas-Hope, E. (1995). 'Island Systems and the Paradox of Freedom: Migration in the Post-Emancipation Leeward Islands.' In *Small Islands, Large Questions*, ed. K.F. Olwig. London, Frank Cass: 161–178.

Thompson, P. and E. Bauer (2001). 'Jamaican Transnational Families: Points of Pain and Resources of Resilience.' *Wadabagei: A Journal of the Caribbean and its Diaspora* **3**(2): 1–36.

Toulis, N.R. (1997). *Believing Identity: Pentacostalism and the Mediation of Jamaican Ethnicity and Gender in England*. New York and Oxford, Berg Press.

Umble, D. (1996). *Holding the Line: The Telephone in Old Order Mennonite and Amish Life*. Baltimore, Johns Hopkins University Press.

USAID/J-CAR (2004). *Sustainable Development Strategy for Jamaica: 2005–2009*. Kingston, Jamaica, USAID.

Vertovec, S. (2004). 'Cheap Calls: The Social Glue of Migrant Transnationalism.' *Global Networks* **4**(2): 219–224.

Wardle, H. (1999). 'Jamaican Adventures: Simmel, Subjectivity and Extra-territoriality in the Caribbean.' *Journal of the Royal Anthropological Institute* **5**: 523–539.

Wardle, H. (2000). *An Ethnography of Cosmopolitanism in Kingston, Jamaica*. Lewiston, Queenstown, Lampeter, The Edward Mellon Press.

Weber, M. (1992 [1930]). *The Protestant Ethic and the Spirit of Capitalism*. London and New York, Routledge.

Weilenmann, A. and C. Larsson (2001). 'Local Use and Sharing of Mobile Phones.' In *Wireless World: Social and Interactional Aspects of the Mobile Age*, ed. B. Brown, N. Green and R. Harper. London, Springer: **92–106**.

Wellman, B. (ed.) (1999). *Networks in the Global Village: Life in Contemporary Communities*. Boulder, Colorado, Westview Press.

Wellman, B. (2002). 'Little Boxes, Glocalization, and Networked Individualism.' In *Digital Cities II: Computational and Sociological Approaches*, ed. M. Tanabe, P. van den Besselaar and T. Ishida. Berlin, Springer: 10–25.

Wellman, B. with B. Wellman (1992). 'Domestic affairs and network relations.' *Journal of Social and Personal Relationships* 9(August): 385–409.

Wengland, R. (1997). 'Alternatives to Gross National Product: A Critical Evaluation.' In *Human Well-being and Economic Goals*, ed. F. Ackerman, F. Kiron, D. Goodwin, N. Harris and H. Gallagher. Washington, Island Press: 373–402.

Whitehorne, R. (2003). 'ADSL Network Capacity Expansion.' In *The Jamaica Internet Forum*, ed. E. Wallace. Kingston, OUR (private circulation).

Wilding, R. (2006). 'Virtual Intimacies: Family Communications across Transnational Borders.' *Global Network 6(2): 125–142*.

Wilk, R. (2003). 'What's Love Got to do with it? Non-Corporate Households and the Legacy of Globalization.' Paper presented at conference on Gender and Globalization, The Maxwell School, Syracuse University.

Wilson, P.J. (1966). *Crab Antics*. Prospect Heights, Illinois, Waveland Press.

Wilson, P.J. (1972). *Oscar: An Inquiry into the Nature of Sanity*. Prospect Heights, Illinois, Waveland Press.

Wint, A. (1996). 'Pioneering Telephone Privatisation: Jamaica.' In *Privatising Monopolies: Lessons from the Telecommunications and Transport Sectors in Latin America*, ed. R. Ramamurti. Baltimore, Johns Hopkins University Press.

World Bank (2002). 'IFC Webpage.' http://www.ifc.org/ifcext/lac.nsf/Content/ SelectedProject?OpenDocument&UNID=2684E69BD7FBB43785256C38006 E2A38, accessed 1 July 2004.

World Bank (2004). *Jamaica: The Road to Sustained Growth*. Geneva, World Bank.

World Bank (2005). *Global Information and Communication Technologies Department*. http://www.info.worldbank.org/ict/, accessed 1 June 2005.

Yawney, C.D. (1979). 'Dread Wasteland: Rastafari Ritual in West Kingston, Jamaica.' In *Ritual, Symbolism, and Ceremonialism in the Americas*, ed. R. Crumrine. Greeley, Colorado, Occasional Publications in Anthropology, University of Northern Colorado.

Yelvington, K. (2001). 'The Anthropology of Afro-Latin America and the Caribbean: Diasporic Dimensions.' *Annual Review of Anthropology* 30: 227–260.

Yelvington, K., ed. (2005). *Afro-Atlantic Dialogues: Anthropology in the Diaspora*. Santa Fe, School of American Research.

Zelizer, V. (1987). *Pricing the Priceless Child: the Changing Social Value of Children*. New York, Basic Books.

Index